S0-BNU-152

The Age of
Participation

The Age of Participation

New Governance for the Workplace and the World

Patricia McLagan & Christo Nel

Foreword by Peter Block

Berrett-Koehler Publishers
San Francisco

Copyright © 1995, 1997 by Patricia McLagan and Christo Nel
All rights reserved. No part of this publication may be reproduced, distributed, or transmitted in any form or by any means, including photocopying, recording, or other electronic or mechanical methods, without the prior written permission of the publisher, except in the case of brief quotations embodied in critical reviews and certain other noncommercial uses permitted by copyright law. For permission requests, write to the publisher, addressed "Attention: Permissions Coordinator" at the address below.

Berrett-Koehler Publishers, Inc.
450 Sansome Street, Suite 1200
San Francisco, CA 94111-3320
Tel: (415) 288-0260   Fax: (415) 362-2512

Ordering Information

Individual sales. Berrett-Koehler publications are available through most bookstores. They can also be ordered direct from Berrett-Koehler at the address above.

Quantity sales. Special discounts are available on quantity purchases by corporations, associations, and others. For details, contact the "Special Sales Department" at the Berrett-Koehler address above.

Orders for college textbook/course adoption use. Please contact Berrett-Koehler Publishers at the address above.

Orders by U.S. trade bookstores and wholesalers. Please contact Publishers Group West, 4065 Hollis Street, Box 8843, Emeryville, CA 94662.
Tel: (510) 658-3453; 1-800-788-3123. Fax: (510) 658-1834

Printed in the United States of America

 Printed on acid-free and recycled paper that is composed of 50% recovered fiber, including 10% post consumer waste.

Library of Congress Cataloging-in-Publication Data
McLagan, Patricia A.
    The age of participation : new governance for the workplace and the world / Patricia McLagan & Christo Nel : foreword by Peter Block.
      p. cm.
    Included bibliographical references and index.
    ISBN 1-881052-56-7 (hardcover: alk. paper)
    ISBN 1-57675-012-4 (paperback: alk. paper)
    1. Management—Employee participation. 2. Decentralization in management. 3. Employee empowerment. I. Nel, Christo, 1954-
II. Title.
HD5650.M378   1995
331.25--dc20   95-35766
                       CIP

First Hardcover Printing: September 1995
First Paperback Printing: January 1997
00 99 98 97   10 9 8 7 6 5 4 3 2 1
This paperback edition contains the complete text of the original hardcover edition.

Editing: David Degener
Indexing: Julie Ryder
Proofreading: Mary Lou Sumberg
Interior Design and Production: Joel Friedlander Publishing Services
Cover Design: Michael Rogondino

Dedication

We offer our maps to our sons Tom, Dan, Andy, and Roark, and to all the young people and generations yet to come. May you complete this voyage of discovery, settle, and find abundance in the new world of participative governance.

Contents

Foreword

IF THE TITLE OF THIS BOOK were a question, the answer would be that the Age of Participation is at least 220 years old. So why write a new book about an old subject? We are still writing books about participation—call it *empowerment,* or *self-management,* or *employee involvement,* or *participative management*—because we are having a very difficult time choosing to put the idea of participation into practice.

We are having a difficult time despite the fact that the idea of participation has impressive credentials, and is closely aligned with the spirit of a democratic society. Our constitution and our system of law and precedent emphasize widespread citizen participation. A generation of experience in the workplace consistently demonstrates that, on the average, participative management strategies improve organizational performance. What's more, the idea of participation has been widely accepted by the business community. A study of Fortune 1,000 companies sponsored by the Association for Quality and Participation found that more than 70 percent had a formal employee involvement strategy.

Despite the entry of the *idea* of participation into mainstream business thought, the *practice* of authentic participation is alive only in small segments of business, education, health care, and government. For example, this same study of Fortune 1,000 companies found that, despite their popularity, participative strategies had affected only 13 percent of the people working for the companies polled.

Bridging the gap between intentions and actions is the challenge of participation. This challenge is a human dilemma, not just a management dilemma. We all know more than we can apply, we each have intentions we have yet to act upon. *The Age of Participation's* contribution to solving this dilemma is that it makes the practice of participation so reasonable, explicit, and concrete that we no longer have an excuse not to implement it.

REFORMING THE WHOLE

Participation is a system of governance that requires all elements of an organization be redesigned in a common direction. Too often we treat management as a menu of techniques that allows us to choose one from column A and one from column B. Every aspect of organizing human effort needs reform. Mission statement, structure, work process, teamwork, the role of the boss, the pay system, information systems, measurements, controls—all the practices and underlying beliefs that we have grown up with, and with which we have succeeded, are now in question.

Moreover, each element affects the others. If we continue to address each element separately, as the province of separate staff specialties, nothing important will change. Here are some simple examples:

» You cannot build teams *and* continue to reward individual performance.

» You cannot advocate self-management and have bosses continue to appraise subordinates.

» You cannot advertise your commitment to customer satisfaction and make building short-term shareholder value your primary statement of purpose.

» You cannot value openness, call everyone an "associate," and have different compensation systems for different organizational levels, still keeping the pay system for those at the top a secret.

» You cannot maintain that management is a system and then assign responsibility for quality improvement, management development, organizational development, reengineering, and customer satisfaction to separate staff units. These are all facets of the same diamond.

The Age of Participation does a good job of mapping the whole landscape of participation, and demonstrating the interconnections among its various pieces. The message is clear: Either begin to revise all the elements of governance, or let things stand as they are. Making piecemeal improvements—often for the sake of being modern—is a waste of effort.

THE RADICAL NATURE OF COMMON SENSE

Another question that this book raises is why common sense has become so radical. What passes for management wisdom seems rather obvious. For example:

» When there are mistakes, stop blaming. Use mistakes for learning.

» Build cooperation, not competition, between departments.

» Share all information.

» Organize around customers.

» Get feedback from customers and subordinates.

» Eliminate activities that do not add value.

» Operate with three levels of management, not seven.

These practices are certainly not rocket science. Why have we become blind to the obvious, and why have we lost faith in our own capacity to act?

Common sense becomes radical when it requires an act of adventure. We are now at risk and our organizations have been so successful and comfortable for so long that we have become cautious and isolated from the reality of the marketplace. Each commonsense participative management practices requires a new path. But because we are still seeking safety, we hold on to control and continue our traditional practices. This wish for safety is also reflected in our love of leadership and our desire to have top management on our side and leading the way. In fact, the more adventure is demanded of us, the more protective we become. If the Age of Participation is beginning, as McLagan and Nel argue, it will come about because our marketplace demands it and our survival is threatened.

Our search for safety also leads us to believe that we need experts to show us the way. We already have the knowledge and skills needed to implement every idea in this book. We do not need consultants or a lot of training to act on what we know. The question is whether we have the will to respond to what is demanded of us—to choose adventure—and allow the protection of familiar habits to fall away. The learning we need to do involves an unburdening--letting go of high-control practices and beliefs. The moment we do, we gain the capacity to adapt and apply the commonsense practices described in this book.

CHOOSING THE ARTIST OVER THE ENGINEER

The underbelly of a practical book like *The Age of Participation* is that it implies a promise that participation can be implemented through a series of rational actions, that organizational change can be engineered. The Age of Participation demands a change in who we think we are. Human beings are not terribly rational; we are not units whose behavior can be predicted by economic theory. We are not cause-and-effect phenomena. Scientific management is an oxymoron. The belief that we can *engineer* a change in the organization of human effort becomes, in itself, an interference to participation.

Listen to the language that we use. We talk about participation and quality improvement efforts as if they were washing machines: We *install* self-management; we *roll out* a new performance management system. Such language and underlying ways of thinking mechanize the process of human development. Mechanical solutions to human problems become cosmetic and ultimately create cynicism.

Governance systems change at the will of those governed. Yes, we can *install* new information systems, production processes, or quality measurement tools, but they need human intervention to make them work. If each individual does not make a personal decision to be accountable for the success of the new process, no amount of automation, appraisal, or pay will produce the results that we require.

The journey toward authentic participation forces us to confront our deepest beliefs about the nature of the person. Historically, our institutions and systems of governance have been based on beliefs that

» people want and need to be controlled,

» clear focus and direction result only from strong leadership,

» people do only the things that they are rewarded for doing, and

» people will not use their personal freedom in service of the organization.

These beliefs are tenets of a mechanical, economist view of human behavior. No wonder, then, that the quickest way to get a quick increase in the price of your stock is to announce a large-scale layoff.

What you see is what you get. When we believe that mechanical intervention will influence organization behavior, we get a mechanical response. When we command people to participate, we get participation in name only. And by and large, what we have received *is* participation in name only: Seventy percent of the Fortune 1,000 companies polled had a program, but only 13 percent of their people were affected.

The only way we truly can enter the Age of Participation is with strategies based on the belief that human systems are by nature self-organizing. Each unit, each team will ultimately have to choose its own path into participation. Participation will have to be invented and customized each time. This is why the artist is required.

Participation—and its political cousin democracy—will come of age when teams of core workers and citizens decide to reclaim the ground on which they live. Workers will treat their unit, their customers, and their funding as their own. Citizens will do the same with their neighborhood and town. Leaders will discover the level of accountability and responsibility that they are looking for when they support the reclamation effort. That is the radical middle ground between monarchy (which we have now) and anarchy (which we fear). Let those in charge launch participation, but only those who do the work can give it form, life, and meaning.

This book, then, becomes an owner's manual for entry into the Age of Participation. If this were the last book written for the next twenty years on creating a workplace, we would save a lot of paper and miss nothing important in the process. The unique contribution that Pat and Christo have made is to integrate so many different theories and practices into one coherent, reader-friendly document. They have collected a hundred different specific actions and framed them in a way that raises the question of participation to the level of societal and philosophical choice. If democracy is to be sustained, and organizations are to serve customers and still be habitable for human beings, we will have to find a way of entering this Age of Participation as quickly and completely as possible.

PETER BLOCK

Acknowledgements

WINSTON CHURCHILL apparently said that writing a book consists of five phases: the first phase is one of enthusiasm and utter belief in what the authors want to communicate. By the last phase, the book has turned into an all-consuming force with its own personality, threatening to devour the authors! These two phases are so overwhelming that they cause us to forget everything that occurred in between!

Perhaps that is the most important reason to write formal acknowledgments for a book-it helps us to reflect and remember the period of creation, those treasured times of discovering new insights, the arguments and concerns, and the inevitable nagging doubts about whether the book really has something of worth to offer. It is the final ritual of an incredible journey that, for us, has been one of remarkable support and friendship from so many people. We want to extend our heartfelt thanks to the many people who have contributed their time, comments, and support in our quest. We received feedback and suggestions that were collectively almost a book in their own right! Without them our book could not have been created. Everyone's help has transformed its potential and quality, and turned it into a truly collective effort.

Working with Steve Piersanti and the team of people at Berrett-Koehler is a rare privilege. The obvious personal interest and time they invest is remarkable, to say the least. Also, the people who read the first draft helped us to make it a more focused book. Thank you Mavis Wilson, Frank Basler, Steve Cohen, Richard Whiteley, Dick Hallstein, Geoff Bellman, Bob Stump, Charlie Bodenstab, and Bonnie Kasten. Then, the very thorough comments we received for the second draft were invaluable for refining and making it more usable. Thank you Tom Blanco, George Lindeque, William Heisler, Nancy Brandwein, Jonathan Charkam, John O'Brien, Mark Curtin, and Steve McMillen. And thank you to our many clients for helping us experience the real world of work during times of dislocation and transformation. Your examples enrich us and our ability to communicate about this very important topic of governance in the world today.

Our colleagues and friends at ITISA provided word processing services, input to graphic design, and professional critique. David Degener instilled discipline and gave valuable advice as editor, and Joel Friedlander has delivered an aesthetically pleasing book. Thank you to all who have become part of this project and helping us to see it through to its final state.

Introduction

POWERFUL SHOCK WAVES are shaking human institutions. The ancient Greeks felt the first tremors. The Renaissance and the Enlightenment felt tremors, too. Like tectonic plates, two views of governance have been grinding against each other for thousands of years. One view recedes reluctantly. The other drives inexorably against it. Although the tremendous tension between them has yet to break the surface, it is increasingly clear that the shock waves associated with this cataclysmic confrontation will forever change our world.

Governance is an important word. It refers to the way in which the stakeholders in an institution—government, community, business, or family—live their power, rights, and responsibilities. Any system of governance rests on a world view—a set of assumptions and values that determines how power, rights, and responsibilities are distributed and expressed.

The authoritarian form of governance has prevailed since people began to organize political, social, and economic institutions. In authoritarian systems, power and rights are concentrated in a small group whose members exercise power over others. This relationship may have made sense in feudal times, when farmers banded together to seek powerful protectors against armed invaders, but authoritarian assumptions and practices are both dangerous and wasteful in today's

1

world. In this century alone, more than 170 million people have been killed as the result of wars, atrocities, and concentration camps. Most of these deaths have been a result of authoritarian assumptions about governance. Authoritarianism has other costs, and they are high: Slavery, ethnic violence, gender discrimination, and the alienation of oppressed people all have roots in authoritarianism.

Participation is emerging as a powerful alternative form of governance. Of course, the idea is not new. Throughout history, humanity has been moving toward increased participation. Athenian democracy in the fourth century B.C., the Magna Carta in thirteenth-century Britain, the Declaration of the Rights of Man in France, the Declaration of Independence in America, the United Nations International Declaration of Human Rights in 1948 were all attempts to spread national and community power, rights, and responsibilities.

In the second half of this century, participation has become a key theme in private and public institutions alike. Some of the emphasis is driven by cost concerns. For example, in medicine we realize that patients must take responsibility for their own health. They must act to stay healthy and to manage their recovery when they are sick. In the community, people have instituted crime watches, because they know that the cost of hiring enough police is too high.

Business organizations are well aware of the costs of rigid, top-heavy hierarchies and oversupervision. Under authoritarianism, the few think, and the many either follow orders or constantly rebel and strike. Clearly, authoritarianism is not cost-effective.

Although the people in business organizations are getting more meaningfully involved, companies have been slow to embrace participation. Chapter One reviews the variety of initiatives that have been tried. Many of these initiatives have failed to deliver. Others have been absorbed over time by the very powerful authoritarian cultures that they were meant to replace. Often, the only result has been a deep cynicism: "We won't try that again."

Participation is not a new topic. But we must see it with fresh eyes. It is not synonymous with teams, or with involving everyone in everything, or with quality circles. It is a system of governance that responds to very powerful and new forces at work in the world today. As

Chapters Two and Three argue, it is also the only viable option for the long-term success of human institutions and the planet itself.

Participation is emerging as a system of governance just as very powerful forces that can either destroy us all or catapult us into a new era of possibilities are converging. The situation is analogous to the discovery of the New World in the fifteenth century and to the conquest of space in the twentieth century. In both cases, insurmountable problems were solved, and the hopes and aspirations of humanity were fulfilled. We had to break through many barriers: Old World views, fear of the unknown, skepticism about the new, lack of resources for exploration and change. But humanity's move into new territory was both inevitable and necessary: inevitable because we were developing the knowledge and had an insatiable curiosity, necessary because stewardship of the world requires us to understand the world and our impact on it.

The shift to participative governance in the workplace is also both inevitable and necessary. It is inevitable because the capacity for participation is widespread. It is necessary because the issues that we face in the workplace are too complex and interdependent to be solved by a few people in authority. Chapter Three reviews the mounting evidence that participative systems outperform authoritarian systems. The emphasis in this chapter is on systems of participation, not on isolated practices or activities. In Chapter Four, we argue that the key to success lies in finding the high-leverage areas and redesigning them. Chapters Five through Thirteen show that, for participation to prevail, not just one or two but a whole array of specific institutional practices must be participative. Chapters Fourteen through Sixteen examine the institution that emerges: It is substantially different from its authoritarian predecessor. And Chapters Seventeen through Nineteen emphasize that it is not easy to create such an institution.

This book is about participation as the emerging dominant form of institutional governance. Its main focus is the workplace, but we argue in Chapter Twenty that its propositions and conclusions are relevant to churches, clubs, educational institutions, and local and national governments—indeed, to any purposeful community or social group.

Our view of participation has emerged from very different perspectives. One of us has lived and worked primarily in the United States, the world's oldest democracy and one of the most productive nations on earth. The other is a citizen of South Africa, until recently one of the world's most authoritarian nations and still one of its least productive. Each author has spent some part of the last ten years working in the other author's world.

Working at the extremes of governance philosophies, we have developed broad and deep perspectives on the issues addressed in this book. Our perspectives are more acute because we have seen the pathologies of governance: the flagrant abuses of apartheid and the discrepancies between the words and actions of leaders and followers in the U.S. system. Understanding the illnesses that afflict governance in these two societies helps us to recognize, understand, and articulate governance health.

Our combined forty years of experience in more than a hundred institutions worldwide have made one thing very clear to us: Although the participative alternative is superior in many ways, authoritarianism still has a tenacious hold on public and private institutions everywhere. In many countries, now including South Africa, people can vote. But the institutions whose members they elect and in which they work are still mainly autocratic. It seems ironic that participative practices are more common today in the new South Africa than they are in the budget committee of the U.S. Congress.

Authoritarian governance is not a viable option for the future. Powerful forces are propelling us toward the alternative: As information technology, global economic and ecological interdependence, stakeholder demands, and other forces converge, participation is really the only viable governance option. Continued autocracy has very high costs. On the macro level, we risk war, nuclear proliferation, ethnic conflict, revolt by the many poor against the affluent few, and ecological disaster. On the micro level, we are threatened by noncompetitiveness, bankruptcy, and the waste of human and other resources.

Fortunately, as virtually every institutional success story tells us, participative governance is the best option available today. Not only does it take the moral high road, it produces results. We are fortunate that this option is available.

This book is about participation. We encourage you to participate in it. First, participate with us in our exploration of the theory and principles of participation that are now emerging. Follow us into client organizations, and think about the examples that we present in each chapter. All the examples come from companies in the United States, Europe, and Africa with which we have worked.

Second, participate by assessing your own organization in the nine areas that have the most leverage on the governance system within a workplace. You can conduct such an assessment at the end of each chapter, starting with Chapter Five. We hope that you will go beyond the brief evaluation suggested by the questionnaires that end the nine chapters in Part Two to start or continue an aggressive governance change program for your organization.

Finally, use the list of books and articles in Suggested Reading, which is organized by topic, to continue your own learning. Participation is the new world of governance. That world has been discovered, and much knowledge about it exists already. But there is much pioneering work to do as people everywhere begin to settle in and develop for the exciting and challenging new age that our discoveries have opened.

PART I

Discovering the
New World of Work

*A*ncient maps reflected myths and assumptions
that inhibited exploration. Do not wander
past the boundaries of the known, they
cautioned. For beyond the known lie unknown threats and
horrible dangers.

That authoritarian governance is familiar terrain makes
many of us captives of our own limited, cautious, even
fearful worldview. Just as the very first maps, which por-
trayed the world as flat, kept mariners from seeking and
finding new worlds, so the maps of authoritarianism will
not help us to find a new world in which governance is
informed by other principles. That new world awaits us. It
is visible on the horizon. In that new world, governance is
participative. Finding it requires new maps and poses
special challenges for today's explorers.

CHAPTER 1

Why Partial Participation Fails

The problem is that we know we have increasingly difficult strategies but less and less likelihood of achieving them unless we do something very different. We've gone through retrenchments. We've run everyone through quality training. We've got visions and values, and we've communicated them through the system. I can't go to our people again and say, "Make this sacrifice for us." Today's actions are falling short, even as fundamental forces are at work that are changing the rules of the game.

— *Executive at a major world airline*

SINCE THE 1950S and increasingly in the 1980s and 1990s, organizations have been trying to break into new performance arenas. Expecting to catapult themselves to new heights of customer favor, quality, and competitiveness, they have launched expensive change efforts. But many of these efforts have failed. They either do not achieve the planned levels, or the effects do not survive the initial excitement. In some cases, change efforts have left an organization in worse shape than it was in before they were begun.

A VARIETY OF INTERVENTIONS

Organizations have tried a variety of interventions. Even with the best intentions, these interventions have had a hard time escaping the gravitational field exerted by an organization's culture and performance. For example, take *strategic planning*. Strategic planning is supposed to position an institution so that it can compete successfully and make the best use of resources for future needs. But it does not take long for what begins as breakthrough planning to become just another bureaucratic process for overburdened management. Even if the plan sets inspiring new directions, there can be many problems. Most organizations are not equipped to deliver on strategies that take them into new performance arenas. Managers soon discover that devising strategies is only the very small first step. Strategies that exceed an organization's ability to act can even be disabling. People become frustrated or cynical. Subsequent plans lose power and credibility.

Improved strategies can even reduce an organization's capacity to act. Ask anyone at American Telephone and Telegraph (AT&T) in the mid 1980s. On one level, the new telecommunications visions bucked a bureaucracy that was used to dictating products to the market. On another, the new visions increased fears within the workforce of obsolescence and redundancy. CEO Bob Allen and his colleagues had to make significant changes in order to give the organization the thrust that it needed if it was to play the field that AT&T had defined long before the divestiture of January 1, 1984.

The same fate haunts companies that use *values and vision* as their main link between management and workers. The best efforts to inspire and create common bonds among all groups and employees within an organization seem unable in the long run to achieve aligned action. And common visions and values do not on their own increase trust between managers and frontline workers. Nor do they ensure that people change their behaviors.

Many organizations have emphasized *employee involvement.* Since the late 1940s, managers have encouraged work teams in production and service settings to solve problems together and recommend ways of improving efficiency or effectiveness. Whether these efforts take the form of quality circles or employee involvement teams, everyone expects revolutionary changes in motivation and productivity. Yet, time and again, energy and effectiveness dwindle. The scope of the problems that teams attempt to address shrinks. And what started as a good idea becomes the target of sarcastic pub talk and proof that involvement does not really work.

Total quality management (TQM) raised the issue of quality to a systemic level. Promoted by the efforts of people like W. Edwards Deming, Kaoru Ishikawa, and Joseph Juran (Walton, 1986; Garvin, 1988)—and by the successful application of TQM methods in Japan—it focused on processes as major levers for significant improvements in performance. Such a focus requires an organization to make a number of changes in the way that it functions. But TQM programs face two dangers: They are often imposed from the top. And they routinely get so entangled in procedures and bureaucracy that the organization ends up losing sight of its customers and their quality needs. As a result, it is not uncommon for what at the outset looks very promising to start with a bang and end with a whimper. It becomes just another training or record-keeping exercise.

For some organizations, the answer lies in *better pay and performance management schemes.* Pay for individual or group performance, gain sharing, profit sharing, and new ways of conducting performance reviews are favored solutions. People reason that, if only the organization can get the rewards and incentives right, the desired behavior will follow. These schemes, too, seem to fall short. Performance review systems work in cycles. New forms replace old ones. Each new system is greeted with hope, but people sooner or later find out how to beat it. Even profit sharing and gain sharing have fair-weather followers. As long as people are making more money, they favor such new schemes. But they are not ready to embrace the downside risk that they face under them.

Another common way of waking up an organization is to call for *cost cutting.* Today's customers will not pay higher prices unless they get greater value. Yet costs routinely rise. Management says to labor, "We have a common cause. We must reduce costs to be competitive. We need your help." Such appeals routinely meet with distrust. Staff members may be reluctant to propose truly powerful actions that they fear may eliminate their own job, or they do not understand the economics of the business well enough to make potent recommendations. Even if a call for cost-cutting ideas is worthwhile, most organizations do not have the capacity to respond. Management leaves the exercise feeling that employees simply do not care. And workers shrug it off as just another attempt by management to squeeze workers.

Restructuring has been an enduring but evolving change technique. In the 1950s and 1960s, it usually meant replacing a functional organization with a market-, location-, or product-focused organization. In the 1970s, thanks to the National Aeronautics and Space Administration (NASA) in the United States and other very complex project-based organizations, the matrix became another option. In recent years, restructuring has undergone another change. Now it focuses on such things as value chains, virtual organizations, and self-organizing and self-managing teams and processes. These new structures seek to emphasize customer and market service by finding the most efficient and effective sequence of value-adding activities from supplier to customer. Start-up plants or operations are generally the most successful users of radical new structures, because they do not have to contend with entrenched habits or traditions. Small software companies and entrepreneurial firms also have good track records with these new, relatively flat structures.

For older organizations, there is less real evidence of sustained success. A recent Wyatt Company (1993) survey of corporate restructuring found that, while 61 percent of the restructured companies reporting that cost reduction had been one their key goals said that they had achieved it, only 21 percent achieved their goal of reduced waste, and only 27 percent felt that customer satisfaction had risen.

The statistics are even more grim when results are tracked over time. Boroughs (1992) noted that share value in reorganized companies tends to be 26 percent lower than in comparable organizations that have not systematically downsized. Of the 850 companies studied, only 41 percent were meeting their profit goals three years after retrenchment.

The 1990s introduced several new solutions to the problem of how to drive fundamental change. One of these solutions, *diversity,* proposes that change will occur naturally if organizations open access to all groups: women as well as men, old as well as young, Black and yellow and red as well as white, physically challenged as well as able-bodied, homosexual as well as heterosexual. The list could go on. But diversity seems to be an elusive goal. Increasing the rate of diversity hires does not seem to change an organization in fundamental ways. Quotas for promotion seem to have no effect on an organization's texture or its ability to be competitive. Many organizations that bring in diverse recruits or accelerate the development of people in targeted populations find either that some of their best new recruits fail or that competitors have an easy time hiring them away. So much for any sense of social responsibility in the diversity area.

The *learning organization* has been viewed as another solution. In its quest for long-term survival, an organization eventually realizes that being the fastest learner in the industry can give it an advantage. But how does one translate this realization into action? Thus far, the value of learning seems to live mostly in rhetoric. While proclaiming that their organization is a learning organization, executives punish the people who challenge their viewpoint. A hidden message permeates employees' career planning: Be sure that what you do looks successful. Any admission of a need to learn is an admission of weakness. Weak people are not promoted. The rhetoric about the learning organization can even be alienating. And as an alienating force, its effect on organizational performance is to increase cynicism, not to add power.

A FUNDAMENTAL SHIFT

Organizations pursue change today under many banners. Some seek to improve strategy, vision, or values. Others espouse employee involvement or total quality management. Still others focus on getting pay, performance management, and cost-cutting processes right. Reengineering, diversity, and learning organization interventions are more adventurous—or at least more recent—ways of propelling organizations into new arenas of short- and long-term success.

But the kind of fundamental change that dramatically increases quality, productivity, and customer retention remains elusive. Successive change initiatives blast into the atmosphere only to return sooner or later to their source, or else they disintegrate as they pull against the very powerful organizational forces that they are trying to escape.

It is useful to ask what these change programs are trying to accomplish and why. The textbook answers focus on such things as becoming the customer's preferred supplier for life; reducing response and action time to as close to absolute zero as possible; innovating at a rate that ensures long-term endurance; becoming the quality and cost leader; becoming the preferred customer to preferred suppliers; becoming the preferred employer for key talent; and having the best cost-benefit performance—that is, adding the best value for the customer and leading the pack in returns on equity and capital.

If these are the goals, then most change efforts have failed, because they have not achieved them. Like the early rockets that could not break loose of the earth's gravitational forces, change programs often cannot escape the prevailing organizational culture. Does this mean that the programs are failures? The answer may be yes—in the sense that NASA's early rockets were failures because they could not escape earth's atmosphere.

But there is another, more important perspective. When we look closely at the aborted, fragmented, or only partly successful efforts of the past, we find many successful, albeit partial, solutions to the competitiveness challenge that we still face, because something much more profound than the individual interventions themselves is taking place. In hindsight, we can see that these partial changes are in fact early attempts to launch a new system of governance. They have had less than spectacular results not because they are wrong but because they have not been propelled by a new vision of institutional governance.

Our thesis is that society's collective vision of institutional governance is undergoing a fundamental shift—a shift that is replacing authoritarianism with participation. Such a shift requires profound changes in our assumptions about how successful organizations must work. It affects values, structures, roles, processes, competencies, and the nature of life and interactions in every institution and in every country of the globe. This emerging new age of participation is as radical a development for human institutions as the discovery of the New World was for Europeans five hundred years ago.

CHAPTER 2

Good-bye, Authoritarianism

SINCE THE PUBLICATION of Alvin Toffler's (1970) *Future Shock* twenty-five years ago, many books about the future have appeared. One conclusion is unavoidable from all the resulting analyses and predictions: Participation is the great governance trend. The strength of this trend is accelerating as we near the end of the twentieth century.

THE FORCES DRIVING US TOWARD PARTICIPATION

There are several powerful reasons why the move toward participation is accelerating. Information is increasingly available in real time and in formats that make it usable. Until recently, we needed people to synthesize, interpret, and format information for the people who were to use it. Hierarchy played such a role within organizations. Today, people get much of their information directly. They can now manage their own activity and participate without layers of interference or direction from authorities. This development will have major impact on public policy as well as on the workplace when people begin to vote on local and national issues via computer and television.

Globalization is another of the forces driving the move toward participation. People, organizations, and even nations that in the past were relatively isolated now find themselves face to face via fax, television, and cellular phone. Companies often design, manufacture, and sell in several different countries. Boundaries within organizations are blurring as functions and levels, customers and suppliers realize that they must bring down the walls between them. Increased interdependence requires increased participation. Global relationships now depend on effective participation and the rapid fall of authoritarianism.

As technology transforms labor, participation receives another boost. Technology is changing the nature of work and freeing up time—time that can be devoted to participation. Because technology reduces the number of people required to produce a given good or service, it increases the scope of production for which each worker is responsible. It increases the size of the individual job and the associated responsibility. As automation and computers take on the routine or dangerous work, the new worker becomes a manager of exceptions. He or she is expected to access information, understand the context of an issue, and respond rapidly and appropriately to satisfy customers. Technology in the work itself makes each person's impact more significant and his or her commitment and involvement more critical. Old-style controls are not appropriate for this situation.

If for no other reason than that the new workforce mandates it, organizations must move toward participation. If workers cannot be guaranteed lifetime employment (and they cannot), then at least they want to be involved and have their opinions heard as long as they are in the organization. The old paternalistic security must be replaced by a new sense of control: "I now have control over my life because I am influential in the decisions that are made around me." This demand to participate will also grow as the new workforce grows increasingly diverse. The participation mandate is already exerting great pressure on authoritarian structures to open up access to governance and opportunity.

The rise of the customer is another important factor driving the move toward participation. Before the Second World War, someone like Henry Ford could say of the cars that his company produced that you can have a car any color you like, as long as it's black. Today, that kind of producer centeredness would mean ruin. Quality is rapidly becoming the minimum prerequisite for customer satisfaction. In the future, customers will increasingly expect to have their individualized needs understood and met—fast. The great mobility of customers today means that their ability to shop around and thus their range of choice have increased exponentially. Organizations must now be in a position to respond almost instantaneously to a customer's request. In practice, the person who receives the customer's request must be empowered to do whatever it takes to get and keep the customer. In other words, people have to be able to think, choose, and participate.

These and other forces of change do not operate in isolation. They converge, simultaneously fueling and being fueled by one another. And the world is becoming increasingly complex as a result. For as the number of interacting forces increases, the number of possible combinations increases, too. Fortunately, the new science of complexity is emerging to help us to understand and deal with the increasing complexity of our world. A megascience, it helps to explain phenomena in physics, biology, sociology—even economics. In simple terms, the science of complexity explores the rules that are relevant to constantly changing, dynamic systems. We now know that the behavior of dynamic systems—for example, the weather, economies, societies, markets, and organizations—cannot be perfectly determined or completely controlled, no matter how perfect our knowledge of them may be.

The new science of complexity is the emerging science of participation. It focuses on what happens when the parts of a complex system interact. It studies and explores the vast information-processing ability of participative systems. It investigates how to influence behavior when a system is too complex to be controllable. The findings of complexity theory are very compatible with the emerging insights about participative governance. Indeed, they are fueling these insights: When both the environment and the organization are complex, authoritarian and centralized governance methods are too brittle and unresponsive to ensure the organization's long-term survival. In white water, we are better off with a flexible raft and twelve alert eyes than with a wooden boat in which one captain "up top" directs a galley of fettered rowers. Complex systems require the alert participation of everyone concerned.

Looking back, it is easy for us to identify the forces that are bringing participation to the fore. But because the forces have emerged gradually, we run the risk of underestimating the magnitude of the shift in governance that they motivate. For the participative institution and the consciously participative way of life represent a dramatic change in how we do things and in what we value about the social, political, and economic systems of which we are part.

THE DOMINANCE AND DEMISE OF AUTHORITARIANISM

The human institutions of recent history can be divided into two broad categories: authoritarian and participative. The participative institutions are emerging from the authoritarian institutions, so it is useless to argue about where one period ends and the other begins. However, we can begin to describe the old authoritarian period and predict the qualities of the new participative era. It is important to do this today because most of us have been—and probably still are—living and working in authoritarian institutions: families, schools, workplaces, governments. Equally important, most of us have not as yet experienced full participation. These facts make it difficult to start and sustain change. We do not as yet have a real perspective on the systems that bred us, and we often lack intimate knowledge of the alternative: participation.

For more than thirty centuries, authoritarianism has been the major form of governance throughout the world. Over that time, its expressions have changed. The methods of authoritarian control in Egyptian and Roman times differed from those of the feudal Middle Ages. The imperial and colonial policies of the eighteenth and nineteenth centuries differed from the authoritarian, capitalist or socialist command-and-control methods of the recent past.

The point is that, no matter where we go in our three-thousand-year trek through history, we are likely to find evidence of authoritarian governance. A small, elite group rules, "thinks," and determines goals and resource use. Its members may even act as institutional parents, while the majority of the population follows orders and implements policies. People serve the law and their leaders. They trade loyalty for protection, entitlements, and rewards. Status symbols, privilege, and patronage abound. People at the top are easily distinguishable from people at the bottom. Those at the top wear togas, jewelry, or neckties. They live in palaces or have plush corner offices. They ride in carriages or in luxury cars provided by their organization, while those at the bottom meet their personal needs on their own. In authoritarian institutions, ethical requirements are often double standards. The people at the top can drink at company lunches to close deals, use company or government supplies and equipment for personal needs, and barter power and sex. The people at the bottom lose their jobs and are jailed for the same behaviors. Finally, coercion, power over others, threats and fears of loss of position or access, and financial carrots and sticks keep people in line and ensure that they implement the leaders' vision of the institution's purpose and goals.

Some of the autocratic practices of the past are defensible but only in the context in which they occurred. Many centuries have been brutal and violent. People needed powerful protectors who could counter violence with violence. The rapid growth of industry in the nineteenth and twentieth centuries resulted partly from the mass production techniques, bureaucracy, and controlled decision processes that were part of the authoritarian package. The middle class grew as a result of these practices, and wealth spread beyond anything that small groups or individuals might have been able to achieve on their own.

Indeed, the authoritarianism of the past may have played a role in the overall increase in living standards and life span observed throughout the world. However, we believe that overt or covert oppression never has a moral justification. Nor is there an economic justification for taking thinking and creativity out of work. In today's world, where affluence, literacy, international and local transport, and information are increasing exponentially; human rights are expanding; and democracy is broadening, authoritarian practices are not only obsolete; they may also be criminal.

Even if some progress did occur under authoritarianism, authoritarianism, like every success, contains the seeds of its own destruction. For authoritarianism has a dark side. There are many signs that the world today is experiencing the cumulative effects of that dark side and that we are reaching the point of diminishing returns on authoritarian forms of governance.

In authoritarian systems, citizens, employees, and even customers are essentially subservient or—worse—disenfranchised and disempowered. The relationships between authoritarian leaders and their constituencies can be either dependent or hostile. In the more benign forms of autocracy, managers are institutional parents, while employees are loyal organizational children. This extension of family dependencies to larger institutional operations is extraordinarily widespread throughout the world. Even today, we hear senior managers complain that employees are not loyal even "after everything we've done for them."

Authorities have also used a variety of less benign methods to encourage subservience. In ancient times, brute force, extermination, and fear were common tools. To our shame, such tools are still used today. More recently, people in power have replaced physical coercion with material rewards and sanctions. In some organizations, it is common for senior officials to peer over their glasses at subordinates in the room and ask, "There are no more questions, are there?" or "Do you know what you are saying and who you are talking to?" Emotional coercion of this sort is just another form of authoritarianism. It sustains the superior-subordinate relationship.

One common way in which the more benign kind of coercion is expressed in corporations is what consultant Albert Koopman (Koopman, Nasser, and Nel, 1987) calls the *corporate cookie jar*. Managers control the manager-employee relationship by dangling an array of goodies—training; company cars; medical benefits; promotions; pay increases; membership in formal and informal social and sports clubs; corner offices; team membership on selected task forces; time with the president, chairman, or managing director; private parking spaces—before employees. The corporate cookie jar enables some managers to use material and financial rewards in ways that ostensibly seek to motivate but that actually promote subservience and ensure control by a few at the top.

Inequalities in organizational life appear to be multiplying, even as the global inequalities between haves and have-nots increase. For example, recent analyses of income levels in major British and

American corporations indicate that chief executives, chairpersons, and main board directors receive as much as a hundred times more than frontline workers. Whether such glaring discrepancies in wealth occur at the corporate, national, or international level, they haunt global and institutional peace and stability.

Authoritarian practices in the productive sector reflect discrimination in the social sector. They are business's own version of the British and French class systems before 1800, the caste systems of India, the Nazism of pre–World War II Germany, the rigid social hierarchies of imperial Japan, slavery and racism in the United States, and apartheid in South Africa. All these systems are expressions of authoritarian coercion and co-option. They coerce when a class, gender, or race is violently oppressed. They co-opt when the collective welfare and wealth of society or the institution are allocated in ways that favor privilege and opportunity and that go beyond appropriate compensation for the value that individuals add.

Business and government institutions all make use of authoritarian rule. Fortunately, business institutions have one built-in control: If they do not adapt, they go bankrupt. The public sector has no such rigorous feedback loops. It can use suboptimal governance methods for decades and still collect public revenues.

Authoritarian governance has another dark side. Its extractive and exploitative economic practices are creating massive problems for future generations. Authoritarian institutions and attitudes are decimating the world's forests, which means that they are reducing the earth's capacity to cleanse the atmosphere. Authoritarian systems have allowed vast tracts of land on all continents to turn into deserts. They have punched holes in the ozone layer and polluted the sky, soil, and sea. Taking only its own current interests into account, not the interests of the community and economy of the future, authoritarian exploitation is eradicating one species every twenty-five minutes. While it is entirely possible that participative institutions may make similar short-sighted decisions, participation at least means that there are legitimate forums where representatives of future generations can and must be heard. According to historian Paul Kennedy (1993), any form of governance that is based on an ethic of extraction and exploitation is not sustainable. He describes earth's sky, soil, seas, and society as a thin layer of life that we cannot exploit endlessly. We may already have gone too far.

Authoritarian governance is bringing about its own demise. The dramatic collapse of bureaucratic, central-command governments in Eastern Europe in the late 1980s and early 1990s signals the death throes of authoritarianism in that part of the world.

At the same time, nonparticipative and bureaucratically run organizations in Western capitalist systems are losing their capacity to survive and succeed. About two hundred of *Fortune* magazine's 1970 list of the 500 top companies have collapsed, disappeared, or been taken over by other organizations. Although some of the changes resulted from acquisitions and mergers, many of these organizations disappeared because they could not sustain their competitive advantage.

Such developments are not restricted to the United States. In Britain, Jaguar (now owned by Ford) and Rolls Royce are losing market share, as is Daimler Benz of Germany. Organizations that used to set the pace, such as Triumph and British Leyland, have all but disappeared from the international scene. Previously untouchable giants like General Motors and International Business Machines (I.B.M.) could follow if their performance does not improve over the poor levels of the early 1990s.

The continuation of authoritarian forms of governance in these institutions has undoubtedly played a role in their economic decline. Authoritarianism may not have caused it, but authoritarian systems are increasingly less able to harness the motivation and commitment of diverse stakeholders. They are less sensitive and responsive to the continuously changing competitive environment, and they are simply not flexible enough to refocus the organization's energies rapidly so as to remain competitive in the long run.

Even Japan, which has its own form of seniority-based authoritarianism, is in economic trouble. Akio Morita, chairman of Sony International, acknowledges that Japanese industry needs a new philosophy of management. Taichi Sakaiya (1991) says pointedly that Japan's inflexibility and its inability to adopt a new form of governance will undermine its international competitiveness, especially against American organizations.

With hindsight, we can see that, since the middle of the twentieth century, it has been increasingly impossible for organizations to succeed unless they renounce coercive management and resource abuse. The only real alternative is to redesign the macro and micro systems for participative governance. The hope is that participation will release the pent-up energy and problem-solving abilities of the masses while breaking the cycles of entitlement and dependency that increase the costs and excesses of authoritarianism.

THE SHIFT TO PARTICIPATION

So conditions as we enter the twenty-first century are ripe both for the decline of authoritarianism and for the rise of participation. This is a crossover time from one form of governance to another. The dynamics of this time resemble the simultaneous destruction and creation that occurs when one tectonic plate moves over another.

Continental masses are always on the move. They grind against each other, one slowly receding while the other moves inexorably upwards and over the submerging plate. The plates vie for space long before there is any disruption on the surface. Eventually, the visible surface begins to change. Upheavals occur, creating new rifts, mountains, and valleys. They make and destroy islands and change the shape of continents. Always, before the major changes, dramatic earthquakes occur.

We are living at the time when the participative plate is beginning to advance over the authoritarian plate. These two forms of governance have been grinding into each other for thousands of years. Records of battles for democracy date back to the Peloponnesian War in 400 B.C. when Sparta attempted to take over Athens. Just as tectonic plates cause great displacement and destruction when they shift, so this shift to participation and democracy will rank high on the Richter scale of human governance.

It is important to understand the deeper dynamics that are responsible for the changes and to see the depth and breadth of the shift. Only then can we understand tremors and aftershocks like those seen in the former Soviet Union early in 1994. Such developments are part of the change process, although they seem to be unstoppable regressions to autocratic values and methods. Aftershocks do not alter the fact that a fundamental change is now under way.

Although longstanding examples of the fully participative organization do not as yet exist, there are enough partial successes that we can start to paint a rough picture of what it will look like. It is not unlike the task that early explorers faced as they traced the shapes of continents. No explorer mapped the entire coastline of Africa or the Americas. Different people at different times gathered information about particular details: coastlines, plains, valleys, and mountains. Over time, long before anyone had entirely explored the new territories, there were remarkably accurate and useful maps that guided further exploration and led to further refinement. The challenge of discovering, describing, and mapping participation is similar to the situation that the early explorers faced.

A GLIMPSE OF PARTICIPATION

In the rest of this book, we will describe and explore the features of participative governance. At this point, it will be useful to examine some of the contrasting features of authoritarianism and participation. This will help to clarify the scope of the challenge. Figure 2.1 shows some of the tensions that result from these contrasts.

In an authoritarian system, managers think, and employees do. Thus, the formulation of strategy and the implementation of strategy are separate activities. In contrast, under participation, people with different roles think at the same time about the same things but not in the same way. Suppose, for example, that an engineer and an operator explore a production problem. The engineer focuses on intricate and long-term design solutions, while the operator points out the practical limitations and suggests operational alternatives. Or suppose that a truck driver and an accountant discuss costs together. The driver contributes thoughts on payloads, timing, and routing. The accountant analyses the costs of leasing or purchasing trucks. Or a company director may manage the process of strategy development, while salespersons discover new market opportunities and bring their insights to the strategy forum for debate.

Figure 2.1 Some Transition Tensions

Authoritarianism	Some Transition Tensions	Participation
Managers *think*, employees *do*.	Powerful forces for change • new information • environment • globalization • production technology • the new workforce • the customer as "boss"	People in various roles think about the same things from different perspectives.
People in senior positions *manage*.		People everywhere are self-managing, with formal leaders using authority-based control as a last resort.
People at the top matter most. Many systems serve them and their information needs.	Imbedded and habitual practices and traditions Resistance to change	Everyone's rights, accountability, and dignity are honored and supported.
Knowledge is an important asset for personal power and gain. Teaching occurs from top to bottom.	Business school reinforcement of authoritarian practices and values Mistaken assumptions that changing one or two practices equals total governance change	Learning and sharing knowledge are key values. People teach each other in all directions.
Formal leaders are superiors.	Use of the language of participation to describe authoritarian practices	Formal leaders are stewards.
Shareholders are primary or exclusion stakeholders.	Time to develop participation skills Time to learn about what moves in participation	Customers, shareholders, employees, and future generations are stakeholders.
Etcetera	Etcetera	Etcetera

In an authoritarian system, people in senior positions are management. They manage the workplace. In a participative environment, most employees are self-managing. They direct their own work flow. There are still formal leaders who are accountable for the organization's strategic positioning, but they are no longer isolated up there far from the bustle of the organization. They are part of a leadership alliance (Peters, 1988). A leadership alliance involves everyone in work and information that traditionally have been the prerogative of management.

In authoritarian systems, people at the top matter most. There are many systems and programs to use and support their skills and brains. In contrast, the participative organization honors and actively supports the dignity, rights, and responsibilities of all.

People in traditional systems often guard and hoard knowledge and use it for power and position. In participative institutions, such behavior is considered to be theft of knowledge capital. Learning and sharing knowledge are two key values. People teach one another, and everyone is a learner. The learning flow can be toward management as well as from it. Formal leaders are stewards, not superiors.

The definitions of performance also vary. In the authoritarian system, performance is often short-term and focused on the financial gain of shareholders. In the participative organization, performance focuses on the customer, on the adding of value, on beneficiation, and on the ability to replenish. The focus of participation is on short- and long-term value and on satisfying multiple stakeholders. People everywhere in the system are equally responsible for creating it. For example, workers have both rights and responsibilities. They can recall leaders who do not lead, and they must accept the personal consequences of their own failure to perform and participate.

THE TENACITY OF AUTHORITARIANISM

The shift to participative governance has been slow, a matter of fits and starts. This should not be surprising. The authoritarian way of life is woven into the very fabric of human existence. Entire subsystems still reflect the old relationships and assumptions. For example, many of the world's business schools still teach theories of management that reinforce authoritarian ways of thinking. Even today, it is not unusual to hear a lecturer (an authoritarian method of education) tout management's prerogative to plan, organize, control, and motivate. The processes themselves have value, but the implicit message of power over others resounds through the ivy-covered halls.

The fact is that governance systems are remarkably tenacious. Every institution that has tried to entrench participative forms of governance can attest to the sheer complexity and turbulence involved in making such a shift. For one thing, no matter how quickly or thoroughly the transition is managed, it is years before old habits, practices, and traditions disappear. It also takes time to learn what works and what does not work and to build the skills that formal leaders and all staff members need in order to contribute fully and responsibly in the participative enterprise.

Institutions have built-in antibodies to major change. They behave like the human body when it receives a transplant: by isolating and then attacking the invader. The new organ often dies before it can begin to function effectively. Pervasive structures, practices, and lines of communication and the thousands of daily interactions that make up the governance of a system together exert a force that is more than capable of overwhelming anything new.

Resistance sometimes takes the form of denial. After one or two participative actions, executives declare the battle won. They and others begin to use the new governance language as though naming it means that the new governance exists. In the meantime, authoritarian practices remain alive and well. Or, if they are not well, the old ways struggle tenaciously to maintain the status quo.

In spite of all this, the move toward participation as the prevailing form of governance in the workplace and the world continues to gain momentum. Its moral superiority and its capacity to outperform authoritarian systems guarantee its advance.

CONCLUSION

It is difficult to say whether institutions in the past would have been better off if participative practices had been used. With hindsight, we can say that the violent, exploitative, and co-optive forms of authoritarian governance that have characterized most of the world's institutions for three thousand years are immoral and fundamentally flawed. Although moral pronouncements may be in order, we are where we are. Human institutions on this planet have developed immense capacities despite the horror of some of their methods. But now, with both hindsight and foresight, we must consciously choose how we will channel resources and govern private and public institutions in the years that lie ahead.

Participation seems to be a desirable option. At least the foundations of participation make sense both in theory and in moral terms. But is participation a wild-eyed ideal, a figment of naive minds? Can participative institutions perform in the real world? And can they outperform the institutions that use authoritarian practices?

Participation as a total system of governance is new to both political and economic institutions. So we cannot answer these questions with tradition or with years of consistent research results. But, as the next chapter shows, there is an increasingly compelling economic case for participation. The bottom line is that participative institutions outperform their authoritarian counterparts.

CHAPTER 3

The Profits
of Participation

PARTICIPATION APPEARS TO BE a logical response to today's conditions and challenges. Many would agree that it has an innate moral and ethical rightness. But does it make economic sense? Do organizations perform better when people are involved than when they are not? As we note later, participation takes time. It encourages conflict, and it must therefore address conflict. It requires meetings and discussions, and it creates a great demand for information and communication. Participation is therefore costly.

However, research conducted since the mid 1980s strongly suggests that participation is worth the price. Companies that constantly and broadly involve their people in what used to be managerial work are more productive and financially successful than companies that do not. Several comprehensive studies provide strong evidence that participation delivers. These studies focus on the use of what researchers call high-performance work practices. As you will see, the work practices that lead to high performance are participative practices.

CROSS-INDUSTRY STUDIES

A number of recent studies across industries show very strong economic reasons for adopting participative work practices. This section summarizes the results of some comprehensive studies.

▪ Research by Dennis Kravetz

In the mid 1980s, management consultant Dennis Kravetz (1988) set out to describe the human resource practices used by financially successful companies. He selected 150 companies and used their financial performance over five years as described in Standard and Poor's Index terms to classify them as most or least successful. Then he interviewed representatives of each company about the company's human resource practices. These were his findings:

» Companies that used the most progressive and participative human resource practices significantly outperformed companies that did not—over five years, they had 1.6 times the growth in sales, 4.15 times the growth in profits, 1.8 times the growth in equity, 1.6 times better current-year profits, 1.09 times greater price-earnings ratios, and 1.46 times better dividend growth.

» High-performing and low-performing firms showed significant differences in work practices—high-performing firms made much greater use of progressive and participative practices.

Table 3.1 shows the differences. Kravetz (1988) did not try to show whether outstanding financial performance caused a company to use the practices listed in Table 3.1 or whether the use of these practices improves performance. But he did show that outstanding financial performance and use of the practices listed are likely to occur together. His research also emphasizes the importance of systems of practices. High-performing organizations make more use of progressive practices than low-performing organizations do.

▪ Research at Columbia University

Columbia University has been investigating the relationship between human resource practices and economic performance since 1986. Assisted financially in the later stages by the Alfred P. Sloan

Table 3.1 Work Practices in High-Performing
and Low-Performing Firms

Work Practice	High-Performing Firms	Low-Performing Firms
Company culture emphasizes people.	90%	20%
Company uses a participative style of management.	70%	4%
Pay is related to group or individual performance.	86%	30%
Employees have clear goals for the firm and for themselves.	80%	26%
Company encourages creativity.	62%	10%
Company gives more than six days of formal management training per year.	60%	12%
Company uses the latest communication technology—teleconferencing, electronic mail (E-mail), fax.	72%	28%
Company encourages employee stock ownership.	96%	56%
Company uses latest workplace technology.	94%	56%
Company uses outside training.	76%	40%
Company has formal and integrated career programs.	66%	30%
Employees work at home.	40%	8%
Company uses technical training.	74%	38%
Jobs are more generalist than specialist.	50%	25%
Company makes deliberate efforts to hire the best people.	54%	30%
Company employs part-time people.	54%	30%
Company is highly decentralized.	82%	62%

Foundation and the Columbia University Center for Japanese Economy and Business, researchers have collaborated with Carnegie Mellon University, the World Bank, and the U.S. Department of Labor to conduct a number of studies. Two studies draw landmark conclusions regarding the economic impact of participative practices. The first, led by David Lewin (1988), covered 495 organizations. It reached several noteworthy conclusions:

» Companies that share profits and gains with employees have significantly better financial performance than companies that do not.

» Companies that share information broadly and that have broad programs of employee involvement (the researchers refer to information sharing and involvement as areas of intellectual participation) perform significantly better than companies that are run autocratically.

» Flexible work design—flexible hours, rotation and job enlargement, multiskilling—is significantly related to financial success.

» Training and development have a positive effect on business financial performance.

» The existence of formal grievance procedures to protect employee rights significantly affects the bottom line in both unionized and nonunionized companies.

» Companies that combine group economic participation, intellectual participation, flexible job design, and training and development get an added productivity boost—two-thirds of the difference observed in bottom-line impact was due to the combined effect of these practices.

Lewin (1988) and Kravetz (1988) studied primarily participative work practices. But Lewin's (1988) research went further, because he and his colleagues used statistical techniques to identify causal relationships between human resource practices and bottom-line performance. Thus, the conclusions just reviewed tell us that participative practices are not just related to financial success. They actually help to cause it.

■ Research by Mark Huselid

Many studies have made clear that participative work practices affect absenteeism, turnover, and productivity, which in turn influence financial performance. Evidence is now accumulating that systems of practices, not individual and isolated practices, make a significant difference on all measures. Nevertheless, many issues remain obscure.

The unanswered questions involve causality—what causes what? Data gathering and data interpretation also pose problems. Mark Huselid and Brian Becker (Huselid and Becker, 1995) decided to do some statistical work to clarify causal relationships and reduce the uncertainties associated with research methods.

Huselid was especially concerned about the possibility that firms with the best financial performance might be more able than others to afford the use of high-involvement work practices. If that were the case, it would inflate the impact of the use of such practices. However, if low-performing firms—firms in crisis—were more apt than others to use high-involvement practices—perhaps in desperation—it would diminish the impact of the use of these practices. He also wanted to resolve such problems as these: interpreting the fact that a firm has a policy as evidence that the firm practices the policy (often it does not), the effects of resource factors—for example, technology—other than human resources, the possibility that the only people who respond to questionnaires are people who are interested in and use progressive work practices (response rates can be as low as 3 percent).

Drawing on U.S. Department of Labor data, Huselid (1995) selected thirteen work practices—information sharing, job analysis, attitude surveys, labor-management participation, group-based incentive pay, formal training, performance appraisals, performance-related pay, promotion on merit (as opposed to promotion by seniority), depth of backup talent for positions, hiring from within, intensity of selection screening, and formal grievance procedures—as his independent variables. He grouped these practices, which are generally associated with participative governance, under three heads: employee skills and organization structures (the first six items), employee motivation (the next three items), and other human resource practices (the last four items).

Huselid (1995) surveyed 826 firms in 1992 about their financial results and work practices, and Huselid and Becker (1995) surveyed 748 firms in 1994. The organizations represented a variety of industries. After the second survey, Huselid and Becker (1995) examined the performance and work practices of the 222 firms that had responded to both surveys. They submitted the resulting data to a variety of statistical corrections and reached six conclusions:

» Participative work practices are significantly associated with decreased turnover, increased productivity, and improved financial performance.

» Participative practices have a substantial impact on financial results; each standard deviation increase in their use increases a company's market value by anywhere between $35,000 and $80,000 per employee.

» High-performance work practices reduce turnover and absenteeism.

» High-performance work practices have strong positive effects on performance even when other policies, practices, and the technology used within an organization are not progressive.

» Firms vary widely in the extent to which they adopt more-progressive work practices; many firms have not yet adopted a range of such practices; the ones that have thus have a definite competitive advantage.

» Implementing participative practices appears to have a short-term cost; increases in their use were associated with temporary drops in cash flow and negative gross return on assets.

One possible explanation of the last finding is that firms in crisis may be more willing than others to invest aggressively in such practices. Another possibility is that progressive firms are more likely than others to make cost-intensive investments in information and work technologies that affect cash position and current ratios. Because performance experts everywhere are asking how to speed the adoption of high-performance work practices and shorten the time needed for changes in work practices to pay off, these possibilities merit further study.

Although the practices in Huselid's (1995) list are predominantly participative, they can be challenged as only partially progressive. Job analyses, performance appraisals, attitude surveys, and the like can indeed be used to increase employee involvement. But they can also be implemented autocratically. Nevertheless, his study is comprehensive, and it does show that firms that attend to human resource issues and increase participation outperform firms that do not. In the future, research will need to define the nature of the practices that it is evaluating more carefully in the future than it has in the past.

■ Lessons from the Automotive Supply Industry

Susan Helper and Laura Leete of the Department of Economics at Case Western Reserve University (Helper and Leete, 1995) studied the impact of twenty-three human resource practices on absenteeism and turnover in 230 manufacturing plants that supplied the U.S. and Canadian auto industry. The range of practices that they investigated and the diversity of the firms that they surveyed—the automotive supply industry in fact includes a broad array of companies that manufacture products ranging from electronics to glass—make their work useful for all companies.

The investigators grouped the twenty-three practices under eight heads: performance-related pay (profit sharing, gain sharing, team pay, job pay), control (quality circles, labor-management committees, extent of union control, extent of cooperation, workers' expectations to make improvements), input (formal improvement process, suggestions made, suggestions implemented), support (workers receive help, supervisors act as coaches), safeguards (productivity increases do not lead to layoffs, managers take pay cuts if there are layoffs, workers are hired for the long term, the organization has formal grievance procedures, layoffs are not used in any circumstance), flexibility (workers make simple repairs, tasks are varied), training, and relative compensation.

The study reached these conclusions: First, job breadth and flexibility, combined with supportive supervisor behaviors, significantly reduced absenteeism. Second, job breadth and flexibility, combined with high relative compensation and work group control over decisions, significantly reduced turnover. Third, team-based pay, not individual incentive or companywide pay schemes, had a positive impact on performance. Fourth, training was associated with low turnover, but the direction of causality was not clear.

The researchers assumed that absenteeism and turnover were related in significant ways to productivity and financial performance. They drew on the generally accepted and long-standing findings of industrial relations research that show a direct and causal connection between financial performance on the one hand and absenteeism and turnover on the other. The studies by Huselid (1994, 1995) validated these connections. The research by Helper and Leete (1995) confirms the need for systems of high-performance, participative work practices. But their conclusions show that certain combinations of practices have especially noteworthy effects.

INDUSTRY-SPECIFIC STUDIES

Some recent work has approached the connection between participative, high-performance work practices and economic performance by investigating specific industries in depth. This section focuses on extensive industry-specific studies that used multiple data-gathering techniques and covered a large proportion of firms and plants within the industry. The lessons that emerge apply to all industries.

■ *The Steel Industry*

Later research at Columbia University dug deeper into the mystery of the causes of a company's financial success. A team of researchers led by Casey Ichniowski of the Columbia University Graduate School of Business and Kathryn Shaw of Carnegie-Mellon University (Ichniowski and Shaw, 1995) conducted a rigorous study of forty-two steel production lines in twenty-six plants and twenty-one companies—80 percent of the lines that still exist in the United States. The study concluded that it is systems of participation, not isolated programs, that have the real impact on a firm's bottom line. Here are some of the study's most remarkable conclusions:

» Isolated and disconnected practices of participation have little or no impact on the bottom line—what makes a difference is the presence of systems of cooperative labor-management relations and participative practice; plants that have such systems are significantly more productive than others.

» Unionization has no effect on performance levels; unionized plants are found among both high- and low-performing plants; performance depends on the human resource management practices that the firm has implemented.

» Units that scored highest on an index of participation (that is, in employing a variety of participative practices) were 7.5 percent more productive than units that used no or only a few involvement practices.

» High-performance work practices had a 13 percent higher yield of prime-quality steel than traditional practices—in other words, high-performance work practices boost quality performance.

Clearly, systems of high-performance work practices make a substantial difference in performance. These findings also remind us that other factors, such as technology, play an important role. Most important, because the investigators controlled rigorously for all potential causes of success except participation, we can generalize their conclusions to other industries.

■ *The Apparel Industry*

Two recent in-depth studies looked at the impact of modular production in the apparel industry. Under the principle of modular production, small groups of people operate in a participative way to produce garments. One study (Berg, Appelbaum, Bailey, and Kalleberg, 1995), which focused on three companies and six plants and which compared performance practices in modular production schemes with the practices in traditional assembly line operations, examined a full array of market, technological, and human resource factors that could have an effect on financial performance. The investigators conducted structured interviews with plant managers, human resource and training staff, union officials, company executives, and employees selected at random from each occupation represented in the plants.

The study found that, at $37.55 per dozen, the total cost of producing a garment was significantly lower for modules than it was for assembly lines, where the total cost was $55.64 per dozen. Workers in modules described significantly greater changes in productivity and quality and better overall product and work group quality than assembly line workers. Workers in modules also reported significantly greater autonomy, ownership, variety, importance, and feedback relative to their job. The employees in modules were significantly more likely than those in traditional structures to participate, rotate jobs, and engage in formal training. These are all high-involvement work practices. Moreover, employees in modules have better labor-management relations than others, and they are more likely to report that they are treated fairly and feel secure in their work.

However, the employees in modules were also more likely to report high levels of stress, and their reports of job satisfaction were no higher than those of employees working under less progressive practices. One plausible explanation is specific to the industry: The work is not very interesting, and the pay is low. However, the relationship between stress and participation is worth further study.

A second investigation of practices in the apparel industry, conducted by John T. Dunlop of Harvard University and David Weil of Boston University (Dunlop and Weil, 1995), provides hard evidence that the participative modular work units have a positive impact on performance. Drawing on a database of eighty-four companies that produced approximately 30 percent of the total value of apparel products, these investigators concluded that participative units performed significantly better than the traditional bundle system in five areas: operating profits as a percentage of sales, work-in-process inventory, stock-outs, speed of production, and lead time to fill orders. Modules did not perform as well as the bundle system in the area of goods delivered on time, but they had an average lead time of fifty-three days, while the assembly lines had an average of ninety-six days.

Despite the significantly improved performance of employees working in modules, the second study found that only 10 percent of all garment assembly in the apparel industry takes place in modules. A second look suggested one possible reason why: Modules and the high-performance practices associated with them are likely to coincide with certain other manufacturing practices in response to product market factors: innovations in information handling (for example, retailers are connected electronically with manufacturers), streamlined and just-in-time distribution operations, and use of computers and automation in design and assembly. The researchers drew four generalizable—and sensible—conclusions:

» Customer-, market-, and product-related factors affect the speed with which innovative work practices are adopted.

» The prevailing production technology influences the selection and implementation of human resource practices.

» Decisions about human resource practices are not the only decisions that affect an organization's ability to be high performing.

» Human resource practices make a significant difference in performance.

The second study shows also that firms are more likely to adopt more-participative practices when market- and technology-related factors require and support them than when they do not.

■ *The Automobile Industry*

Jean Paul MacDuffie (1995) of the University of Pennsylvania has been tracking the use of so-called lean production practices in the automobile industry since 1986. His research, which involved eighty-six plants spread around the world, has focused on high-performance work practices and on a variety of other, related technological and productivity practices: use of problem-solving groups, team-based production, and robotics; low use of in-process buffers, such as inventory; low incoming parts inventories; job rotation; training; contingent compensation, including pay for knowledge; general automation; high model mix; and complexity of parts.

MacDuffie (1995) identifies five performance groups distinguished by performance indexes ranging from 15.8 (best) through 21.8, 22.7, and 30.3 to 93.6 (worst). Here are his conclusions:

» The best-performing plants perform well in all practice areas and make significantly more use of high-performance practices than low-performing plants.

» Plants that recently implemented team approaches had consistently lower productivity than others, but plants that had a long history of teams had the best performance of all.

» Most plants in the industry are using at least some elements of lean production or high-performance work practices; as a result, performance is converging across regions around the globe—the inescapable inference being that high-performance practices are becoming not a key differentiator but a necessary condition simply for staying in the game.

» The relationship between high-performance work practices and performance is not linear for any single practice; the evidence suggests that sets of interrelated practices, not one single best practice, are most effective.

» Regions differ in their readiness to adopt innovative practices.

To expand on the last point, the use of teams is increasing rapidly in Europe, but the United States and Australia are still relatively low in this area. Performance-related compensation and training are rising rapidly in Europe and Australia, but they have made little headway in the United States. U.S. and European plants have made large reductions in incoming inventory, while in Japan and Australia inventory is increasing. This finding indicates that regional and cultural factors do play a role but that they do not override the positive effects of high-performance practices across regions.

OTHER RESEARCH RESULTS

The discovery of the impact on productivity of systems of participation carries a vital lesson that has been echoed in other quarters. A 1990 conference on pay and productivity sponsored by the Brookings Institution investigated the relationship between pay and bottom-line performance. The organizers did not intend to focus on participation. Yet when all the results were in, the conference leader, Alan S. Blinder, was forced to conclude that "changing the way workers are treated may boost productivity more than changing the way they are paid, although profit sharing or employee stock ownership combined with worker participation may be the best system of all" (Blinder, 1990, p. 13). Moreover, "worker participation apparently helps make alternative compensation plans like profit sharing, gain sharing, and [employee stock ownership plans] work better and also has beneficial effects of its own. This theme, which was totally unexpected when I organized the conference, runs strongly through all papers" (Blinder, 1990, p. 13).

David I. Levine and Laura D'Andrea Tyson (1990) offer one possible explanation. Their contribution to the Brookings Institution conference concludes: "Psychologists, other behavioral scientists, and some economists stress a complementary link between participatory arrangements and cooperative behavior among firm members. This link focuses on the possible effects of participation on such factors as the workers' commitment to the firm's goals, their trust in the firm's managers, and their sense of goodwill toward other firm members. One broad interpretation is that participation may actually change the goals of the workers so that they more closely conform to the goals of the firm" (Levine and Tyson, 1990, p. 187). No matter what the reason may be, contributions to the Brookings Institution conference support the position that systems or collections of high-involvement work practices have a significant effect on performance.

Sam Stern (1992) picks up on participation as a cause of productivity in a different but important way in a study of people practices and corporate creativity. His study focused on the human resource practices associated with corporate creativity in Japan. The first and second most cited sources of corporate creativity were fellow employees and customers. Innovation thus grows out of involvement and free exchange of information.

A five-year study by John Kotter and James Heskett (Kotter and Heskett, 1992) of 207 U.S. companies in twenty-two industries found that the financially successful companies focused first on fulfilling customer and employee needs and only secondarily on profits. This research indicates that when companies focus on all key stakeholders and when they expect leadership from all employee levels, they outperform their competitors by wide margins. As Table 3.2 shows, the performance gap between representatives of the high-performance and low-performance cultures is enormous.

Table 3.2 Financial Performance of High-Performance and Low-Performance Cultures

Increase over Eleven Years	High-Performance Cultures	Low-Performance Cultures
Revenue growth	682%	166%
Employment growth	282%	36%
Stock price growth	901%	74%
Net income growth	756%	1%

After investigating the state of governance in five nations—Japan, Germany, United Kingdom, United States, and France—Jonathan Charkham (1994) came to similar conclusions. He relates the economic success of companies to two qualities: their dynamism and their accountability. He acknowledges that many external factors—national policy, culture, and so forth—affect these qualities. But he also concludes that the most successful institutions tend to be networked. That is, their operations tend to be cooperative rather than confrontational, well informed rather than ill informed, and collegiate rather than individualistic. While the author's main concern is executive- and board-level operations, these values are those of more participative systems.

CONCLUSION

Evidence is building that the shift toward increasing involvement is not just morally right and not just a response to pressures from the masses. Participation shows positive impacts on productivity. Practices in the highest-performing organizations across industries are practices that optimize involvement.

The research on high-performance work practices and organizational performance justifies the following conclusions: First, high-performance practices are participative practices. Although researchers have yet to identify the full set of practices that causes high performance, it is clear that the formal and informal work practices that lead to high performance are practices that provide structure and support for involvement by all employees.

Second, systems of practices, not isolated practices, make the difference. Until the late 1980s, research focused on finding the practice or practices that "really" made a difference in performance. Research studies show clearly that success is not the result of individual practices. Organizations need a critical mass of mutually reinforcing practices in order to get significant performance gains.

Third, systems of participative practices have a strong impact on performance. Studies show that the amount of impact differs in individual cases, but they agree that systems of high-performance practices have a very strong impact on financial performance and on factors like absenteeism and turnover that have proven implications for the bottom line.

Fourth, the context of product and market is important—especially for decisions to adopt new work practices. Business strategies, customer requirements, and industry competitiveness are some of the factors that affect the types of human resource practices that a firm requires. They also seem to play a role in determining how quickly and thoroughly a firm adopts participative, high-performance work practices. However, this factor of strategic fit seems to affect the form and the magnitude of various governance practices, not the nature of the practices themselves. Practices that support, reflect, and structure high involvement are emerging as best practices regardless of external, industry, and strategic conditions. Research shows that participative, high-performance work practices have positive effects on performance whether work is complex or simple, repetitive or intellectual, proceduralized or unique.

CHAPTER 4

Bringing Together
the Essential Levers
for Change

TODAY'S RESEARCH on productive organizations is beginning to make a very important point: One or two participative actions do not make an organization effective. The move to participative governance requires a broad and fundamental change in the genetic code of our institutions. Such a change in turn affects how virtually everything operates. Until now, the genetic code in organizations has been authoritarian. Authoritarian genes are everywhere—in all systems, practices, and interactions. The shift to the new governance paradigm requires the equivalent of a genetic reengineering of the organization. The changes may not happen all at once, but the institution will be propelled into the new era only if sufficient changes occur simultaneously. And early "transplants" of participation into an alien authoritarian culture will require lots of support if they are to escape rejection.

The chapters in Part Two of this book describe nine high-leverage areas on which the genetic reengineering for participation must focus: values, structures, leadership, management processes, information, relationships, competencies, controls, and pay practices. We have not chosen these nine areas because they account for all facets of an organization. Rather, they are important because they have leverage: They send powerful messages throughout the system, and they influence other systems, practices, and interactions. By bringing the principles of participative governance to these nine areas, we can create a context within which the organization's deep-seated genetic code has a good chance of changing.

These nine areas exist now in every institution. They reinforce one another. Together, they entrench authoritarian governance in ways that no organization chart can reflect. Their interweaving creates a very durable and resistant organizational fabric. Any attempt to introduce ad hoc or isolated participative practices in such an environment is bound to fail. It is like putting water on a waterproof fabric. The water cannot penetrate. It beads and rolls off. The fabric has been designed to be waterproof. Every part works together to make it so. That is why so many well-intended but partial change efforts have failed or had disappointing results. They simply cannot sink in under the existing governance rules.

Our work, learning, and research lead us to conclude that the nine elements that we have identified are the primary carriers of the organization's genetic code. By focusing on these few levers, we use an important insight from the science of complexity: Because organizations are dynamic and complicated systems, they cannot be perfectly controlled. But there are major forces—scientists call them *attractors*—that consistently influence a system's behavior. If you can influence these forces, then you can affect the whole system. Influence them all or most of them, and the system will change. The key, of course, is to reengineer them all, weaving them into a tight and resistant web of self-reinforcing and participative governance.

VALUES

Values are deep and often invisible controlling forces within an organization. More than any other element, they determine the nature of governance. They are often grounded in unconscious and deeply embedded assumptions about the world in which we work. Governance values have been shaped over decades, even centuries of experience, learning, and reinforcement. The deeply ingrained governance values often become conscious only when they are challenged or threatened. In the absence of challenge or threat, we act and respond without asking whether the underlying values are valid or acceptable.

An organization's values are a key thread in its governance system. If the values are authoritarian, then we create hierarchies, disempower people, insist that managers have prerogatives without responsibilities, create rigid control mechanisms, underline authority with status symbols and patronage, restrict access to information, and treat people as subordinates.

Participative values invalidate such practices and drive us to different responses. If the old values, which are remarkably tenacious, are allowed to survive, then it is impossible to sustain change. Ultimately, the old values will digest and absorb any new initiatives. The new governance requires new reference points guiding what we do, what we accept, and what we will not tolerate.

STRUCTURES

Structures express our philosophy of governance. Participative governance cannot live in structures that were designed to support authoritarianism. The participative enterprise values empowerment, personal accountability, open access to information, and a focus on the customer. These values cannot thrive in an authoritarian hierarchy under chains of command. Therefore, an organization's structures must be redesigned to reflect and reinforce transparency, to ease access across levels and functions, to organize work as a flow from the customer through the organization to suppliers, and to help people operate in a variety of self-managing teams.

LEADERSHIP

Leadership is about breaking new ground, going beyond the known, and creating the future. It is also about helping people to settle into new territory that gives them hope for the future. The new governance requires leadership to create it. The new governance also requires a new kind of leadership that does not depend on the superiority and subordination that supported leadership in the past. New leaders help to create capacity in their people. They give up their need to be treated as customers and instead become the stewards of all the organization's stakeholders. If leaders do not make their behavior congruent with the needs of the participative enterprise, then no real change in governance is possible. Anyone who has tried to help an organization change knows this is true: People who have formal power must operate according to participative values. Old-style leaders cannot have a changed organization unless they themselves change.

MANAGEMENT PROCESSES

Management processes include all the major actions that relate to the formulation and implementation of strategy. Management processes are vital threads in the participative fabric because they are central to the organization's economic success and because they are powerful determinants of the organization's culture. If strategy, plans, budgets, goals, decisions, and feedback occur in authoritarian ways, then participation can only be theoretical. If strategy, plans, budgets, goals, decisions, and feedback occur in participative ways, then the values of the new governance will come alive and take root. Any organization that wants to make participation the norm must deliberately redesign these management process events and help everyone to develop the skills and disciplines needed to make them work according to the new rules.

INFORMATION

Information provides the context in which people work. If access to information is narrow, fragmented, and controlled by authorities, then this context creates the conditions of authoritarian governance. If access is broad, integrated, and open to all, then the context enables participative governance. People need to be able to access and use information in order to take charge of their own work life. Such access and use go hand in hand with empowerment, high-performance teams, and accountability.

Access to information and the ability to use it to influence decisions are the ultimate determinants of power. Whoever has information has power. Those who do not have information are disempowered.

Without it, leaders cannot be accountable, structures become hopelessly bureaucratic, and relationships turn brittle with suspicion. Authoritarian institutions restrict access to information. Participative institutions expand it. No organization can become truly participative unless it restructures and rechannels information so that everyone has what he or she needs for empowered performance.

RELATIONSHIPS

Relationships are both the building blocks and probably the most telling indicators of the new governance. In fact, the genetic code of the organization is embedded in the thousands of interactions that occur every day between people everywhere in the organization. This fact gives relationships a unique power. At their heart are observable and describable human behaviors. These behaviors are the smallest expressions of participation or authoritarianism within an enterprise. As such, they are very manageable units of change. In the authoritarian organization, relationship behaviors are hierarchical and dependent. They are often also manipulative. In the participative organization, relationship behaviors are interdependent.

That formal authority continues to have levels even under participative governance does not mean perpetual subordination. In the new governance, people work together as necessary to serve customers. They respect each other, and they tell the truth, regardless of level or status. In the new governance, it is common to see people with lesser authority coaching their organizational "superiors" in the areas in which they have special expertise. Without this kind of reversibility, there can be no real participation.

In spite of what the organization's vision, values, and mission statements say, the interactions that people have with each other—their relationships—are the best indicators of the real governance of an organization. As an old African saying wisely observes: People see what you say long before the words leave your mouth.

COMPETENCIES

Competencies are the personal resources that help to make a system of governance work. Authoritarian organizations focus on the competencies of the people in authority. People in control need to be able to plan, organize, control, motivate, and deal with the alienation among employees that often results from dependency, secrecy, and lack of responsibility. They must develop the human resource systems that keep people loyal and tied to the organization.

Because the new governance asks everyone to become a responsible partner in the effort to make the business successful, it requires everyone to broaden his or her competencies. Without a broadened business knowledge and the array of skills needed for self-management and participation, the general worker or the professional in an organization cannot perform new roles. Without new leadership competencies, authorities do not know how to use power differently. Participative governance is impossible if all parties cannot perform their new roles. The organization will revert to authoritarian ways.

CONTROLS

Regardless of the form of governance, every organization needs controls. Controls are the checks and balances that keep things on track and prevent costly errors. They provide the criteria and the warning systems that establish replicable processes, create stability, and prevent anarchy.

Controls can be external or internal, imposed or self-generated. How they are developed and enforced reflects and reinforces the values of the prevailing governance system. In the authoritarian organization, management creates the controls, mandates their use, then often has to keep close watch in order to ensure compliance. In the participative organization, people help to develop the goals and indicators that underlie the controls. They help to decide on the consequences of nonconformance. Beyond this, in the participative organization, participation promotes the individual's sense of commitment and heightens his or her responsibility for the success of the enterprise. It creates conditions for increased self-control.

The organization's control mechanisms are therefore important levers for authoritarianism or participation. How they are developed and enforced creates a powerful force that pulls the organization toward one or the other form of governance.

PAY

Pay is a tangible signal about what is important in an organization. It is an exceptionally powerful message about governance because it is very personal: People see their pay as feedback about their individual worth and about what is valued at work. Pay is an emotive and generally a "hot" issue. It has little proven ability to motivate and great ability to demotivate. It unmistakably directs people's attention to specific areas of performance. But if people feel manipulated by the pay system or if they are not deeply committed to the values that it has been designed to support, they may subvert it for their own ends.

The pay system plays an important part in creating and sustaining an institution's governance. Pay cannot effectively develop relationships, but it can undermine them. It has limited capacity to control, but it can help to link activity with output. If pay systems are secretive and manipulative, if they reward competitiveness and punish mistakes, and if the organization has no or few other sources of feedback and reward, then pay will help to sustain authoritarianism. However, if pay encourages teamwork and learning and if it has clear links to the overall success of the enterprise and its customers, it will encourage participation.

THE NEED FOR CONGRUENCE

The shift from authoritarian to participative governance is a fundamental one. It affects and transforms thousands of behaviors and assumptions. What organization has the time and ingenuity to make all those changes? Probably none. What we suggest is to simplify the solution: Go for leverage. Focus on the major organizational elements that, if changed, will have repercussions on virtually every aspect of the institution's interactions and life.

Are the nine areas that we have just reviewed the only high-leverage areas? We cannot say. There may be others. Each of these nine areas is mentioned regularly in the literature on transforming change. Our own experience shows that the failure of any of the nine areas to change consistently drains energy away from the larger change process. Authoritarianism is a tenacious form of governance. As long as any of the nine areas remains authoritarian, it remains an outpost from which the old system can attack and discredit the new. We have seen this happen when pay systems do not change, when structures remain rigidly hierarchic, when management processes remain exclusive and authoritarian, and when leaders behave as they did in the past while asking others in the organization to behave in new ways. Commitment to the new governance is not a matter of picking and choosing what we want to change. It means a commitment to transformation.

As for the sequence of the nine areas, there are no absolute answers. In this book, we present the pieces in the order that makes sense to us. That is, we suggest that values, structures, and leadership should be addressed early. We think that pay systems (because they raise many emotional issues) should be addressed later when people know more about the relatively intrinsic rewards associated with other aspects of participative governance.

We argue in Chapter Eighteen that there must be enough change going on at any time to ensure a critical mass. Both authors have been involved in change efforts in which things happened so slowly or in such isolation that they never took root. Doing several things at once may seem risky, but it is the only way to get the momentum and benefit that give you any chance of success.

No one can yet point to a situation in which an organization has changed in all nine areas of governance and lived with the changes on a sustained basis. But as was true for fifteenth-century explorers, we do have the outlines of a valid governance map. It may still be a bit rough and imprecise in areas, but the map is accurate enough to keep us from getting hopelessly lost. And by using the map to find our way, we will undoubtedly perfect it quite rapidly.

We have many converging reasons for presenting a systems view of participation in which the nine areas are the key outline of the governance map. Here are three: First, as Chapter Three shows, research into effective organizations is beginning to point out that participation needs systems. One or a few participative practices simply do not make that much difference in performance. Second, in our work with organizations to change various of the nine areas, we have found that the others invariably interfere and must be addressed. Third, as sociologists and scientists clarify their understanding about how complex organizations work, the notion of change by changing key levers or attractors is becoming increasingly credible. The chapters in Part Two of this book discuss each of these nine high-leverage areas in detail.

We have found that, if people are to initiate and sustain the transition from authoritarian to participative governance, they need to have a clear and complete understanding of what has to change. Such an understanding has two components:

» The practices and mind-sets that have to be abandoned.

» The practices and mind-sets that have to be constructed, nurtured, and maintained until they are strong enough to resist any residual authoritarian habits or tendencies.

Each of the chapters that discusses one of the nine high-leverage areas ends with a list of governance practices—authoritarian practices and participative practices—related to the area. The authoritarian practices need to be abandoned, and the participative practices need to be constructed.

These lists are presented in the form of assessment checklists. You can use the checklists to assess current governance practices within your organization. We encourage you to complete each end-of-chapter checklist as you complete the chapter. Appendix I contains a scoring sheet that will help you to analyze the results. Appendix II gathers the individual end-of-chapter questionnaires together into a single comprehensive document that gives you a complete picture of the two worlds of governance in easy-to-use format. We hope that Appendix II will be useful as you prepare for the long road to participative governance and that it will continue to guide you as you advance along that road.

CONCLUSION

The participative organization, like the authoritarian organization, is internally consistent. The parts fit together and express mutually supportive assumptions and values. This congruence makes it possible for the organization to perform. We have identified nine essential elements that must become participative if an organization's governance is to be transformed: values, structures, leadership, management processes, information, relationships, competencies, controls, and pay. These are key levers for change that in turn can affect other areas of the organization.

As we saw in Chapter Three, evidence is accumulating that when these pieces are all participative, their congruence can help the organization to reach new heights of performance. When the nine governance areas converge, they create a self-sustaining system. The pieces interact in ways that feed and fuel one another. Consequently, when the nine pieces are all brought into play, they create a system that is much more than the sum of its parts. The chapters in Part Two examine each of the nine areas and show how they can and must be redesigned to carry the new participative genetic code.

PART II

The New Governance Map Takes Shape

*L*ong before we used airplanes and spacecraft to gain a true and accurate picture of the world, people had very useful maps. Explorers of the fifteenth and sixteenth centuries did a remarkable job of drawing the broad silhouette of the world's continents. Each explorer contributed new details or information that modified the known contour.

That is where we now are in the Age of Participation. Most of its elements have been discovered, but they have not yet been thoroughly explored. For example, we know the continent of values, but we have not traced all its rivers to their sources. The land of structures is now being mapped, but its highest peaks have yet to be climbed. New plateaus of leadership beckon. The paths are well trodden, but the forests have not been explored. We sail the oceans of relationships, but we have yet to sound their depths. And the voyages of true discovery are only now beginning.

CHAPTER 5

Values:
The New
Genetic Code

VALUES HAVE BEEN a major focal point for companies making the shift to participative governance. When we walk the halls of such organizations, we hear statements like these: "Our values help us control from a distance." "That wasn't consistent with our agreed values." "We may not want the unions to know that we will close that operation until after our peak season, but our values require us to tell them now."

The fact is that people in organizations do share values. Over time, an organization always evolves a culture with deeply entrenched norms and assumptions. These norms and assumptions determine the texture of relationships among all stakeholders as well as the organization's orientation to quality, productivity, people and their importance to competitiveness, and other factors of business success.

Values are the principles and ethics that reside in everyone and that guide their actions and choices even when no one is looking. Thus, values are much more powerful in ensuring consistent behavior than procedures, rules, or close supervision. Procedures and rules are effective as long as someone is there to enforce them. Most decisions and actions cannot be supervised that closely. Values operate at a distance—always present and always crafting how people respond to situations, with or without the external control of others.

Think of a ship on a voyage across the ocean. It moves toward its destination (its strategic goals), and it constantly adjusts its course as conditions change. However, its successful voyage relies on the subtle shared values to which all the stakeholders subscribe. The builders of the ship, the owners of its cargos, the national and international shareholders whose investments fund it, the people guiding it from shore during storms, the captain and crew, the technical experts who stand ready to deal with problems—all these crucial players must have a common set of assumptions, ethics, and principles to avert catastrophe and ensure success. These ethics and principles cannot be altered to suit operational or environmental conditions. Moreover, these values develop over time and with everyone's overt or covert participation and agreement.

It is important to distinguish the values that an organization espouses and the values that the people in it use. In the 1970s and 1980s, it was fashionable for organizations to develop new values. Such development usually occurred at special meetings of senior managers who discussed changes affecting their organization and then crafted a new set of values to guide the organization's decisions and activities. The new set of values was typically expressed as a vision, a mission, a code of ethics, or some combination thereof. Whatever form these newly espoused values took, they then found their way into company newspapers, posters for the shop floor, and plaques on boardroom walls. In the meantime, the old values continued to guide day-to-day behavior. In most cases, the newly espoused values only deepened the cynicism about the organization's ability to adjust to dramatic changes in the world around it.

It is not easy to change an organization's value system. As we have said, such a system evolves over time and becomes the worldview, the mind-set, the spectacles through which people interpret what happens and screen options and alternatives. Moreover, these real organizational values determine the way in which people react to surprise and change. Thus, if employees expect to be taken care of, they react emotionally and even violently to retrenchments that break the values contract that they thought they had with the organization.

Another reason why it is not easy to change an organization's values is that they usually mirror the values of the larger political and social system. International, national, and local public institutions have historically operated according to authoritarian values. This predisposition has reinforced the autocracy within private and public institutions and families. In fact, each system has reinforced the other, thereby creating a mutually sustaining authoritarian system of governance in the world.

This reinforcement raises a particularly important point regarding values. The majority of people within any system of governance share the same values about how the organization and its relationships should work. However, the fact that they share values does not necessarily mean that there will be consensus on issues. For example, stakeholders who operate within an authoritarian system are likely to view one another as adversaries. Thus, management and trade unions express a shared worldview when they treat each other as adversaries. Their shared values emphasize mutual mistrust, secrecy, and win-lose conflict.

For these reasons, moving to a shared worldview of participation necessitates a fundamental value shift that draws all stakeholders into a shared process of, first, rejecting the values of authoritarian governance and, second, working mutually to develop the values on which participative governance will be based.

The forces affecting institutions are changing at a rapid pace that exposes the major inadequacies of the value system that we all have shared. But we are still early in the change cycle. Any attempt to change the values that guide behavior in an organization is still an uphill battle. But values can be changed.

There are several conditions that enable a deliberate move to participative values. First, people throughout the organization must understand the systems of values that underlie both authoritarian and participative systems. Second, everyone must be involved in identifying the organization's own values and the types of behavior that will express the desired values. Third, there must be checks and balances to ensure that people act on the values that are key to the organization's success.

AUTHORITARIAN VALUES

Authoritarian systems began with values that helped them to survive in a world in which many external forces were unmanaged and people were highly vulnerable. Without modern infrastructures, people were subject to natural disaster, raids, decimation by enemy tribes and invaders, and plague. These external conditions seemed to require authoritarian responses, so most people bought into, or at least submitted to, the authoritarian values that enhanced their chances for survival: mutual protection, loyalty, clarity of role and social class, leadership by the fittest and most powerful, single-point decision making.

As time went on, these values became hard to defend. Their use today has more negative than positive consequences. In the modern world, which is dominated by the forces discussed in Chapter Two, authoritarian values actually impede the attempts of humanity to move forward. In the meantime, many institutions still operate according to the old values. They continue their coercive and dependent practices beyond the point at which these behaviors have any real survival value.

Most institutions in the productive sector are still guided by authoritarian values. This is troubling, because the workplace has a large influence on our daily lives. If we fail to bring participative governance to the workplace, then it is unlikely that society as a whole will ever make democracy an enduring success. At the same time, large and small organizations across the entire spectrum of the productive system—business, government institutions, local and regional authorities, and organized labor—are now in a historically unique position to shape the worldviews, beliefs, and practices that will determine the quality of human life and relationships in the future.

When values continue to drive behavior even after they have outlived their usefulness, they have severe negative effects. Yet old values often do persist, because the individuals and groups who have become powerful under the old values are reluctant to give up their power. These groups often impose harsh sanctions on anyone who wants to change the rules. For evidence, look to the recent history of the former Soviet Union. Look to General Motors: Ross Perot challenged the old values and was removed from the board. Look to families: Children question their parents and are disinherited.

The point is, authoritarian values that had some purpose in the past remain in many institutions today, albeit in atrophied form. In some cases, power-seeking leaders and dependent followers are exploiting them for personal gain. Whatever the reason for their use and whether it is conscious or unconscious, authoritarian values are not relevant to today's environment and problems. The continued use of such values for personal gain is, in fact, a special form of evil that requires a new look at morality. The key question becomes, What is the moral institution, given the circumstances in which humanity finds itself today? It is the key question because the values of the participative organization must not only guide decisions for the future but also help to redress the excesses of the past.

PARTICIPATIVE VALUES

At least ten key values are emerging as guiding principles for the participative institution: customer focus; commitment to participation; shared power, rights, and responsibilities; access; internalized control; respect for the balance of rational and nonrational; thinking close to doing; broad legitimacy; diversity; and learning. Organizations can express these values in different ways and use a variety of diverse behaviors to express them. But these values are important in the successful participative enterprise, whether they emerge through trial and error or conscious planning.

■ *Customer Focus*

It may be a cliché to say that organizations must be customer driven. But in a participative workplace, the customer takes on an entirely new meaning and becomes a part of the ultimate purpose of work. When people are clear about their role in serving the organization's ultimate customers, the intrinsic meaning in work increases. Delighting the customer and having raving fans, as Ken Blanchard (Blanchard, Carew, and Parisi-Carew, 1990) says, serves as a force that enables people to transcend the immediate activities of their work. Daily tasks achieve greater worth by being seen as the delivery of service that delights others. A reciprocal feeling can develop between customer and supplier: "I'm delighted as a customer, and my delight raises the worth of any task." "I'm delighted as a supplier because my work has purpose that others value." In the participative enterprise, customers are the economic electorate, the commercial voters who determine whether the organization has delivered satisfactory service and whether it deserves ongoing support. Everyone in the organization becomes a steward of satisfaction and customer care.

■ Commitment to Performance

Participation is not an end in itself. It is a means of directing the energy in the organization toward accomplishment. Truly great organizations are committed to performance. Their people know that they must add value, eliminate waste, and get and keep customers. They see participation as a vehicle for getting the work done with quality, continuous improvement, and innovation. The quest to involve people is thus more than something that is nice to do for them. It relates to the economic well-being of the enterprise and all its stakeholders. It has a higher purpose.

■ Shared Power, Rights, and Responsibilities

Power is access and ability to mobilize money, people, technology, and other assets. In authoritarian organizations, power is treated as a scarce resource and restricted to those at the top. *Rights* are claims that individuals can make regarding power and how they are treated by others. In authoritarian organizations, rights are often assumed at the top and negotiated at the bottom. The belief in universal and unalienable human rights challenges these notions and is absolutely fundamental to participation. *Responsibilities* refers to people's duties and commitments—what various stakeholders can legitimately expect of them.

> *One large insurance company decided to involve all employees in creating a set of values. At first, the managers resisted. They saw participation as eroding their managerial prerogatives.*
> *Meanwhile, most of the employees gave their vocal support to the principle of participative governance. Slowly, management became convinced of the economic superiority and good commercial sense*

of participation. But then the employees started resisting. They had thought that participation was mainly a matter of broadly distributing the rights and benefits of the organization. They were not quite as ready to take on the burden of accountability for performance and decisions. A period of education was required. The moral is simple: Both management and employees need to relinquish the traditions of authoritarian governance before participation can be successful.

The participative organization must be designed to ensure that everyone is accountable and has appropriate power and that his or her rights are respected. The balance of these three elements is key. As accountability is extended to everyone, so must power and rights. As power and rights increase, so must people's accountability for the results. Participation is not an easy response. It acknowledges the choice-making capacity of human beings, and it demands that everyone consciously take responsibility for and accept the power of this gift.

■ *Access*

The participative organization equips as many of its people as possible with information. It encourages people with problems and ideas to contact those who can solve them or implement them. Workers who design and make the product talk to customers who use it. People work with each other based on need, not on their position within the organization. Suppliers and customers are treated like partners. They receive information, and they are acknowledged members of the team. They have access at all points and levels, determined by their need and potential contributions.

There are no psychological walls in the participative enterprise. Every effort occurs to minimize buck-passing and not taking personal responsibility for activities that do not add value. People attend meetings because they have information to share or something to contribute, not because of their title, the place they occupy on the organization chart, or their insider or outsider status. Access is power, but it is not power for its own sake. Access does not exist independent of the work that must be done or of the decisions that must be made. Access is a value that permeates the organization.

■ *Internalized Control*

Internal controls—for example, common values, shared goals—are often more comprehensive than external controls. That is, internal controls can affect all, not just some, behaviors in ways that are appropriate to the situation. For example, if I value quality, I will bring that value to everything that I do. If I am controlled for quality, I will pay attention only to those aspects of the product or service that are controlled, and I am likely to overlook any problem that the quality controllers have not anticipated. In the participative organization, people work toward quality and customer retention because they want to do so. The organization is designed to help make sure that this happens.

■ *Respect for the Balance of Rational and Nonrational*

The authoritarian institution primarily acknowledges the rational, the linear, and the scientific. It often denies the emotional, intuitive, messy, and nonlinear qualities of the world, institutions, and people. Recently, we have begun to see the tremendous cost of such denial. Creativity, long-range impact, complex problem solving across boundaries, total customer service, and employee dedication all require people to go beyond the planned and the rational in their work. People must increase their caring, their passion, their willingness to take risks. The formality and rationality of the organization chart and all it implies are at once too cumbersome and too brittle to support responses to many of the daily issues with which the informal, human organization must deal. Today's organizations must value the emotions, intuitions, and boundary-breaking behavior that bring true quality to the fore.

■ *Thinking Close to Doing*

Participative organizations create whole jobs. People both think and do. Implementers help to develop strategy. Strategists stay close to what people do on the ground. Specialists know the total business, and people everywhere do much of their own staff work. Ivory towers are vacated, and factory doors carry signs saying *Thinking Welcome and Required Here.* Staff groups refuse to monopolize policy and strategy in human resources, finance, sales and marketing, information systems, or any other specialty area. In the participative organization, learning and work are totally intertwined. Learning is part of the operational work stream and one of the highest expressions of the organization's commitment to creating whole jobs.

■ Broad Legitimacy

In authoritarian companies, formal leadership is legitimate if it has direct financial control of the business or if those with such control—stockholders or the government—confer legitimacy. In participative organizations, workers, customers, and the community also confer power. Executives and managers lead by the consent of the governed. They are legitimate only as long as the institution that they lead adds value for the customer and the community as well as for the more traditional equity stakeholders. In some cases, leaders can be recalled by employees as well as by shareholders.

■ Diversity

Inbred institutions risk the same fate as inbred families. They lose their robustness, versatility, and adaptability. Diversity is the antidote. Participative institutions encourage diversity because, despite the increased possibility of conflict, the array of possible solutions also increases. Nations and institutions that ignore the demand for what evolutionary biologists call *requisite variety* do so at their own peril.

■ Learning

The participative world exalts learning. The participative organization is set up to stimulate learning. People are encouraged to try new things and to do old things in new ways. There is no blame for any problems that ensue if mistakes are analyzed and relevant learnings are shared. People everywhere in the organization have personal learning agendas, and they learn from one another regardless of position or age. Those who share their special knowledge and skills are appreciated. Those who do not are considered thieves of knowledge capital.

The accountability for personal learning and development of competencies is pervasive in participation. The right to participate requires everyone to learn and be aware of issues as part of his or her admission to decision making. It is not enough just to be there. The fact that one is on a team or affected by a decision does not give one the right to question or reject a decision merely on the basis of personal opinion or views. Everyone always has the right to express his or her own interests and desires. But participation requires people to be informed and to respect levels of knowledge and experience that are greater than their own. In the participative organization, access to learning is open, and people take responsibility for learning and for becoming informed.

VALUES RECONSTRUCTION: A PARTICIPATIVE PROCESS

The ten values surveyed in the preceding section reflect a new organizational morality, a new guiding framework for institutional success. They are not soft. They place real pressure on organizations to come to terms with how they exist in the world today.

Values for a participative organization that are not developed participatively are likely to fail. At a minimum, such values will be merely decorative, and the real values that still reinforce the old ways of doing things will continue to determine the organization's daily practice.

The main challenge facing institutions that want to reconstruct their values is to ensure that the espoused values become the values used in the organization. Successful entrenchment of values means that peoples' intentions and behaviors become very closely connected. Making such a connection requires several things.

First, people must understand and articulate the organization's current value system. People must understand and accept their history and the forces that have formed them before they can create a future that is fundamentally different from the one they have. Thus, the first step is to say, "This is how we have been doing things here."

Second, people from the entire organization and from stakeholder groups outside the organization must collaborate directly in creating the new values. While such collaboration can occur through representatives, representation is not the ideal. Eventually, every individual must feel that his or her interests and ideas have been represented. The best way of achieving this aim is to use processes that actively involve all employees in the process of creating the values of participative governance.

Third, the values must be expressed in terms of specific behaviors that enable everyone to grasp the values as tangibles. Both the responsibilities and the rights associated with a value must also be expressed. Behaviors will necessarily be representative and descriptive, not prescriptive for every situation. There are thousands of behaviors that can occur to support or break a value on any given day. Concrete examples give stakeholders a powerful framework within which they can evaluate and continuously shape their understanding of and adherence to a common values foundation. The last thing the participative organization needs is a new bureaucracy or new sets of procedures.

It is quite natural for managers to resist a participative approach to the formation of values. They can fear that employees will create values that serve their own self-interest, not the interest of the organization. Employees, too, often resist a collaborative development of values. They do so out of suspicion and passivity bred during years of authoritarian rule.

A major manufacturer and distributor of automobiles wanted to empower its workforce. But company managers realized that they could do so only if people shared core values about the company and its work. The CEO invited senior managers, middle managers, staff representatives, union representatives, and shop stewards to explore options openly. A diverse group of approximately fifty people met for two days. Together they identified a set of key focus areas that needed to be addressed. They also agreed that 100 percent of the employees should be involved in creating the core values.

How did they achieve such participation? First, a representative group of management and the workforce published an invitation for people to be trained as values workshop facilitators. The response was overwhelming, and the members of a core team were selected for training. Over a period of three months, facilitators involved hundreds of employees in workshops. Each workshop brought together between twenty and thirty people: a mixture of senior managers, professional staff, technicians, administrative staff, and frontline workers. The literally thousands of contributions and inputs that resulted were consolidated into: ten core values; seven strategic focus areas with quality requirements for successful implementation; descriptions of day-to-day practices that exemplified the values in terms of reciprocal rights and responsibilities; and an unfolding strategy that defined the organizational practices that need to be dismantled, maintained, or initiated in order for the values to be lived and the strategic focus areas to be achieved. Finally, multilevel and multifunctional task groups were formed to drive each of the strategic focus areas and to facilitate the entrenchment of the values and their related rights and responsibilities.

The company knew that it was making headway when virtually the entire industry went on strike and the company's workers continued to work as usual. As one union representative put it, "We already have achieved what others still need to use strike action for."

Once people overcome their initial resistance, the values that they create usually read like those described in a standard business school text on globally competitive practices. In every such process in which we have participated, the collective workforce—management, employees, and organized labor—has created a set of values that expresses the best sentiments of world-class organizations and global competitiveness. Working together, these groups create lists that essentially duplicate the ten values reviewed in this chapter. There is nothing mystical or strange about this. Managers and employees have a vested interest in the organization's survival and success. In the past, few people have had a real opportunity to contribute consciously to the long-term shaping of their institution. When they do have a chance to exert such influence, most people are serious and accountable. Few interventions are quite as powerful for this purpose as the communal development of shared values.

VISIBLE CHECKS AND BALANCES

Creating and having shared values is a key step in the process of creating a participative organization. But since it is easy to espouse one set of values and live another, organizations need also to have visible checks and balances so they can ensure that the stated values are practiced. There are many ways of doing this. Here are five:

» People make open, public commitments regarding what they will stop doing, start doing, and continue to do to bring the values to life.

» Custodians are appointed for each value; their job is to keep the organization's attention focused on the value, help to address breaches of the value, advise people on improved values-related action, and help to resolve problems caused by larger systems issues; values custodians are usually line people; they are not values custodians full-time but do this work as part of their day-to-day responsibilities.

» Values discussions occur as part of individual or team performance reviews.

» Recruitment and selection processes include values-related questions; people are selected because they share the principles that guide the institution.

» A creed of responsibilities, rights, and empowerment defines the parameters, behaviors, and practices that underpin day-to-day value-based behavior.

The values that are supposed to guide behavior and decisions in the organization must have clear support and sanction. In the absence of such support and sanction, changing the values that people say they pursue will not change the organization's entrenched norms, especially if these norms are authoritarian values that punish any real attempt at participation in subtle ways.

CONCLUSION

Values exist and guide behavior in organizations, whether we plan them or not. In most organizations, the values that act as norms and assumptions continue to be authoritarian. This pattern cannot continue if we want to shift to participation. While it is not easy to change values, new norms can emerge if several conditions are met.

First, everyone in the organization must acknowledge the values that have guided behavior and assumptions in the past. They must recognize the difference between authoritarian and participative values and accept and own their own history and desire to change.

Second, everyone must work together to explore and define the important values that will help the organization to be efficient, effective, and enduring. The needs and perspectives of all stakeholders are important in these deliberations.

Finally, the organization must put into place checks and balances that will nurture the new values to ensure that they are not overcome by the old norms and habits. This process requires discussions, follow-up, and sanctions—conditions that may seem to contradict the image of laissez-faire freedom traditionally associated with participation. But participatively developed values bind everyone to them. If people choose not to comply, the organization has a right to require conformance or to take corrective action. For with values like the ten reviewed in this chapter, there is very little likelihood that a new authoritarianism will occur.

Think about the values in your organization. Figure 5.1 contains five pairs of items. Allocate ten points between the two items in each pair. The points awarded reflect the extent to which each statement is true. Allocate five or more points to an item only if you can say that at least 75 percent of the people in your organization would agree that the statement closely reflects their views and experiences. Nine or ten points indicate that your organization is really a case study example of the statement. The points that you award to each pair of items must total ten. When you have finished rating the statements, add up the numbers in the A column and the B column, and record them on the VALUES row of the Governance Assessment Score Sheet in Appendix I.

Figure 5.1 Assess the Values in Your Organization

☐ **1A.** Values are not used in any explicit way in our human resource practices (for example, selection, recruitment, orientation / induction, performance review, and so on).

☐ **1B.** Our human resource practices were (re)designed and are evaluated to reflect and reinforce our values.

☐ **2A.** Our stated values were developed by people at the top of the organization and communicated to the people who must align their behavior with the values.

☐ **2B.** Our values were developed participatively. All people and stakeholder groups were involved.

☐ **3A.** We have no formal way of enforcing our values or evaluating day-to-day behaviors and decisions against values.

☐ **3B.** People everywhere in the organization are evaluated against our values. They are part of our explicit employment contract.

☐ **4A.** The values we say that we stand for are very different from the values that we practice.

☐ **4B.** The values that we say we stand for are taken very seriously as mandates and criteria for action and decisions at all levels.

☐ **5A.** The values that are really important here generally support authoritarian and dependent behaviors.

☐ **5B.** The values that are really important here require participative behaviors from all people.

CHAPTER 6

Structures:
Flow, Not Boxes

STRUCTURE CREATES THE FRAMEWORK for values and relationships. It functions much like the walls, doors, and windows of a house or like the channel that a meandering river follows across the countryside. It creates the pathways for the formal flow of information, and it guides peoples' assumptions about the actions that the institution considers legitimate. If an organization's structures support and require participation, then the organization has taken a giant step toward participation as a way of life.

One reason why it is good to attend to this area early is that old-style, authoritarian structures and work designs are particularly powerful barriers to the evolution and development of participative governance. Any organization that wants to move to participation must redesign itself in order to become participative and reap all the benefits of a higher-involvement style of operation.

Think about the profound and yet simple changes that must occur. They are so fundamental that even children see the discrepancies between authoritarian designs and what we need in order to have a more responsive workplace. This story illustrates that point:

One of our sons, Roark, and his friend Tanashi were playing in the study while Christo struggled to draw pictures of both the old and the emerging organization structures. The little boys became interested in the drawings and took one from the desk. It happened to be a drawing of a traditional, hierarchical organization chart: a pyramid of boxes connected by lines. Figure 6.1 shows the chart that the boys discussed.

Figure 6.1 The Traditional, Hierarchical Organization

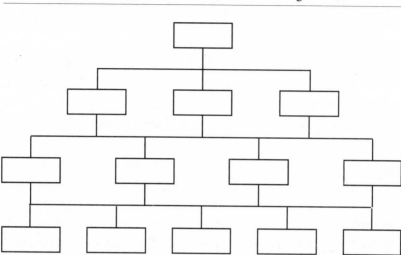

"That's one of those drawings of an organization," said one.

"There's a picture like that in the headmaster's office at school, with pictures of the teachers in all the little boxes," observed the other.

Christo asked the boys what they thought of the drawings and how they felt about the organizations that the drawings reflected. The boys' comments were perceptive.

"It looks all sticky. If you take away one piece, then lots of pieces fall with it."

"It's not nice at all. You cannot move it around. If you push it, it will fall over."

"The people here," said Roark, pointing to the boxes at the lower levels, "can never really talk to the people there." He pointed to the boxes at the higher levels.

"This one," said Tanashi, touching the box at the very top of the chart, "is always telling everybody else what to do. He must be pretty lonely."

"There are no paths for any of these to talk to one another. They are so separated," remarked one of the boys, pointing to the boxes at the bottom of the pyramid.

The children drew the same conclusions from the traditional organization chart as many redesign experts: Authoritarian structures entrench superior-subordinate relationships among people. They create fiefdoms, territories, and chains of command that isolate people and that often make position more important than performance. The rigidity and dependence that they support make it difficult for an organization to respond to exceptions flexibly and quickly.

The organization chart and its underlying values have been the standard blueprint for organizations throughout this century. It reflects the values of the authoritarian world as refined for use in the productive sector by Frederick Taylor and Henry Ford. It assumes that organizations are more effective when thinking is separated from doing; when work is divided into small, specialized chunks; and when job and group boundaries are clear and relatively discrete.

It is clear that such an approach to work design and organizational structure had enormous benefits in the past. In boosting productivity, it helped to raise the standard of living for the middle class and create massive wealth for stockholders.

Pyramid-style organizations have been the norm in the public and private sectors for most of this century. Until very recently, the nation-state has been the basic political unit, and it has always entailed massive bureaucracy. Two world wars, hundreds of local and regional clashes, ideological conflict between capitalism and communism, and the Cold War have all affected the choice of institutional structures everywhere. Thus, until very recently, both the macro- and micro-systems have nurtured hierarchy, specialization, discrete jobs, and clear authority structures.

Steep pyramidal structures create major problems for today's organizations. Information moves too slowly within them, customers are too far away from those who serve them, and people are too busy taking care of their bosses to care. Nor do they have the flexibility needed to compete in a rapidly changing global market.

In all fairness, the picture that we have just painted is probably not quite as bad in practice as we have made it out to be. Deep hierarchies and functional silos have been eroding for the last several decades. For one thing, when individuals move from one box on the chart to another, they often change the definition and the content of the job that it represents. Their skills, energy, and political ingenuity enable them to redesign the job—often extensively—while they are in it. The job's title may stay the same, and its position on the chart may not change, but the real content of the work may be quite different in practice from what it seems to be on paper.

The informal structures have also been growing in influence and importance. Communication, informal work teams, and social networks often form around emerging customer and institutional needs that the organization as defined by the chart is not meeting. For many people, work on task forces, project teams, and advisory groups takes up more of their time than work done through and with their boss and others with whom the organization chart connects them.

The old structures are rupturing despite the stability that the chart seems to imply. Yet people still spend a great deal of energy maintaining the facade, as if the direct reporting structure were all that existed. The boss above still controls important personnel decisions, such as those involving pay and promotion. The people in the organization— a precious and expensive resource—live split lives as the organization pretends to be more rational and in charge than it is.

The old, authoritarian worldview maintained that the whole equals the sum of its parts, and each part is a separate, discrete fragment of the whole. While we made progress under the directive styles of the past, we know now that reality is hardly fragmented, mechanistic, or predictable. Rather, the new worldview asserts that the whole is reflected by and contained within each of its parts, and each part is a microcosm of the whole. These worldviews are about as mutually exclusive as one can imagine. And the contrast has dramatic implications for the design of organizational structures.

The point is that there is an acute need to revisualize the organization. New pictures that show the desirable interplay among people will help to break the stranglehold of old mind-sets. Of course, this new vision must reflect the configuration of work most effective in promoting productivity, quality, and customer service. We will return to the issue of how the new organization charts may look after we discuss the new types of interaction that they must depict.

THE EMERGING FORM
OF THE NEW ORGANIZATION

Participative structures and work designs are still emerging. In some cases, as in many manufacturing organizations, they take the form of flexible, relatively permanent work teams whose most important relationships are horizontal: with suppliers and customers, including the people within their own organization with whom they must cooperate in the stream of work that adds value for the customer.

Other structures are totally flexible and have no fixed teams or relationships. People may be on many teams and work on each team for a different period of time. They may operate as consultants, temporary team members, or full-time employees. Things have come a long way since the days of quality circles and ad hoc problem-solving teams.

The relatively fixed core team of people who work together day after day is one structural unit that remains common in participative designs. However, in a totally flexible work design, there are no fixed teams. People move flexibly among teams, and they may be on many teams at the same time. These teams may be part of the new "virtual organization" where some or all team members are temporary and not even employees. The fixed core teams of employees and the temporary teams of self-employed people occupy the two ends of a continuum that is beginning to hold many design options.

Participative structures have two basic building blocks: teams and value-adding work streams. The number of ways in which these two basic elements can be combined is almost limitless. It is like playing with Tinker Toys. Any number of flexible designs are possible when we combine the round blocks—teams—with the rods—value-adding work streams.

■ *The New Core Work Teams*

Whenever there is a sequence of activities that occurs over time and that benefits from consistent and reliable work processes, there is an opportunity to establish a core work team. Such teams have relatively fixed places on the organization chart. But in the participative organization, they influence decisions in and around their work about what will be produced, about how it will be produced, about the resources required, and so on. Their ability to influence and their relative permanence enable them to achieve a combination of continuous improvement, productivity, built-in quality, reliability, and flexibility in their work. The new core teams are very different from the shift workers who used to be buried at the bottom of the old hierarchical heap.

The ongoing decision processes of core work teams are mostly consensual and collaborative. Leaders and team members jointly set goals, determine targets, and agree on the quality requirements that need to be met. Team members are given and accept full accountability for accomplishing the work, and they can deploy the resources needed to get the work done. Together with the team leader, team members define what they will produce. They monitor, evaluate, and learn by doing. Thus, team members are never alienated from either the formulation or the implementation of goals related to their work.

The first priority of the fully functioning and productive core work team is uncompromising performance through small improvements every day. This priority requires a shift in the attitudes and the mind-set of both members and leaders. The relationship between them is not a vertical, superior-subordinate, power-over relationship based on threat and fear. Rather, it is a horizontal, peer-to-peer, power-with relationship based on partnership.

Without a shift both in attitude and in mind-set, it is not possible to sustain the continuous improvement ethic and focus on uncompromising performance. Since performance is the primary purpose of participation in the productive sector, these shifts in relationships are key.

■ *Temporary Teams*

Organizations or parts of organizations often require even more flexibility than relatively permanent core work teams can give. This is especially true for work that is focused on projects, as it is for consulting firms, internal staff groups, customer service teams, and sales teams. It is also true for organizations pursuing strategies of so-called mass customization. Mass customization is an increasingly popular response to the need to meet unique customer requirements with products or services that have a core of standard components or that use a common base of skills and capabilities. Modular shelving—Benetton's practice of combining standard clothing styles with the ability to adjust stock and colors immediately to local needs—is one example.

Both project-based and mass-customizing organizations are constantly assembling, disassembling, and reassembling teams. People can be on many temporary teams and have no real home base at any one time. An individual can play a lead role on one or two teams and be a support player on others. It is difficult to draw pictures of organizations with temporary teams, because the people in them move and shift.

In these situations, the organization must know how to keep track of skills and of those who have them. The Minnesota Mining and Manufacturing Company (3M) keeps a list of the skills that their technical people possess. The entire organization uses this list to identify potential team members and to find technical advisers for special situations. A few years ago, Deloitte, Haskins and Sells adopted the same technique. Computers and broad access to databases make such lists a powerful and inexpensive option.

■ *Value-Adding Work Streams*

Except in very special cases, both the core and the temporary teams operate as part of a value-adding work stream that flows through them from internal and external suppliers to internal and external customers. Thus, the team is never an end in itself. It transcends its own performance actions by incorporating customers' requirements and suppliers' ideas, outputs, and capabilities. It is becoming clear that being boundaryless—both horizontal and vertical—is the desired end state.

HORIZONTAL BOUNDARYLESSNESS. Horizontal boundarylessness centers on the main value chains within the organization. The main value chains are those through which the work flows that adds the value for which the end customer is willing to pay. For example, in automobile manufacture, the main value chains consist of the work done to design the car, procure and assemble its parts, test its safety and reliability, make it look and feel good, teach customers how to use and care for it, deliver it to customers, and maintain it. It does not include such things as developing staff, preparing reports for senior management, complying with internal budgeting processes, or working to develop supplier contracts. This is not to say that such work is not important, because it is. It enables and supports performance along the main value chain. But the distinction between direct and indirect work does introduce a requirement: Activities that are not part of the main value chain must either clearly support the primary customer-satisfying activities of the organization, or they must be stopped. They are the tributaries that flow into and add value to the main stream of work.

The teams that are part of the main value stream have four requirements, which we can call the four Ds:

» Delight the customer.

» Deliver added value.

» Do the work proactively and consciously.

» Define what the team needs in order to get the job done and sustain continuous improvement.

These are the requirements for all teams, core or temporary. When a team possesses this ethic and the skills that go with it, there is no need for old-style job descriptions, bureaucratic controls and procedures, or layers of supervision and management control.

The focus throughout is on the customer or the stream of customers who will pay for and use the final product or service. The organization aligns all activities and intentions with one goal: creating and keeping customers. Such a focus significantly reduces the uncertainties and complexities of work, the messiness and inevitable conflicts.

Of course, if the paying customer is the unifier, then the vast majority of employees inside the value stream, as well as those who serve it, must be in constant touch with the customer. There are two key reasons why. First, it increases the organization's knowledge of what the customer wants. Second, constant contact with customers helps to transform the customer-supplier relationship from an authoritarian one in which the customer is "always right" to one characterized by mutual learning and respect. Within this new, more participative relationship, it is possible to separate real wants from desires that do not add real value for the customer and for which he or she is not really willing to pay.

Horizontal boundarylessness also requires the people who used to be external suppliers and external customers to become part of the organization's vision of itself. This element is a subtle but very important form of globalization for the business. When external customers and suppliers move inside the organization, customers train suppliers, who in turn train their customers. Whether suppliers are inside or outside the traditional organizational boundaries, they decide when and what to stock. They become their customers' warehouses, their customers' partners in strategic planning, their customers' R&D laboratory.

Employees in one of our client companies—it manufactured wood-based materials—were very critical of their supply of raw materials and spare parts. A group of employees suggested to management that they work directly with suppliers to determine stock levels, quality requirements, and timing of deliveries.

At first, management resisted the suggestion, on the grounds that the organization needed to keep strong budgetary control over such purchases, because they cost the organization millions of dollars each year. Acknowledging this concern, the employees suggested that the purchasing manager remain the arbitrator between themselves and the suppliers but that the arbitrator have the power to overturn a proposal only if he could prove that the old way of doing things would improve productivity and performance.

Management accepted the team's proposition, and team members set up meetings with suppliers. But a new problem arose. Traditionally, the supplier's representatives had worked with middle and senior managers. Moreover, as the years wore on, increasing numbers of the operational workforce were people for whom English was a second language. In this case, several could not speak English at all. Traditionally, the English-speaking suppliers had interacted with English-speaking managers. An inability to communicate now jeopardized the new plan. The operational team came up with a simple solution: They brought a translator to facilitate operator-supplier interactions.

Within six months, productivity had increased by 30 percent, equipment breakdowns had decreased by 80 percent, and unplanned overtime was virtually nonexistent. Moreover, the organization's initiative had encouraged the supplier organization to get its own operational staff involved. Soon, teams of operational staff from both the customer and the supplier organizations were paying regular visits to each other's plants. Long-service supervisors from the customer organization were seconded to the supplier organization. Within a matter of months, this alliance of worker-level people had succeeded in removing many activities that did not add value from their interactions with one another. It also significantly reduced inventories and eradicated the tendency to overengineer certain components.

An external customer can become its supplier's assembler, delivery system, and source of new product ideas. A supplier's computers can move inside the customer's workplace, with the customer's own data flowing into the supplier's databases. As the following story shows, additional options emerge when the supplier's employees are also customers of the supplier's customers.

Over the years, a large brewery had established a very successful distribution network of local bars, restaurants, liquor stores, and hotels. To meet one of its primary service requirements—that none of the outlets would stock beer past the targeted shelf life— the company printed the date for maximum aging on the label. Nevertheless, many outlets still served old beer.

What appeared to be a large logistical problem was resolved when the brewer realized that most of the outlets had its own employees as customers. Brewery staff could ask for a bottle of beer and check its age whenever they visited one of the outlets. This solution emerged, by the way, when a truck driver came to the brewery one day with a case of outdated beer. He had gone to his favorite pub, asked for a beer, and found that the beer had aged beyond the target date. He asked the bartender whether any of that stock was still available. The bartender found a few dozen bottles of the aged beer. The brewery employee immediately bought it all and returned it to the brewery. The brewery reimbursed him, he collected a new case of beer, and he delivered it to the bar the next day.

Ultimately, there are no real horizontal boundaries related to the conception, design, creation, delivery, or use of products and services. There is only a partnership among all parties, including the paying customer, to ensure that the product or service delights and retains those who finally pay for it.

VERTICAL BOUNDARYLESSNESS. Vertical boundaries also soften and become transparent in the participative system. This does not mean that everyone does everything or that there are no levels of authority. People have different skills, energy, and experience, and they have different work responsibilities. The organization needs to have individual focus on the various levels of work, which range from developing strategy to serving the customer.

Two factors require the vertical boundaries that we have known in authoritarian systems to disappear. First, in participative systems, the people who do the work must also think about it and help to strategize for it, while the people whose primary role is vision and strategy must retain a strong link with the work itself. Why? As Henry Mintzberg (1994) explains, the best strategy is a combination of planning and learning from experience. Reliance on old-style planning processes, which assumed that it was possible for the top to think how to act strategically and which then expected the bottom to do without thinking or involvement, simply do not work. The participative organization does not separate thinking from doing. It involves operational staff in strategic decision making, and it requires those who guide the organization's broader and longer-term planning to keep in close touch with what happens on the ground. Second, any person in a participative organization must be able to contact anyone, anywhere, anytime in pursuit of uncompromising performance and customer satisfaction and delight.

Although executives, managers, and staff are accountable for different types of work, people everywhere need seamless contact and access. After all, the whole product or service is the work of the entire organization. The separation and isolation of levels, common in authoritarian organizations, is probably one of the major reasons for low productivity and waste. No organization today can afford the costs that result when people do not have contextual or specific information or rapid and truthful feedback. Nor can an organization afford the costs of the excessive patronage, political gamesmanship and second-guessing, and career-motivated posturing that occur because level is more important than getting the work done with uncompromising quality. Replacing the goal of delighting the boss with the goal of delighting the customer is one of the greatest challenges facing the participation-bound institution.

One challenge that many organizations face is eliminating work that does not add value from the main value-adding stream. One structural solution that helps them to do so is to bring as many functional activities into the main work stream as possible. For example, work teams can develop their own budgets and do their own staffing and performance management. The support staff for these activities should be very small, and its members should not have power to create work or reporting requirements that expand their influence without adding value. Assuming such functions may at first seem to distract teams from their main job of producing a product or service. But it has some major benefits: The team makes better decisions, and it owns them. In the past, they belonged to functional staff.

THE NEW STRUCTURES AND TEAM OPERATIONS

The new structures shine the spotlight on the main value-adding stream. They also bring customers and suppliers who traditionally were outside the organization's boundaries into the organization's activities.

While these things are happening, the structures within teams are changing, becoming more flexible. Hierarchy is systematically eroded, and role flexibility focused on the goals to which stakeholders have agreed increases.

In the participative organization, old-style and vertical chains of command and lines of communication give way to horizontal interaction and participation. The team leader, who is primarily a coordinator, not a controller, is a flexible performance facilitator who has a relatively high level of technical and group process expertise. His or her job is to facilitate higher levels of performance in the short and long term, not to control and boss or to keep all the visibility and customer contact to him- or herself.

In the participative organization, the relationships between team members and team leaders are constantly changing. When team members have little skill and experience, they listen, learn, and relate to the leader and more experienced members. They are then trainees, and the others are their mentors or coaches. Under these conditions, they move into a healthy dependency. But it is only a temporary state, for their goal is to progress to levels at which they can take full responsibility for doing the things that have to be done to ensure high levels of performance. In a mature team, in which most members are highly competent in key skills areas, the team's members and its leader or leaders operate as peers.

In the fully participative and high-performance team, roles shift as a function of task, the skills and development needs of individual members, and the availability of team members for different amounts of work.

For a number of reasons, teams are becoming an increasingly important performance unit. First, much work is complex and requires several people with diverse skills and experience to contribute parts of the solution. Work to develop a truly creative and comprehensive product or service often requires diverse views. Second, a lot of productivity is lost when people or teams hand over work from one section or phase to the people or team in charge of another section or phase. For example, the handover of a machine problem from an operator to an engineer often means that the operator has to wait for the engineer to come in from a central location. It also encourages operators to do quick fixes rather than work with the engineer in order to solve the problem once and for all. Such a solution can only be reached if the engineer and the operator see themselves as members of the same team, not as isolated boxes on the production chart and the engineering chart. Inefficiencies also occur when one shift hands work over to another shift. Often, rather than solve problems in its own time, a team passes its problems on to the next shift. Such behavior is a sign that people in the organization do not view and value one another as continuous service partners in pursuit of a common purpose.

ENVISAGING THE PARTICIPATIVE ORGANIZATION

How will the participative organization look, or at least how can we draw it?

The micro views for individuals and teams are perhaps the easiest to depict. Figure 6.2 shows the relationships between an individual's team and individual roles and accountability.

Figure 6.2 The Roles and Accountability
of an Individual in a Team

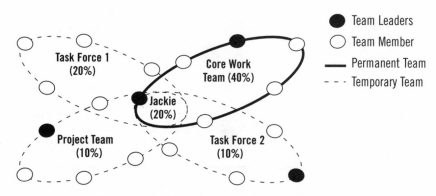

Jackie is on four teams: the core team, led by her "manager," two task forces, and a project team. She is the team leader for one of the task forces. Forty percent of her work is done on temporary teams, 40% with her core team, and 20% as an individual contributor.

The individual is at the center of the "flower" depicted in Figure 6.2. Each team of which the individual is an active member is represented by a "petal." In some cases, the individual may be the team's overall leader. In others, he or she is a general member. However, even in these teams, he or she may sometimes take a lead role for parts of the work. One important conclusion emerges from this individual perspective: When individuals are on more than one team, their ability to self-manage becomes very important. This is true because they themselves are the only ones who are fully aware of their total job.

Figure 6.3 shows the structure of a team. It somewhat resembles that of an atom. Figure 6.3 shows the team spinning because the roles of individual members change from task to task. The leadership role takes on different meanings as the task changes or as team members move into and out of the leadership role. For example, when the work is unfamiliar to most team members, the leader for the task will temporarily assume a "superior" position from which he or she coaches, directs, and educates. If the work is such that the skills of team

Figure 6.3 The Team as Atom

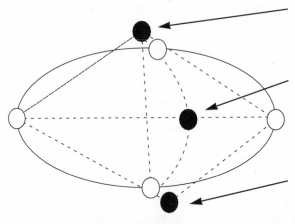

Team leader takes "superior" position to coach, direct, and educate an inexperienced group.

Team leader takes a "collaborative member" role with an experienced group of people with complementary skills—where he/she has a technical role to play.

Team leader takes a process support role providing only coordination.

members are complementary, then the leader's role becomes one of fellow expert and peer coordinator. If the task is one in which members have expertise and the leader needs only to coordinate, then the leader takes a process support role. The leader may even be a learner or one of several people doing the work.

Figure 6.4 shows another way of depicting the operations of a team within a participative organization. Figure 6.4 depicts a role chart. Here, you change the structure simply by moving the Ls (for *leads*), the Ss (for *supports*), and the As (for *approves* or *coaches*) from one person to another.

The entire participative organization is more difficult to depict. One could, as Figure 6.5 does, show a pipeline carrying decisions and actions that have long-term, medium-term, and short-term implica-

Figure 6.4 The Team as Role Chart

TASK	Carol (Team Leader)	Sam	April	Johann	George
1	L			S	S
2	S			L	S
3	A		L		
4		L	S	S	

L - Leads
S - Supports
A - Approves

tions. The people in the pipeline have one purpose: to remain consciously committed to the four Ds—delight, deliver, do, define—and to seek continuously for ways of refining these interrelated imperatives for attracting and keeping customers.

The depiction of the participative organization as a value-adding work stream is a very useful way of describing the roles and contributions of various functions and areas of expertise. Figure 6.6 shows the participative organization as a value-adding work stream. In both cases, the graphic representation of the organization depicts roles, not people. The same individual can appear at several different places on the same diagram. For example, operational workers can be part of a

Figure 6.5 The Participative Organization as Pipeline

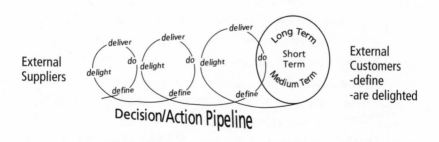

External Suppliers

External Customers
-define
-are delighted

Decision/Action Pipeline

vision or strategy team as well as active members of several work teams. As Figure 6.6 shows, external customers and suppliers can appear anywhere within the main stream, even in several places at once.

Figure 6.6 The Participative Organization
as Value-Adding Work Stream

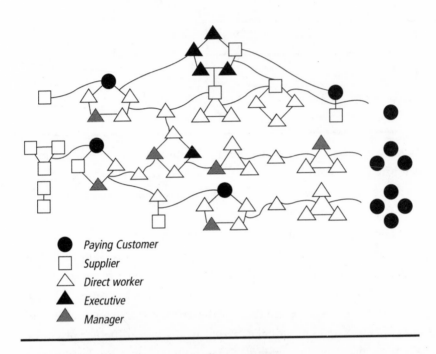

● Paying Customer
□ Supplier
△ Direct worker
▲ Executive
▲ Manager

CONCLUSION

The rigid box-and-line organization chart of the past can no longer be used to describe the roles and relationships within organizations today. Even if companies draw themselves in the traditional way, they can no longer operate exclusively along the well-defined paths and finite responsibilities that these charts depict. It is true that some work is stable enough to be managed within defined structures and responsibilities; that is, it benefits from hierarchy and relatively firm boundaries. But even in organizations in which the work is largely routine, the hierarchy must at least flatten if not give way to increasingly flexible structures. And no matter what the organization's work, roles within work groups must be able to change to ensure the best use and development of skills. Continuous improvement, attention to quality, and successful handling of exceptions cannot occur without such changes.

Think about the structures in your organization. Figure 6.7 contains five pairs of items. Allocate ten points between the two items in each pair. The points awarded reflect the extent to which each statement is true. Allocate five or more points to an item only if you can say that at least 75 percent of the people in your organization would agree that the statement closely reflects their views and experiences. Nine or ten points indicate that your organization is really a case study example of the statement. The points that you award to each pair of items must total ten. When you have finished rating the statements, add up the numbers in the A column and the B column, and record them on the STRUCTURES row of the Governance Assessment Score Sheet in Appendix I.

Figure 6.7 Assess the Structures in Your Organization

6A. *We are a hierarchical organization in which one's position on the organization chart makes a lot of difference in what one does and is allowed to do.*

6B. *We are a flat organization. The organization's structure makes it easy to meet customer needs because anyone has open access to anyone else at any time.*

7A. *Departments and teams are structured functionally, and work is divided up to make it easy to manage and coordinate.*

7B. *Departments and teams are structured in the best way to get the work done, even if that means mixing levels and functions.*

8A. *The formal, administrative boss is the key decision maker in performance reviews.*

8B. *The people who must use what individuals or teams produce or deliver participate directly in performance reviews and have real influence in them.*

9A. *Job descriptions define what people can and cannot do. Team roles are relatively fixed.*

9B. *Work and group structures allow and support multiskilling and flexible work assignments for team members. Assignments are based on current workload, skills, and development priorities.*

10A. *People doing the day-to-day work report to supervisors and managers, who make and control the final decisions.*

10B. *Teams are designed and empowered to manage their own day-to-day activities and make their own operational decisions.*

CHAPTER 7

Leadership:
Four Imperatives

LEADERSHIP IS ONE of the most popular topics in the literature on governance. This is not surprising, because the shift to increased participation changes our view of effective leadership. And because we are in the midst of a major shift, leadership as a concept is unstable. Moreover, notions of the formal leadership that we expect from appointed and elected leaders are being confused with notions of the informal leadership that we expect of everyone in the institution.

In this chapter, we focus primarily on formal leaders—people who have been appointed or elected to power, who are authorized to represent and make decisions on behalf of others, and who can rely on institutional mechanisms to enforce their decisions. This focus should not be interpreted as meaning that informal leaders are not important. It simply acknowledges that formal leaders are a crucial design focus for any institution that wants to change.

Formal leadership is concerned primarily with organizational survival over the long term. It must create the conditions needed for innovation, continuous improvement, and adaptation. Formal leaders must also maintain the appropriate internal tension between forces for stability and forces for change. Formal leadership is thus inextricably intertwined with an organization's optimism, youthfulness, and creativity.

In authoritarian systems, formal leaders are often those who can acquire and hold the most power by any means—charisma, force, fear, patronage, promises of safety, or manipulation of external rewards. Because authoritarianism has been the prevailing mode of governance for many centuries, followers as well as leaders have come to expect leadership of this kind. Both leaders and followers have colluded in coercive and dependent relationships for so long that the dependency and subordination of followers and the supremacy of leaders have become unquestioned principles.

However, there is a great deal of evidence that the old assumptions about leadership are cracking, as they must. The forces for change described in Chapter Two provide the background. But, as many public and private institutions are now discovering, it is not easy to shift to new assumptions about leadership and followership. Neither side has the experience, skills, or mind-sets needed to perform the new roles and relationships that shifting forms of governance require.

Many years of authoritarian operation have created undercurrents of alienation, anger, and distrust. Authoritarian controls and collusion kept these forces underground in the past. But attempts to move to increasingly participative modes often release these pressures before the skills, values, and mechanisms of participation have taken root. When this happens in nations, there are violent eruptions like those in the former Soviet Union, Bosnia-Herzegovina, China, and South Africa.

Conservative leadership and a frightened and ill-equipped populace do not readily give up the habits of boss rule and dependency. When participation is introduced into companies, employees sometimes seem to "take advantage" of the new freedom by making new demands. Or they take a wait-and-see attitude that reinforces management's old suspicions about employees' "laziness."

These are among the many dynamics of transition that we will examine in Chapter Eighteen. These dynamics, plus the fact that new models of leadership and followership are only just emerging, make today's leadership requirements unique.

Leaders face four main challenges as institutions move from authoritarianism to participation. First, leaders must let go of authoritarian assumptions and behaviors. Most people who have or who seek formal authority are themselves a product of the authoritarian era. They have been in the authoritarian swimming pool, and they are therefore wet, even if they decry authoritarian assumptions and modes. They must go through the painful process of leaving old habits and expectations behind.

Second, today's leaders must manage the transition from authoritarianism to participation. This transition has its own dynamics, which are quite separate from those of either authoritarian or participative governance systems.

Third, formal leaders must be accountable stewards of participative processes, planting these processes and helping them to take root.

Fourth, every formal leader must expect and encourage everyone to be a leader in some aspect of his or her work. Leadership for the future is no longer a position located only at the top of the organizational pyramid. It is a function that everyone can perform with customers, in teams, when faced with problems and decisions. It is the living expression of the belief that everyone has a unique contribution to make in an area or at a task at which he or she is better than anyone else. In their own special areas and with their own unique energy, all people can lead.

Any of these four leadership challenges could absorb one person for an entire career. When they are combined, as they are now, leaders face a truly formidable set of challenges.

LETTING GO OF AUTHORITARIAN PERSPECTIVES AND BEHAVIORS

Years of authoritarianism have bred many assumptions about formal leadership. In authoritarian systems, the people at the top are expected to be the thinkers, the strategists, the people with the answers. They are expected to make no mistakes, never to change their minds, and not show the weaknesses that in others would be judged evidence of human frailty. Under the old rules—or at least under the fantasies that supported the old rules—leaders must appear to be faultless.

Old-style leaders are used to being treated like customers. People in authoritarian systems spend a lot of time and energy trying to please those above them. In businesses, these efforts take the form of elaborate presentations to the boss, pandering and positioning, passing the good news on, leaving the bad news behind, and so on.

In most institutions, the people at the top have also become used to their privileges and perquisites. Mahogany-paneled offices, gold-plated office accessories, corner suites with beautiful views, limousines, and first-class travel combine with deferential treatment from those below them to give them an aura of aristocracy. With the exception of the deferential treatment, which is arguably a negative under any circumstances, people who have heavy leadership responsibilities deserve to be rewarded for them. But for many leaders in authoritarian systems, the rewards breed aristocratic attitudes that in turn lead to paternalism and abuse of privilege.

Recent studies indicate that the excesses of authority increased significantly during the 1980s and early 1990s. In 1980, CEOs in the largest American companies were paid about thirty times more than the operational worker. By 1990, the multiple had increased to more than ninety. This increase occurred during a period of relatively flat growth in productivity and sharp staffing cuts. Today's leaders must let go of this type of abuse of privilege.

Richard Hallstein (1993, p. 2) talks about the personal journey that he took in letting go of his own authoritarian assumptions and behaviors. A difficult journey, it requires a lifelong commitment to new views of self and others: "This feeling that we are constantly in charge grows in its addictiveness. The more we accomplish, the more we're convinced that we can make things happen. We get increasingly addicted to activity, excitement, being in charge, and being successful. We believe that we are a superior kind of human being who can handle anything. Such a burden this can all become!"

We must not underestimate the powerful legacy of authoritarian programming. Anyone who has grown up in or around an authoritarian system, even if he or she rebelled against it, has at least in part been formed, perhaps even tainted, by its values and views. The leader's first task today is to recognize his or her own part in the history that belongs to us all. He or she must explore the case for moving from authoritarian to participative governance. If the case makes sense, he or she must be willing to leave old behaviors and mind-sets behind in order to enter the next generation of human institutions.

At a minimum, today's leaders must conduct a very thorough and critical self-examination to find the autocrat in themselves. There are many questionnaires on leadership style, and a leader can use any one of these to get structured feedback from work colleagues and from the people whom they lead. It is also helpful to get professional feedback from a specialist in leadership development. Many powerful people do not have a clear and accurate awareness of their impact on other people. They do not realize that when they speak, people hear a roar. When they walk, others feel the earth shake. When they look at something, others see a laser burn. Such fantasies of followers as these are part of the strange legacy of years of authoritarianism. People with power who truly want to lead acknowledge this legacy. They begin their own development by carefully exploring how their own behaviors and attitudes sustain abuses of power.

LEADING THE EMOTIONAL TRANSITION

The second task of today's leader is to guide the emotional transition from authoritarianism to participation. This transition has many complexities and dangers. It has at least two phases: the phase of recognizing and setting up for change and the phase of managing the dynamics that are unleashed as people and systems establish the conditions needed for a new form of governance. These phases can take several years.

The former Soviet Union provides ample evidence that both phases are inevitable and needed. Gorbachev was clearly the leader who set the stage for change. World economic and political dynamics assisted him, and events that occurred before his term laid some of the necessary foundations. But he began the talk about glasnost—openness—and perestroika—democratic structures—before Boris Yeltsin took power. In the next phase, Yeltsin tried to construct the mechanisms of a new, participative economy, but he did not invest enough in the task of helping the Russian people and Russian institutions acquire the mind-sets needed for a new way of living and governing. Nor did he help people to see that the ups and downs of transition were indicators of progress, not of failure. The West is partly responsible for the resulting problems, for it has failed to deliver the massive investments of aid needed for the transition.

Major changes like the shift from autocracy to participation take time and require personal changes that can be traumatic. These changes are archetypal. That is, they tap basic human emotions of the kind explored and expressed in myth.

Many Biblical stories and ancient myths are stories about transition, which may indicate that transition is more common than we admit. Jonah had to spend days in the belly of the whale in order to become enlightened. Noah spent years on the Ark. Moses and the Israelites wandered in the desert, often without hope, for years. Christ fasted for forty days in the desert, agonized for hours on the cross, and rested for three days in the tomb before he moved into his new, glorified state. According to Buddhists, we all spend many transitory lives in various stages of ignorance and enlightenment before we attain nirvana.

Transition and transformation often help us to forge a new life and way of living. It may be that the greatest gift in the current age is the gift of living in the explosive turmoil of transition.

Whether a gift or a curse, transition is a reality of governance today. Leaders must somehow help others to assume new roles, make new assumptions, and shoulder new responsibilities even when they are afraid that taking such steps will destroy their own ability to lead.

BEING ACCOUNTABLE STEWARDS OF PARTICIPATION

At the other end of transition is the world of high performance and involvement that many organizations have only begun to enter. In that world, formal leaders must exchange the roles of bossing and parenting for the role of stewardship. Stewardship places the formal leader in a position of service to the organization's many current and future stakeholders. As Peter Block (1993, p. 22) says, "Stewardship in an institutional setting means attending to the service brought to each employee, customer, supplier, and community. To be accountable to those we have power over. This is accountability congruent with the redistribution of power, privilege, and purpose."

The principle of stewardship, under which leaders are the supporters of others, not their controllers, is not new. The ancient Chinese writings collected in the *Tao Te Ching* are attributed to Lao-tzu, a contemporary of Confucius (551-479 B.C.). The *Tao Te Ching* describes four levels of leaders: those who are despised, those who are feared, those who are loved and revered, and those—at the highest level—who are "barely known by men" or who have "but a shadowy presence" (Lao-tzu, 1963, p. 73; 1972, Chapter Seventeen). The highest level of leadership enables people to claim that *they* did it themselves or that it happened to them naturally. All the world's great religions express the same sentiment. Its essence is that true leaders involve others in ways that enable and empower these others to achieve much more than they could alone. True leaders also make sure that these others get the credit for their achievements.

The work of stewardship for participation begins with the redesign of assumptions, systems, and processes in ways that eliminate bureaucracy and other barriers to high performance and involvement. We have suggested that leadership is one of the nine critical areas on which design and redesign can focus. The others are values, structure, management processes, information, relationships, competencies, controls, and pay.

Formal leaders must put their full weight behind changes in these areas and be willing to do the personal learning and support the organizational trial and error that are part of this massive governance shift. As an expression of their belief in the value of the new governance principles, leaders must also be willing to accomplish this redesign work participatively. Such a willingness makes the move to participation much faster than it is if the change is a movement coming in without the support of formal leaders.

This does not mean that an organization cannot become more participative without the active support and guidance of the institution's leaders. But, as we all know, changes that do not have the support of the formal leaders in chronically authoritarian systems are more costly and difficult to implement than changes that do have their support. If the institution's formal leaders do not support the governance shift, activism, adversarial politics, and even revolutions to remove those at the top may be the only alternatives. These alternatives increase the costs, lengthen the time frame, and add to the pain and difficulty of the change.

In many cases, the energy required to unseat or change the current authorities is more than the organization can muster, and the change effort dies. Many total quality management and customer focus programs have died for just this reason. When key people refuse to make the personal power shifts and system changes that are needed if these programs are to work, the efforts collapse unless a very strong subversive element supports the change.

ENCOURAGING A LEADERSHIP ALLIANCE

In the participative world, everyone shares the leadership role. In its broadest sense, leadership is no longer just a seat in the boardroom, the box at the top of the organizational pyramid, or a title bestowed on a few. It is a role in which anyone engages whenever he or she attempts to redirect resources or attention in order to accomplish a larger goal. Leadership acts can occur whenever problems are solved, decisions are made, or information is acted on. When someone attempts to change things or to influence others to take new or different directions that will better serve multiple stakeholders for the future, he or she performs a leadership act.

Ordinary people can and must perform leadership acts in the new organization. Organizations that will be successful in the future create what Tom Peters (1988) calls *leadership alliances*—environments in which people at all levels take innovative, creative, and courageous action toward the fulfillment of common purposes.

Traditionalists often reject such notions as idealistic, claiming that most people are just followers who need to be led. But such a view denies the very real innovative and creative capacity of every human being. We are all lifelong learners. We all have the capacity not only to live with but to cherish discontinuity. Procreating; giving birth to a child; raising a family; growing up and moving through the traumas of childhood, puberty, adolescence, and adulthood; moving from one home to another; losing loved ones and overcoming grief; being attracted to other human beings; falling in love; getting married; changing jobs; getting divorced; leading church groups and voluntary organizations—these and a myriad of other activities help ordinary people to develop a capacity for leadership.

It may take a bit of tweaking and molding, but every organization has a treasure chest of untapped leadership capacity just below the surface. All that it really takes to reveal it is to jettison some of the authoritarian attitudes of the past and to value the capacities of people who, after all, are managing to survive and even be happy in a pretty complex world.

> *Isaac was a driver whose main job was delivering small items by car or acting as a chauffeur to company visitors. He had worked in this position for more than a decade, and he was well liked by everyone who met him. He wanted to do more—to take on a real challenge. But, despite his outgoing personality and his ability to talk about a wide range of subjects, his managers always maintained that he was not promotable beyond his existing position.*
>
> *Meanwhile, Isaac developed another career. He played lead saxophone at a popular nightclub. As the years went by, his band developed a fair international reputation. It toured the United States and worked in several European Community countries. Isaac both set up the tours and managed the money for the band.*
>
> *As the band's reputation increased, many of Isaac's day job colleagues and managers expressed great surprise at his success. Their organization had no room for leadership alliances. Isaac took his creative energies elsewhere.*

Isaac's story shows that the key question is not whether people have the inherent capacity and drive for leadership but whether organizations are governed in ways that continuously celebrate and encourage creative and courageous action by all members: employees, suppliers, customers, even stockholders.

Anyone who has tried to help to create a participative workplace has encountered a dilemma in this area. There may be verbal acknowledgement that everyone can lead. There may even be enlightened management that wants to encourage the spread of leadership. But decades and centuries of prescriptive and old-style management practices have created a counterculture of subordination and apathy. People may not know that they have the skills, and they are often reluctant to take charge of anything at work.

Although everyone is responsible for this disempowerment—employees and management, followers and leaders alike—it is up to formal leaders to take the most responsibility for changing it. Formal leaders still have access to the largest share of the power and resources within their organization, and they must do something about these centuries of subordination as part of their formal stewardship role.

That formal leaders have this responsibility does not absolve employees from the responsibility of breaking the shackles of subordination and moving to new levels of empowerment and accountability. It does, however, point to one of the great tasks facing stewardship in our time: creating the conditions under which all people accept and activate their own leadership energies whenever and wherever they are relevant and needed. This means that people who are not used to power must take the initiative, be responsible, and stand up for unpopular and unsupported ideas—even against the boss. The new leader supports, encourages, and requires people to take such stances.

CONCLUSION

Leaders today are caught in a cusp, a state of transition between the old era and the new. Expectations are high; models are few and unproven; the old rewards and perquisites are slipping away; and dissatisfaction, finger-pointing, and even violence toward leaders are common.

Nevertheless, the task of facilitating this governance shift and then managing under the new requirements is the work of leaders in our time. It is either a crisis or an opportunity for those who would take formal leadership roles today. Wherever the individual stands, at least four major challenges are putting today's leaders to the test. First, they must give up their personal stake in authoritarianism. They must learn to forego the customer-like treatment, the abuses of privilege, the aristocratic attitudes, and the exploitive perquisites associated with leadership in the past. These patterns are difficult to break because followers reinforce them: They expect leaders to be superhuman, to be customer and judge, to be their royalty.

Second, they must lead the transition. Transition is a long, frustrating, and yet very creative time in which all groups change their assumptions about roles and relationships and all the elements of organizational governance ratchet to new forms and connections. As Chapter Eighteen shows, it is not a smooth period.

Third, once the transition has been negotiated, leaders must govern under the new rules of the Age of Participation. These rules focus on both high performance and high involvement. This governing task is a particularly interesting one today, because we are in the early stages of participation. There are few comprehensive success stories and little information about reliable practices.

Fourth, formal leaders must give leadership away. They must help every member of their organization to recognize the leadership capacity that he or she possesses and to use it in ways that help to make the organization great.

It is not an easy task. People who take on a formal leadership role today deserve to be paid well and well supported. But no amount of compensation can offset the real personal costs that leaders must be willing to assume or the very real chance that they may not see the full effects of their efforts.

Perhaps what must attract leaders is the belief that they can make a difference for the future. But the calling is one to stewardship—stewardship motivated by the opportunity for service and impact. The calling is to be a change leader who is stimulated rather than paralyzed by uncertainty, paradox, resistance, and alienation. The calling is also to be a psychological leader whose personal hope and optimism help to energize others and give them space for risk and united action.

For those who respond to such a calling and the promised legacy that it implies, the years ahead will be exciting, and life will have tremendous meaning. Those who do not wish to accept the challenge and endure the uncertainty and anger expected in the times ahead should follow another path.

Think about the leadership in your organization. Figure 7.1 contains five pairs of items. Allocate ten points between the two items in each pair. The points awarded reflect the extent to which each statement is true. Allocate five or more points to an item only if you can say that at least 75 percent of the people in your organization would agree that the statement closely reflects their views and experiences. Nine or ten points indicate that your organization is really a case study example of the statement. The points that you award to each pair of items must total ten. When you have finished rating the statements, add up the numbers in the A column and the B column, and record them on the LEADERSHIP row of the Governance Assessment Score Sheet in Appendix I.

Figure 7.1 Assess the Leadership in Your Organization

☐ **11A**. *Formal leaders use their positions for personal gain, power, and prestige.*

☐ **11B**. *Formal leaders are stewards of the organization's stakeholders and work actively to optimize the interests of all stakeholders.*

☐ **12A**. *Formal leaders expect people and systems to adapt quickly and rationally to change.*

☐ **12B**. *Formal leaders expect people to go through a period of adjustment, even of resistance, as part of any change process. They facilitate and guide emotional transitions.*

☐ **13A**. *Formal leaders behave autocratically. When others work with them, it is clear who is boss and who is subordinate.*

☐ **13B**. *Formal leaders behave participatively. They involve other people and readily defer to better ideas and expertise.*

☐ **14A**. *Formal leaders have an attitude of "I know" or "I have the answers."*

☐ **14B**. *Formal leaders admit when they don't have answers or when they need to learn, even from those "below" them.*

☐ **15A**. *Leadership is static. It is the prerogative of people who have formal authority.*

☐ **15B**. *Leadership in day-to-day work moves from person to person, depending on the task and the competencies required.*

CHAPTER 8

Management Processes: Everyone a Manager

IN THE AUTHORITARIAN ORGANIZATION, managing is the responsibility of managers. Management decisions are made by managers and communicated—or not communicated—to the people who must do the work. Thinking is separated from doing, power is disconnected from accountability, control is imposed on people from without rather than from within, and measurement supports evaluation, not improvement. The major decisions on the business calendar—strategic planning, budgets, business reviews—are generally made by people at the top with little consultation.

At most companies, authoritarian assumptions and values have been built into key management events and business calendars. Authoritarian values saturate the strategic and business planning processes, team management processes, budgeting, communication of plans, individual goal setting, day-to-day decision making, business reviews, and performance review discussions. All these management processes need to be redesigned to broaden involvement.

Management processes, which range from the development of strategy to performance reviews, are the backbone of the operation of any business. They are the vehicles first for determining what the performance of the business should be, then for ensuring that the organization's resources are applied efficiently to carry out the strategic intent. These processes are such central and powerful factors of business success that how they occur becomes the real culture of the business. If they occur coercively, the culture is coercive. If they operate dependently, the culture is dependent. If independence or interdependence characterize them, then the culture is independent or interdependent.

Management processes may be the ultimate key to the shift from autocracy to participation. They are an expression of the organization's values that affects every person in the business. These processes must become participative, or the organization cannot be a high-involvement institution.

STRATEGY DEVELOPMENT

Even in authoritarian organizations, a great deal of strategy is developed by people during their day-to-day work, because what people do every day actually becomes the strategy of the business. Henry Mintzberg (1989, p. 29), professor of management at McGill University, calls upward strategy development the "emergent" strategy of the business. He encourages organizations to scan the activities that are occurring in the workplace and to bring the innovations and successes that emerge from these activities into the more formal strategic planning process so they can be spread to a wider audience. Such scanning is one of the ways in which people can be helped to become involved in setting a company's direction.

However, the participative organization involves a broad audience in its more formal strategic planning activities, because it knows that every stakeholder can have some insights to contribute. One of the main business purposes of participation is to ensure that relevant knowledge and ideas come to the fore, no matter what their source. Employees, customers, suppliers, trade union representatives and members, and financial stakeholders are all candidates for involvement. For organizations in which strategy traditionally develops in secret and at sessions to which access is restricted, such involvement clearly requires a substantial change.

There are many ways of involving people formally in strategy development. Some organizations conduct large sessions for perhaps hundreds of people at which environmental and competitive information is presented and discussed in small groups. Facilitators ensure that everyone gets involved and provides ideas. Another way of involving people is through computer networking, which uses electronic mail (E-mail) to air critical business issues. Individuals respond with their ideas or other perspectives. Decentralized discussion groups organized especially for the purpose of strategy development or occurring in natural work groups are other avenues for input and discussion.

If people have been excluded from strategy discussions in the past, it is important to expect an initial period of testing and even of naïveté. Participants must expand their understanding of relevant business issues and develop confidence in their own perceptions, insights, and ideas. Only then can they become full participants in the strategic thinking of the business. Managers must also get used to asking questions, listening, and examining diverse views and perspectives. This, too, takes time.

STRATEGY COMMUNICATION

If people have been involved in the development of the organization's larger goals and plans, the work of strategy communication is already half done. However, how people learn about the organization's strategic intent and begin to translate it into terms meaningful for their own work is a second key management process, even if strategy is a participative product.

Participative communication about strategy is two-way, not just a video presentation or a talk in a large hall. Rather, responsibility is shared in dialogue that gives everyone a chance to ask why and to discuss the operational implications of decisions to move in some directions and not in others.

Ichak Adizes (1988) tells a delightful story to illustrate the difference between intended strategy and actual strategy. He says that a consultant had been working with the executives of a shoe-manufacturing company. During a three-day workshop, they formulated a wonderfully ambitious new strategy. It focused on everything—market niches, technological adjustments, export opportunities, new designs, unions. Two weeks later, the consultant was working with a team of production people. He asked them how they planned to make their mark in the company. "Easy," replied one worker. "We will take size 4 shoes and size 8 shoes and put them into boxes together."

Once strategic decisions have been made, it is vital for the organization's formal leaders to talk and write about the decisions in terms that are relevant to the people who must implement them. Those people—employees, suppliers, key customers, trade union representatives—must then be able to discuss, clarify, and translate the decisions for themselves. Open dialogue, questions, and even challenges help people to internalize the strategic intent so that they can and want to implement it and make the strategy work.

> *A shipbuilding company in the northeastern United States holds a series of leadership conferences annually at which all employees review and discuss the business strategies. The annual conferences are supplemented by quarterly lunchtime business awareness sessions. At these lunches, employees learn and exchange ideas about key business projects and new product developments.*

It makes no sense to have a strategy that no one understands, commits to, or acts on. Interdependent communication has many benefits, including a strengthened connection between individual and organizational goals, a shared context for action throughout the organization, and increased confidence that leaders have really thought about and taken advice on the best direction for the company to follow. Confidence in leaders is an interesting by-product that occurs because people know the company has a direction. They may not agree with it, but participative communication will enable them to understand what it is and why it exists.

TEAM GOALS

Work today increasingly occurs in teams. Every department, work group, task force, and project team must therefore align itself with the organization's larger goals. When teams are aligned, their understanding and commitment increase, and the organization can speed implementation of its key goals.

The means by which a team selects its goals, determines its roles, and creates commitment is thus the third management process that we need to target for change. Teams must learn how to decide participatively what they will do, who will do what, and how the team will manage itself in order to accomplish its goals. By participating in teams, people can develop the confidence, processes, and skills that they need in order to become involved in the larger arena. The participative team becomes a microcosm of the participative organization.

There are many benefits when teams determine their goals participatively. There is deliberate integration with customers and other key stakeholders. The team overtly decides what it will and will not do. People are clear about their roles, responsibility devolves, and the strategy becomes action that can be taken.

> *A New York-based financial services company has representatives in every major financial center of the world. The global team in charge of securities transactions meets at least once a year. Using a simple but structured process, team members examine the larger business strategy and explore how they can optimize their role within it. They use the discussions about team goals to help spread responsibility among team members and to ensure that all ideas and questions have been addressed.*

BUDGETS AND ACTION PLANS

Many participative processes break down because budgets are often developed before goals have been set or because budgets are developed and controlled outside the team. Thus, new ideas often cannot and do not get funded.

But participation often increases the ideas and the range of actions available to a firm. So participation can raise serious questions and create confusion about priorities and resource allocation. In a participative organization, these questions must be resolved through debate and meaningful influence. Participation is a sham if the people who are accountable for their actions cannot influence the allocation of resources to their functions.

Devolving budget power is a frightening thought for many managers and financial staff. They do not trust the motives or knowledge of others sufficiently to turn control over to them. Their concerns may be well-founded. Many teams and individuals may indeed lack the knowledge or skill needed to make informed decisions about the allocation of resources. Thus, a transition period in which teams and individuals learn how to conduct cost-benefit analyses may be needed. Some amount of financial education and coaching may also be needed before full budget power can diffuse throughout the organization.

One of the best ways of achieving such education is to change the job descriptions of financial and data-processing staff. Part of their valuable expertise must be transferred to operational people. During real-time interaction, the staff specialists can coach and educate front-line workers to assume increased functional responsibilities.

A strong case can be made for taking bold steps in this area. Most people are reluctant to examine the financial implications of their ideas. It is hard to break out of one's financial naïveté and dependency. There is thus a compelling reason for devolving authority quickly and for providing coaching and education after financial authority and responsibility have been moved down. Most people learn faster when they know that they must be accountable for how they spend money and other resources. Chances are that there will not be any real increase in poor decisions. In fact, resource stewardship often increases overall when budget responsibility spreads to everyone.

A processing plant that employed seven hundred people was notorious for its autocratic management style. But new leadership wanted to make substantial changes. An important opportunity came along when expansion and new crate technologies required the purchase of several new forklift trucks.

The plant production manager and his team decided to take a chance. They asked the operators to decide what forklifts to buy. In spite of the 40 percent illiteracy rate among operators, a remarkable process ensued. The forklift team, coached by both a financial and a technical adviser, developed quality criteria for the trucks. They identified suppliers and invited them to submit proposals. They screened the suppliers and, with the help of the financial adviser, reviewed the financial implications of the suppliers' proposals. Ultimately, the team recommended a special design that would be easy to operate and that would enable them to carry more crates per load.

The forklifts purchased in this way continue to be the best cared for in the company. And everyone agrees that no one could have made a better decision.

INDIVIDUAL GOALS

Participation implies that individuals make choices and have influence over their own affairs. For this reason, the participative organization must maintain a vital and participative individual goal-setting process. Personal goals become an individual's vehicle for influencing his or her own work, for making commitments, and for negotiating support and resources.

The participative organization respects the individual's unique perspectives on his or her job. It invites the individual to bring those perspectives into the process of deciding on his or her own goals. In the past, goals were ends. They established what an individual would do or accomplish. In the participative organization, individual goals are a key means of involvement. They are the focal point for discussion and debate with stakeholders, the place at which strategies become specific deliverables and actions, and the rallying point at which an individual can shape and express his or her view of quality and innovation.

If there is no discussion and debate about individual goals, there can be no real participation. In goal-setting sessions, the individual's ideas and issues matter, and he or she takes time to align with larger strategies and customer needs. Goal-setting time is also an opportunity to take stock of various team commitments and to make trade-offs if the job has gotten too big for one person to do.

Regular, participative individual goal setting helps everyone to become a partner in the business. But individual goal setting must have the legitimacy of budgeting and business planning. It must be a protected requirement that involves everyone everywhere as part of the business calendar.

DECISION MAKING

Decisions are made everywhere every day within an organization. In authoritarian organizations, people at the top make a broad array of strategic, operational, and even tactical decisions. In participative organizations, there are levels of decision-making authority—for example, senior management is responsible for determining the organization's long-range strategic direction—but there is broad involvement and consultation. Moreover, people everywhere in a participative organization have more authority than they would in an authoritarian organization, and they require fewer levels of approval to get their day-to-day work done. The role of the leader is to decide the direction. The rest is up to the people who must do the work.

There is a lot of confusion about the decision-making processes that are appropriate in a participative institution. The issue is an emotional one, because many managers fear that the devolving of decision-making authority will lead to loss of control and anarchy. They interpret participation as meaning that all the people must be involved all the time. But participation does not imply reckless involvement. Everyone does not have to be involved in everything. Involvement must be purposeful. It must add value either by improving the quality of the decisions made or by enhancing commitment to them. Few people, no matter what their level, want to spend their time in endless meetings and decision processes.

Nonetheless, participative organizations do pay more attention than authoritarian institutions to the ways in which decisions are made and to whom is involved. First, participative governance recognizes everyone to be a decision maker. The person who sweeps the floor must decide which broom to use, where to start sweeping, and what to suggest as long-term solutions when persistent or dangerous spillage causes problems. An insurance salesperson must decide which policies to offer a client. An executive must decide which strategies the company will adopt and which it will not.

When a situation arises in which a decision must be made, the individual or team who owns the decision must decide how to decide. This decision is often more important than the decision itself. Involving other people can lengthen the time that it takes to make the decision. It can also open the door to conflict and dissent, which lengthen the time required to reach closure. However, failing to involve others can result either in a bad or in an incomplete decision. It can also lead to a solution that others either do not understand or do not want to support.

The quality of the decisions that are made and acceptance of these decisions are two key issues. Decisions about the individuals to involve in a decision-making process should depend on one or both of two things: their ability to improve the quality of the decision and the importance of their acceptance of the decision for its successful implementation. These two key issues underline that a decision is more than the making of a decision. The complete decision cycle has at least four key elements: gathering data, deliberating, making the decision, and implementing the decision. A slow, conflict-filled, participative decision can sometimes be implemented in less time than a fast autocratic decision. If the total time required for the former is less than the total time required for the latter, it seems obvious that more involvement is better than less.

Victor H. Vroom and Philip W. Yetton (Vroom and Yetton, 1973) describe a decision-making model that is very relevant for the participative organization today. These authors say that there are four ways of making a decision: independently, consultatively, by consensus, and through delegation.

A decision can be made independently when the person who makes it has the necessary information and when the commitment of others to it is either assured or unnecessary. For example, a decision by a manager about the color that his office will be painted or by a technical expert about a very technical issue could fall into this category. Of course, an independent decision might be needed in an emergency: for example, by a fire marshall or a refinery manager when there has been an explosion.

A decision is consultative when the decision maker asks others for possible solutions but makes the decision him- or herself. This type of decision is especially appropriate when the person who makes the decision needs more information and ideas than he or she has in order to make a good decision. Others may need to be committed to the decision, but major differences of opinion among others and time pressures may mean that there is no time to work the differences out through consensus. In the case of a consultative decision, the decision maker must make it clear that he or she will make the decision after hearing others' views. Otherwise, people may expect their advice to prevail and decline to support the plan that ultimately results.

Consensus decisions are decisions that the decision maker and others make together. Here, the decision maker becomes one among equals and does not use his or her status, if it is greater, to pressure for a particular view. The person in whose domain the decision is must be sure that the consensus-making process exacts the best ideas from all participants. Consensus decisions are best when input from others is required in order to reach a good decision and strong commitment from others is essential for its success. It is also best when the problem is complex and none of the possible choices is clearly superior.

A decision is delegative when a person who has authority to make a decision passes the power and accountability for making it to another person or to a group. The delegated decision represents an expansion of power and accountability for the person or group that is to make it. Delegation is an appropriate decision-making method when the success of the decision depends on the commitment of the new decision maker to it and when making the decision will help to broaden and develop the capabilities of the individual to whom the task has been delegated. A delegative decision can be made independently, consultatively, or by consensus, depending on the method that the new decision maker chooses. The person who delegates the decision can play a consultative or consensual role, acting as coach, resource, or adviser on quality.

One of the best ways of developing the organization's capacity for participation is to involve people consultatively, consensually, and delegatively in decisions. In the early stages of a shift toward participation, decision makers should as a general rule choose the participative level that is one step higher than the decision seems to require. That is, if the decision could be made independently, a consultative method should be used. If it calls for consultation, use consensus. If consensus is the best option, delegate the decision to a group.

As people acquire experience in decision making, they must learn more about the business and about what it takes to work successfully with others—skill areas that are important for making participation work in the long run.

Clearly, everyone in the organization must become more aware of him- or herself as a decision maker. Everyone must also be more conscious that his or her choice of decision-making method will affect the quality of the decision and its chances of being implemented. It is also important for everyone to become as competent as possible in the various methods of decision making.

It is important to strike a good balance between independent, consultative, consensual, and delegative decisions. Many very complex decisions require increased involvement, both because it improves the quality of the decisions made and because it makes the decisions more likely to be carried out. But independent decisions should be taken when they are appropriate so that the organization is not cluttered with meaningless consultation and collaboration. To be overly collaborative can be as damaging to the spirit of participation as autocracy is when involvement is needed.

In the early stages of building an organization's capacity to participate, it is wise to get people more rather than less involved. Involvement can develop the skills of effective participative decision making and expand the ability of everyone to decide in all four ways.

BUSINESS REVIEWS

Participative organizations make voracious use of business information. People everywhere receive and analyze it: How happy are customers? What are the current business performance statistics? What is working, and what is not working? How well are we doing against our competitors? What is happening in the economy? These are all questions that employees and even suppliers must be able to answer.

More important, in participative organizations, individuals and teams talk about the implications of data on business performance for their own goals and work. In participative organizations, everyone knows that implementation of strategy and ultimately the success of the business as a whole are their responsibility. No matter how big or small the job may be, it affects performance.

For these reasons, information about business performance is broadly available in the participative organization. It is available in print, at meetings, and in large-group forums. These communications are also dynamic. There is dialogue, exploration, and questioning. Interaction deepens the participants' understandings of what is and is not happening, what is and is not working. People meet in small groups to discuss implications. They meet in large groups and across levels to talk about the performance of an organization in which they all have an emotional and tangible financial or career stake.

> *In the early 1980s, the vice president of manufacturing at one of the world's largest cosmetics companies decided to get all his staff involved in running the manufacturing operation. One of the main ways in which he accomplished this aim was through monthly meetings of the entire manufacturing team, top to bottom. Personnel met in a large hall for an hour during the overlap between two shifts. The vice president presented performance data both for manufacturing alone and for the company as a whole and then deferred to the floor for discussion. Anyone could raise an issue, offer an idea, ask a question, or describe a problem. In the course of the discussion, people in the group often identified projects that they thought might help to make improvements. On the spot, individuals volunteered to manage these projects. It was not unusual to have assembly people take charge of a project for the entire line. Immediately, the vice president entered information about the project into a computerized project tracking system, together with the project team's list of steps to be completed by the next group meeting.*
>
> *The combination of total communication, good facilitation, systems support, and trust enabled the group operation to beat the industry on every key measure.*
>
> *Of course, the high involvement in business communication and problem solving did not exist in a vacuum. Among other things, every senior manufacturing executive spent one week a year working on the line, performing tasks assigned at the discretion of frontline supervisors. This helped to build the trust and rapport that made broad involvement in business decision making possible.*

PERFORMANCE REVIEW DISCUSSIONS

The eighth important management process area that must become participative is performance review. This is an interesting and controversial arena, especially since the proponents of total quality management, have condemned performance reviews as enemies of quality. The case that can be made against performance reviews is pretty strong. Years of coercion and dependency have turned individual feedback processes into blaming, game playing, and punitive activities. Performance reviews have also become ineffective tools of the pay and promotion system.

But frustration caused by abuse of feedback systems is not a reason to abandon them. Individuals in participative organizations need personal feedback, and teams need it. Feedback keeps things on track, and it is crucial to learning. Direct and respectful feedback is also important in the building of trust and relationships. Personal and team feedback and performance reviews have important roles to play, but we must eliminate the effects that have resulted from past abuses.

In the participative organization, performance review is participative. Individuals and teams manage their own process. They ask for feedback and contribute information to the feedback process. They use multiple sources, seeking the views of customers, colleagues, suppliers, and relevant people in management. Feedback focuses on the quality of performance and on ideas for improvement and future innovation.

A growing body of evidence suggests that performance reviews should focus on development and improvement, not on pay and promotion. Such a focus can emerge only if pay for performance occurs across the board through total company schemes like profit sharing and gain sharing. The emerging insights indicate that individual pay differentials should depend on skill and job differences, not on individuals' success or failure in accomplishing specific goals.

Chapter Thirteen examines pay in some detail. The important point for now is that performance review is a key management process that, when participative, helps to create the new governance. Since participative reviews tend to raise trust levels, they can also play a role in entrenching participation for the long term.

CONCLUSION

Eight management processes carry the genetic code for an organization's culture. If these processes occur autocratically, the organization will be authoritarian. If the organization involves people meaningfully in these processes, it will be participative.

In the participative organization, everyone is involved in all eight processes. The processes also have the status of events on the business calendar. In most organizations, strategic and business planning, budgeting, and business reviews already have such status. In the participative institution, this status extends also to team goals, individual goals, day-to-day decision making, and performance reviews.

Because these eight processes occur at the main interfaces between individual employees and the business as a whole, it is crucial to make them participative. In a very real sense, participation has a good chance of becoming the organization's overall style if people are meaningfully involved in these eight processes. Meaningful participation in these areas will inevitably spill over into others.

Think about the management processes in your organization. Figure 8.1 contains five pairs of items. Allocate ten points between the two items in each pair. The points awarded reflect the extent to which each statement is true. Allocate five or more points to an item only if you can say that at least 75 percent of the people in your organization would agree that the statement closely reflects their views and experiences. Nine or ten points indicate that your organization is really a case study example of the statement. The points that you award to each pair of items must total ten. When you have finished rating the statements, add up the numbers in the A column and the B column, and record them on the MANAGEMENT PROCESSES row of the Governance Assessment Score Sheet in Appendix I.

Figure 8.1 Assess the Management Processes
in Your Organization

☐ **16A**. Managers do the business planning and budgeting and conduct the business reviews.

☐ **16B**. Staff at all levels are actively involved in business planning, budgets, and business reviews.

☐ **17A**. Personal and team performance management—goal setting and performance feedback—are primarily processes for the personnel department. People play games with them in order to get better pay, recognition, and promotion.

☐ **17B**. Personal and team performance management—goal setting and performance feedback—are credible business processes that are applied with the same nonnegotiable discipline and consistency as budgets and business plans.

☐ **18A**. Decisions at all levels are highly controlled. Senior management often overrides decisions or requires approvals.

☐ **18B**. Everyone is considered a decision maker within his or her area of performance. Approval levels exist only when they add value.

☐ **19A**. Financial staff and senior management determine and control budgets.

☐ **19B**. People everywhere have meaningful influence in the development of their own budgets. Senior management and financial staff play a supportive and coaching role.

☐ **20A**. Senior management restricts distribution of business plans and strategies and provides information selectively to those who "need to know."

☐ **20B**. Business plans and strategies are broadly distributed and widely discussed.

CHAPTER 9

Information:
No Secrets

IN ORDER FOR PEOPLE who do the work to participate effectively, they need information that can guide their action. Giving them such information requires a dramatic reversal of authoritarian practices. In traditional organizations, the people who must implement strategy often know very little about the organization's larger goals and plans. Nor do they get enough timely feedback to make corrections as they work. At the same time, senior managers often do not have real and useful information about what is really going on in and around the organization.

Curiously, when computer data processing became widely available in the 1960s, very few of the assumptions about who would get information and what information they would get changed in most organizations. The computer makes it possible to bring information to many people and to process it and present it in ways that make it useful for a variety of audiences. But the early use of computers was based on authoritarian assumptions about right to know and need to know. Most organizations need a new vision of information as a decision tool for everyone within the organization.

"Our biggest learning in the past decade," says a senior director of a large bank, "is that computers really enable participation. Initially, computers did little for productivity and customer service. We used them largely to speed up what we were already doing. They enabled us to process significantly larger volumes of data with fewer errors and greater efficiency. Now we are empowering people by putting information at their fingertips. Telephone enquiry clerks are authorizing payouts that used to go to supervisors and even branch managers for approval. It has meant a mind-shift for us all."

Information technology is one of the major forces that makes participation possible. Before the computer, companies needed a hierarchy of managers to gather, sort, summarize, and pass information up, down, and around the organization. This information channeling function of the organizational hierarchy is no longer needed. Superimposing sophisticated information systems on old hierarchies is a wasteful redundancy.

There are at least four qualities of information that make true participation possible. First, the people who do the work must have access to information about strategies, vision, and the work itself. Second, everyone must learn to be a skilled user of information. Third, information is positioned for learning and continuous improvement rather than for punishment. Fourth, relevant functional information is integrated into everyone's job.

MAKE INFORMATION AVAILABLE TO PEOPLE WHO DO THE WORK

People need two kinds of information in order to be able to think, make decisions, and solve problems in their work: strategic information about the larger vision and context and tactical information to help them do their day-to-day work.

Vision and context information helps people to understand the why of their work. It is information about the big picture: the market, the customer, the competition, the organization's goals, its strengths, and its weaknesses. It is also information about what is going on in the organization itself.

Everyone has a vision, and everyone operates in a context. In the absence of a shared vision and a shared context, people will make them up. This means that such important questions as, Why do we have to reduce costs? will find answers, even if the answers are based on rumor or fantasy. The issue is whether the answers will be informed (the competition has come out with a better and cheaper product) or speculative (managers want to increase their salaries).

The participative organization makes a special effort to keep everyone well informed and to give everyone an up-to-date view of the vision and the context. It uses newsletters and newspapers for this purpose. More important, it also uses dialogue: dialogue about the environment, about the organization's own business strategies, its activities and performance, and its values. In authoritarian organizations, such dialogue occurs only at the highest levels. In participative companies, everyone has a chance to discuss what is going on around them, and these discussions take place regularly. They ensure that, when decisions and problems arise, there is a base of common knowledge and values on which everyone can draw.

A senior executive of an international airline made an important remark about context and participation. He said that he can count on any of thousands of airline employees to do the right thing with customers because all employees share a vision of what the airline is trying to do and to be.

In addition to knowing the organization's vision and context, every worker also needs information in order to do his or her job. Thanks to computers, we can now access a much broader range of information than we did in the past. Through electronic mail and voice mail, information can be channeled to many people with virtually no delay. These methods can also be used to provide just-in-time education.

For example, insurance salespeople no longer need to know the detailed features and uses of a variety of policies. They can list a customer's needs and then have the computer supply information about relevant policies and their features within seconds. Electronic scanning of credit cards brings instant credit approval right to the sales clerk. It no longer takes a supervisor to conduct a credit check. In many companies today, an order clerk can call up information about his or her current customer and use the information about buying history that the computer displays to suggest additional purchases.

Every industry has examples of the job and productivity improvements that are possible because information can now go directly to the worker without time delays or distortion.

A general principle for information systems is thus emerging: Bring information to everyone. But the principle goes even farther: Bring information to the customer if possible. Make the customer a part of the business, just as American Hospital Supply did when it put terminals into hospitals from which supplies could be ordered directly. Bring information to suppliers, as WalMart has, so that suppliers can decide on their own when to restock.

This thinking obliterates company walls and moves information out beyond them. It also sounds a death knell for the hoarding of information, the secrecy, and the punitive uses to which information has often been put in authoritarian systems.

TEACH PEOPLE TO BE SKILLED USERS OF INFORMATION

Today's information environment requires new skills and attitudes. People at all levels within an organization must be able to articulate their information needs, think deductively and inductively from data, know how to evaluate data, and understand the various ways in which information can and should be presented. Yet very few people are prepared to thrive in this data-saturated world.

Even today, information systems specialists who know very little about the operating needs of their organization continue to create information systems for users who cannot knowledgeably articulate their own needs. Left to their own devices, information specialists often just create computerized versions of manual reports. They put profit-and-loss statements and balance sheets into electronic spreadsheets without helping users to understand how to use the power of the computer to create financial scenarios and test assumptions. They put information about inventory and receivables into the computer without harnessing the computer's ability to highlight exceptions, shifting patterns, and trends. Aggregation and averaging remain the main ways of manipulating data, although much more powerful statistical techniques are now within reach.

Users must articulate their needs. They must recognize the difference between reports of averages and reports that highlight areas to be managed. And they must take responsibility for identifying the really vital indicators that they want to track. Without such action by users, the power of self-management that the computer gives us will pass people by.

> *A large manufacturer of consumer goods decided to make real-time information available to machine operators. The financial and programming specialists spent a significant amount of time with the operators discussing how the production and performance information would be displayed. One of the accountants commented, "For the first time, I realize that information is an essential input and supply to manufacturing. In the past, we financial people always saw it as our right to receive information for control and analysis. Now we see ourselves as the accountable supplier of an essential commodity."*
>
> *Today operational staff receive updates on information related to material usage, waste, throughput, and productivity on virtually a real-time basis. One worker, who runs marathons, says, "It is our stopwatch for the race we run every day. In the past, management watched the stopwatch, and we looked at the road just in front of us. Now, we use the stopwatch as part of our work. Together with management, we discuss how to improve our running times every week."*

Users must also learn to see information as a key management and self-management tool, not as a technical Big Brother that manages them. Such a learning process requires a questioning and analytical attitude. Everyone must continually ask whether he or she is being served by the data that he or she receives. Are these data helping them to recognize and solve problems more quickly than they could in the past? Are these data providing the information that they need and that they can actually use in decision making? Do reports stimulate thinking, or do they suppress it? On a more basic level, do people even have the basic reading, computing, questioning, and analysis skills that they need in order to work at and beyond the surface of the data that they receive?

In the United States, companies have used information technology to reduce the thinking required on the job. In Japan, companies have done just the opposite. People in Japan aspire to greater knowledge and skill because they have the computer as a thinking tool. In the United States, the use of computers has often had the effect of deskilling workers. This trend means that the increasingly large investments that companies are making in people and in technology are having poor returns.

The new information environment requires new skills and opens new opportunities. It demands that everyone everywhere in the organization become a more astute manager of information.

USE INFORMATION FOR LEARNING RATHER THAN PUNISHMENT

One legacy of authoritarianism is the tendency to use negative information to punish and blame. In this way, authoritarian systems are like dysfunctional families: Everyone colludes in a myth of perfection. When the myth inevitably breaks down, someone has to be blamed.

The new information systems (IS) director in a steel company developed a new labor efficiency report for the rolling mills. The report, which replaced several reports filled with almost incomprehensible and unusable statistics, was designed to identify critical areas for management attention and action. One superintendent was not impressed. "If I understand this right, it's impossible for a mill to have 69 percent efficiency and not be on this report." The IS director agreed but pointed out that the list of areas for action included only those areas in which problems were not being solved. If the 69 percent efficiency problem was being addressed, it would not appear on the report. "I don't care," the superintendent replied. "I'll be damned if someone with a 69 percent efficiency isn't going to be on this report." The superintendent's reaction showed only too well that he continued to think of the report as a hit list, not as a repository of information that could be used for identifying and solving problems and improving overall performance.

The punitive use of data in companies is so prevalent that it is often difficult to find or discuss the truth. As a consequence, problems are often hidden until they turn into disasters, or they are solved in isolation in ways that have little learning value for the rest of the organization. Worse, people may manipulate data to show what the boss wants to hear and see. Needless to say, learning and fast correction in such organizations are exceptions rather than the rule.

It is easy to talk about what should happen. What should and must happen in a truly participative organization is open, improvement-oriented use of information. People should expose their own errors and learnings, using them to correct themselves and to help others avoid learning the same lesson the hard way. This is the only way in which resources can really be used effectively.

Few people realize that a rocket in space or a ship on the sea is more often off than on course. Even the most sophisticated programming before such a vehicle is launched cannot set it on a path that will never need adjustment. What actually keeps a rocket or a ship headed toward its goal is countless thousands of little self-corrections that respond to feedback about where the vessel is, where it is headed, and how much it is off course. Without constant negative as well as positive information, it would be impossible to carry a cargo to any predetermined goal.

The fact is that the authoritarian organization does not create the conditions for continuous correction of this sort. It does not because these systems closely connect self-worth and performance. Authoritarian systems constantly convey the messages: You Are Your Performance; Promotion Requires Perfection; Once You Make a Mistake, You Are Branded; Watch Out for Career-Limiting Moves.

Of course, it is not just authoritarianism at work here. Organizations are collections of human beings. And human beings have emotions and fears that prevent them from being perfectly rational. But authoritarianism feeds these fears. Indeed, it can raise them to levels that can be destructive to the organization and to the people in it.

Once the managers of a production plant accepted that they needed valid information, they introduced performance and productivity accounting systems that could help them to evaluate the full use of their assets. But they worked hard to position the information as a tool for learning and continuous improvement. They asked people to tell the truth. The truth was startling and unpleasant. Production efficiencies were below 40 percent. (The managers had thought that they were above 60 percent.) And waste was above 50 percent if material use, overtime, unplanned maintenance, and absenteeism were also considered. They began to use information to guide performance improvement on both counts. Workers and managers got together regularly to discuss and resolve ongoing problems. Care was taken not to blame anyone for any problem. Everyone became dedicated to the use of information and problems as a way of stimulating learning and improvement.

Within eighteen months, the production plant had become the international benchmark for performance in its field.

W. Edwards Deming (Walton, 1986) often observed that the evaluative and blaming cultures of the past have great tenacity. So he and others who teach quality through participation claim that all uses of information to blame and punish individuals must stop. These uses include individual performance appraisals, surveys that point fingers, and incentive schemes that reward individuals rather than teams. Only after eliminating such uses of information can an organization use it for real improvement and learning.

Many organizations today say that they want to become learning organizations. Open and nonpunitive use of information is one implicit tenet of this goal. Achieving it requires a long, dedicated period of reeducation as well as the active and public use of information for learning rather than punishment. Some companies encourage increased openness and problem solving by giving awards for the mistake that produces the most learning.

Executives play a key role in the detoxifying of information. Leaders must be models of openness, admitting mistakes, talking about their own learning, and supporting early identification of problems. They must stop destructive competition among departments, and they must make it clear that information is to be used for improvement and learning. Executives also help to set the tone when they position problems and mistakes as opportunities to improve the organization, not to punish individuals.

INTEGRATE FUNCTIONAL INFORMATION INTO THE WORK

Finally, participation can live in the organization if all relevant functional expertise and information have been integrated into individual and team work. Years of institutional fragmentation have removed the financial, human resources, marketing, technical, and other functional expertise from individual jobs. In most companies, budget and other financial decisions are made by finance and accounting specialists. Staffing, coaching, and other people management functions are the responsibilities of staff specialists and unions. Customer service and satisfaction fall to marketing and sales. The list could go on. The point is that the jobs in authoritarian companies are not whole.

Participation requires all kinds of expertise to be reintegrated into every job. Everyone is responsible for the budget and for the financial success of the organization. Everyone must play an active role in his or her own personnel decisions. Teams and individuals must take an active role in hiring, developing, and giving feedback to colleagues. Everyone must understand his or her own role in getting and keeping customers. Information management itself is moving to all individuals.

As people thus reintegrate functional expertise into their job, they need access to functional information. This does not mean that every employee must be an expert in every function or that he or she needs to pore over detailed functional data. But it does mean that everyone must have the basic information that he or she needs to set and manage his or her own budget, make relevant personnel decisions and recommendations, and so on. This may mean that business financial and wage data and information about customer feedback and competitors that was once kept secret must be disclosed to line employees. It is a risk that is worth taking if increased commitment and improved day-to-day decisions are the result.

CONCLUSION

As responsibilities move out in the organization, information must also move, or people will not be able to perform their increasingly responsible roles. Appropriately decentralized information systems give people the access that they need. Restrictions, confidential data, and secrets may still be needed to protect some patentable ideas and competitive information, but information must be available to those who need to know it, not just to those whose position within the hierarchy designates them as its recipients. Decentralizing information gives people the information that they need in order to think effectively and make decisions about their work.

Four qualities distinguish the use that the participative organization makes of information. First, people everywhere have access to information about the larger vision, the work context, and their own job. Second, all employees develop skills as information users. Third, information feeds learning, not punishment and blame. Fourth, day-to-day functional information is integrated into the core work of the business.

When these conditions have been met, work can begin to be done in a different way. Work structures are shaped to needs and expertise, not determined by hierarchical reporting arrangements. When this occurs and when information is widely and instantly available, an organization can never be the same. As a study of information networks in seventy-five companies conducted in 1993 by CSC Research and Advertising Services concluded (Stewart, 1994, p. 20), "When work is carried out through networks, an organization's structure changes whether you want it to or not. I can't find a single case where it doesn't happen."

Open information is one of the main transforming forces for participation. Once information becomes open, the organization itself changes. But such change requires many new habits and many system changes. And it requires leaps forward in trust and new forms of control at all levels. The next chapters examine some of the complementary changes in relationships, skills, and controls.

Think about the use of information within your organization. Figure 9.1 contains five pairs of items. Allocate ten points between the two items in each pair. The points awarded reflect the extent to which each statement is true. Allocate five or more points to an item only if you can say that at least 75 percent of the people in your organization would agree that the statement closely reflects their views and experiences. Nine or ten points indicate that your organization is really a case study example of the statement. The points that you award to each pair of items must total ten. When you have finished rating the statements, add up the numbers in the A column and the B column, and record them on the INFORMATION row of the Governance Assessment Score Sheet in Appendix I.

Figure 9.1 Assess the Use of Information in Your Organization

21A. Executives treat business strategy and performance data as confidential, to be discussed and known only by a select few.

21B. Information about the bigger business picture is available to and openly discussed with everyone in the organization.

22A. Job performance data are designed for management use. Managers use the information to determine the areas that workers will act on and improve.

22B. Information systems and reports are designed to help the people who do the work to take action and solve problems.

23A. Data-processing and information systems specialists define information system requirements. Workers and line managers rely on them to determine the information that will be provided and how it will be formatted.

23B. People actively and deliberately define their own information needs. They actively use data for continuous improvement.

24A. People either try to hide their mistakes, or they look for someone on whom they can blame them.

24B. People openly admit their mistakes and use information and experiences for learning and improvement, not for punishment and blame.

25A. Functional staff manage and use most of the information related to their specialty. Workers and line managers depend on staff for decisions about budgets; human resource decisions, such as staffing; and the like.

25B. Everyone has access to basic financial, human resource, and marketing data and uses the data to make decisions in day-to-day work.

CHAPTER 10

Relationships: Partnerships with Purpose

THE TUMULTUOUS 1960S AND 1970S—the era in the United States of antiwar protests, student revolts, Woodstock, and flower children; in Europe, of student uprisings and social change; in Africa, of the exodus of colonial powers; in Japan, of the quality revolution—also helped to raise relationships in organizations to a new level of concern. The Theory Y view of management (McGregor, 1960), which was introduced at the beginning of that period, altered forever the way in which we talk about management and organizational governance. But this humanistic approach also had a downside. It created the impression that a soft and warm, touchy-feely approach was all that was needed to improve the well-being of an organization. Perhaps it reflected a pent-up need for attention to the human factor after a long history of authoritarian practices. But it also made us aware that relationships are a key factor for the success of participative organizations.

Today, our view of organizational relationships has matured. We now see that quality, customer retention, and productivity depend on effective relationships—relationships among managers and staff, team members, union and management, the organization and its suppliers, the organization and its customers, and the organization and its regulators, to name only a few.

Interactions and relationships between people occur in thousands of events every day. Because relationships are the smallest and most personal unit in which participation occurs, they are at the heart of governance. When they are adversarial, coercive, and dependent, they create the foundations of authoritarianism. But when people acknowledge one another's independence and work together interdependently, there is participation.

In some ways, relationships are the most manageable area on which our efforts to create a participative enterprise can focus. For example, relationships are observable. They exist in the visible interactions that occur between and among people. We can thus describe what we see, shape it, and help to formulate alternatives. When we see or hear a "superior" criticize or even humiliate a "subordinate" before peers, we can react. When we see a worker ignore a problem because it is "not his responsibility," we can coach him to higher levels of partnership and accountability for the whole.

Relationships are human. People can relate readily to relationship issues. Such issues can be discussed in everyday terms. No strange terminology is needed. And people need little training or guidance to take personal action that can change their relationship behaviors.

Finally, relationships are immediate. We experience them personally in the here and now. There is little lag between impulse and response. And there are relatively few ways in which it is appropriate to respond. We may accept the interaction as it is and not register any conscious response. We may get some pleasure from it and want to tell the other person about it. Or we may not like it at all. But because the emotions occur in the here and now, they give us daily, even hourly opportunities to make changes that can foster participation.

Participative relationships can either be the cause of a move to new governance or the effect of such a move. But no fundamental change is possible unless people's day-to-day behaviors are participative. When you can stand over at the side of the room and see consistently interdependent behavior across levels and groups, then you can be sure that participative governance has won.

Trust is at the heart of the relationship shift. As recent research funded by the Sloan Foundation and the Columbia University Center for Japanese Economy and Business shows (Ichniowski and Shaw,

1995), participative and interdependent practices can occur only when trust is high. Investigations by the Forum Corporation (1991) confirm this finding. The Forum Corporation (1991) investigators envision trust as a quality that we attribute to people. Their research identifies three conditions that make people trustworthy: First, others see them as skilled and knowledgeable. To put this condition in personal terms: I trust you when I believe that you will fulfill your responsibilities. Second, people cooperate rather than compete. In personal terms: I believe that you will involve me in any decisions that will affect my work life. Third, people admit their own mistakes and uncertainties and work to learn and improve, not to blame. In personal terms: I know that you have the humility to learn from me.

Trust works both ways in a relationship. All stakeholders—management, employees, unions, functional staff, suppliers, customers, regulators—must work together to build trust and cast off the conflictual, adversarial, dependent, and counterdependent behaviors of the past. To accomplish this goal, they must make a conscious effort to define and abandon the relationship behaviors from the past that still linger on.

Where do we start? Core teams provide the best opportunity for reconstructing trust. Together, team members can identify the behaviors between them that reflect the past. This process can take some time. Normally, it requires all team members to have a heightened sense of awareness to identify inappropriate behavior the moment when it occurs and to make one another aware of the inappropriate behavior. A professional facilitator can help during the initial stages. He or she can act as the team's alter ego. The skills of the alter ego are not all that difficult for team members to acquire, which means that the organization can develop sufficient line and staff people to speed up the process of learning in relatively little time.

Marthie, a trained facilitator who works in a major multinational organization helping managers to become more participative and effective, remarks, "In earlier years, I used to rely on traditional training and team-building methods to try and help people change the way in which they related to others. But no matter how good the training program was, we didn't achieve much. Now I spend most of my time sitting in management and team meetings or even just accompanying individuals through their day."

She continues: "Whenever they interact with someone in a way that does not support the desired relationships, I intervene. I ask the individual and others in the relationship—right there, not in a classroom—to describe how they could have interacted differently. How could the one have restructured his or her interaction to be more participative? How could the other have been more active and constructive in responding? What will they do in the future to promote the desired participative relationship? Fortunately, this observing skill is quite easy to pass on to others, so the team or individual does not once more become dependent on me. At first and quite understandably, people are a bit uncomfortable with the forthrightness and honesty that this approach requires. But they soon agree to use it as an important way of personal and team learning. They rapidly become their own tutors, reinforcing one another's learning and new interaction habits."

Relationships play such a powerful role in the establishment of participative governance because they are human in a fundamental way. Anyone can improve and change how he or she works with and relates to others. We have all spent a lifetime in relationships. Most of us have a pretty clear understanding of what we like, what makes us feel less or more dignified, happy, or sad. Most of us would prefer to be in respectful, mutually responsible relationships. It just remains to do the work to build the trust and habits that make such relationships possible.

In our experience, changes in relationship should take place almost exclusively within day-to-day interactions in the workplace. Past practice has approached changes in relationship from an almost exclusively psychological or therapeutic position. This bias is unfortunate. Some relationships may indeed be so poor that they require professional, even therapeutic intervention. But these relationships are the exception, not the rule. Most of the time, all that is needed is to help people become aware of their own needs and of their own capacity to develop constructive relationships.

CREATING PARTICIPATIVE RELATIONSHIPS

Participative relationships can be created quite rapidly if we follow four simple guidelines: intend to change, commit to a blend of independence and interdependence, manage relationships consciously, and put formal processes and structures in place.

■ *Intend to Change*

People at all levels must intend to establish new relationships. It cannot be left to chance, and it will not occur spontaneously. Everyone needs to accept that the habits and traditions instilled by years of authoritarianism do not disappear overnight just because someone decrees that they shall. Instead, people across levels and functions must consciously identify the relationship practices that need to be discontinued and the relationship practices that need to be constructed to take their place. People can start by describing these practices in writing. Making the process conscious makes people aware of their own and of others' behaviors and contributes to the development of new relationships. These new agreements on how we will conduct relationships in the future become a new contract that can be developed in workshops and meetings among multiple stakeholders.

■ *Commit to a Blend of Independence and Interdependence*

Participative relationships require us to blend independence and interdependence. That is, on the one hand, we must take personal responsibility. On the other hand, we must share responsibility in ways that are appropriate to the work.

Independence establishes the strong personal foundation for collaboration. People first honor each other's individual worth and right to exist. They also develop the basic skills needed for taking charge of and responsibility for their own decisions and lives. When people feel that their independence is threatened, it is easy for them to retreat to the relative security of authoritarianism and bureaucracy. The parties to relationships in a participative environment must take great care to respect the independent right of the others to exist and contribute constructively to their own well-being and to the well-being of the organization.

Independence without interdependence can become counter-dependence. That is, one party must lose in order for the other party to win. Some managers, employees, union leaders, functional staff, or customers may believe that participation means the ability to be individualistic: "My point of view must always be accepted. Otherwise it is clear that they are not really serious about participation." Ralph Stayer (1990, p. 68), former CEO of Johnsonville Foods, reveals that he first had to overcome his own desire to have his individualism confirmed. At first, he viewed participation as a matter of getting other people to make the decisions that he would have made: "Worst of all, I now see that . . . they were right [to be suspicious of my motives]. I didn't really *want* them to make independent decisions. I wanted them to make the decisions I would have made. Deep down, I was still in love with my own control; I was just making people guess what I wanted instead of telling them."

Interdependence occurs when all parties to a relationship contribute what they can to help accomplish a common goal without playing games, abusing power, or violating morality and values. Interdependence occurs when everyone checks his or her behavior against two standards to which Gandhi dedicated his life: truth and nonviolence (Nair, 1994). These two standards combine with the three elements of trust—trust in each other's ability to deliver on agreements, trust that meaningful involvement will occur, and trust that people can admit their own mistakes and learn from one another—to define the conditions for true interdependence. Think about it: Interdependence can exist only when we can rely on one another for truth, nonviolence, and trustworthiness.

The commitment to a blend of independence and interdependence is a commitment to personal responsibility and trustworthiness. We may never be perfect in these areas, but we can go far beyond the unhealthy superiorities and dependencies of the past. In fact, if we are going to establish a participative enterprise, we must make these rather dramatic changes in our day-to-day interactions.

■ Manage Relationships Consciously

Participation calls for increasingly conscious living. This is true for people on both sides of a relationship: managers and workers, union officials and management, customers and suppliers, experts and learners. When an interaction occurs, each party can act in ways that reinforce authoritarianism or that reinforce participation. And both parties are responsible for the way in which the relationship plays out. The next three paragraphs examine the authoritarian and the participative responses to three situations.

SITUATION 1. A customer calls a manager to complain about the quality of the service that he or she has received. The authoritarian response is for the manager to blame customer service staff and take on the responsibility for resolving the problem. Customer service staff blame the customer and allow the manager to solve the problem. The participative response is for the manager to tell staff that the customer has complained and then either work with staff to clarify the problem and devise a solution that will maintain and perhaps even improve the company's relationship with the customer or to ask customer service staff to work as a team to solve the problem. Customer service staff take a problem-solving approach and assure the manager that they will take care of the issue and involve the manager if needed.

SITUATION 2. Performance goals have to be set. The authoritarian response is for the manager to have expectations that he or she makes known only when an employee fails to live up to them. As an alternative, the manager tells an employee what his or her goals are. The employee waits to be told by the manager what to do. When the response to this situation is participative, the manager talks with the employee in broad terms about customer needs and business issues and asks the employee to set his or her own goals—getting the manager's and other stakeholders' agreement. The employee takes steps to find out what the challenges of the new work are and proposes ways in which he or she can contribute to them.

SITUATION 3. The business is performing poorly, and there is a chance that cutbacks may have to be made. In an authoritarian response, management assesses the situation and makes the decision. It keeps its deliberations secret until the final course of action has become clear. Meanwhile, rumors circulate among employees, who shun any controversial work or comments that could jeopardize their jobs. The union prepares to strike. In a participative response, management assembles a representative group of stakeholders and presents the organization's case and business reasons for large cost cuts. Management opens up the books for all to see. Management asks workers to form a task force that will investigate the issues and propose solutions. If management retains the prerogative to make the final decision, it makes this clear from the outset. Employees take time to understand the larger business issues and make it clear either that they want to take part in making the decision or that they support their representatives in advising about the decision. The union makes it clear that it wants to participate and that it will have the larger, ongoing interests of the business in mind even as it represents its members.

No matter what the situation, all stakeholders can shape the interactions involved. This realization is one of the most vital that people need to come to: The transformation of relationships is not a one-way process. All stakeholders are responsible for either perpetuating or changing the nature of existing relationships. Employees perpetuate autocracy when they consistently adopt blaming and dependent behavior. Management perpetuates autocracy by reserving the right to make all the decisions and by relying on position rather than on expertise and relationships. Unions perpetuate old governance patterns by remaining adversarial and by refusing to take shared responsibility for the performance of the organization as a whole. Customers reinforce old patterns by squeezing and bashing suppliers and by treating them like servants, not like partners whose goodwill is necessary if a better product or service is to be produced more efficiently.

Any player can set in motion the events that change the relationships in which he or she is engaged. It is difficult for a manager to abuse an employee who is informed and who repeatedly makes creative contributions. It is hard for an employee to remain passive when a manager creates space and allows the employee to experience the consequences of his or her actions directly. And a labor union whose officials are included in open, candid, and respectful business discussions finds it difficult to say no on principle.

■ Put Formal Processes and Structures in Place

Any attempt by management to force people to develop participative relationships is bound to fail if it does not give people direct and personal access to senior levels or alternative controls. Especially during the early stages, it is common for some people to feel threatened by the impending change and to fall back on coercive tactics.

The most successful efforts rely on formal processes and structures to create the space needed for people to deal with the new demands of participation. This does not mean that you have to start with a clean slate. There never is a clean slate. Even in a start-up operation (where, admittedly, it is easier to create participative relationships), people bring their own past experiences and relationship traumas with them. But it does require exerting sufficient pressure and creating sufficient opportunity for people to voice their concerns without any fear of victimization.

> *A giant railway company suffered severe strikes in the late 1980s. By the mid 1990s, relationships between management and workers had reached an all-time low. Attempts to repair the situation by asking all parties to show mutual trust and respect failed to produce any change.*
>
> *At a certain point, the general manager realized two things: First, 'trust' and 'respect' are both verbs. They require action. Second, you cannot develop them in a theoretical way. You have to start with the conditions that prevail.*
>
> *In his own environment, the general manager was plagued with daily labor issues that really should have been resolved at operational levels. During a workshop for workers and senior managers, the question of poor relationships was raised for the umpteenth time. People tried to think up ways of solving the problem. Both managers and workers were reluctant to act. Both sides claimed that they had too many experiences of broken promises and of agreements to which only lip service had been paid. Clearly, the bad experiences built up over time had contaminated the relationships at operational levels.*
>
> *The general manager got tired of the seemingly endless debates about the issue. He invited the union to meet with him to discuss any problem. At first, the issues that they raised related to day-to-day work problems. Although he was the most senior manager in the region, the general manager assumed personal responsibility for following up on even the most minor of issues.*

This visible demonstration of the company's willingness to resolve problems rapidly built trust between the general manager and union leadership.

Then the next layer of management was brought into the process. These managers were asked to commit to quarterly meetings with worker representatives. Quite quickly, the quality of the discussions between the general manager and the unions changed. They no longer focused on the larger operational issues, since these were being resolved at the quarterly meetings. Instead, they focused on getting rid of bottlenecks and on problems with suppliers.

Next, operational management began to hold monthly meetings with representatives of the shop floor workers. Once again, the nature of the meetings between general manager and unions changed. The day-to-day issues that he and the union leaders had always discussed and resolved at top levels were now being addressed on the ground at the monthly operational meetings. Moreover, the quarterly sessions between middle management and worker representatives focused increasingly on planning issues, which meant that they were removed from the agenda of the general manager and the labor leaders. Today, the meetings among top leaders focus on strategic issues related to overall financial performance, customer service, and deployment of resources.

In the short span of twelve months, railroad management and the unions established a web of participative relationships that had real and positive impact on the hard business issues. But, as the general manager observed, it required setting up processes that everyone could see, that made a real difference, and that gave people with different interests an opportunity to interact with one another on a formal basis.

He insists that this change in relationships would never have occurred by chance or if the change had been viewed as optional. He also emphasizes the need for ongoing interaction: Constructive relationships cannot be developed and then left alone. It is like any business practice. The financial and information systems require new input every day. Procurement and quality control are never ending processes. Why should relationships be any different?

The general manager sums up the experience in these terms: "At first we made the error of thinking that relationships were something that you did at workshops or social events. Now we realize that they need as much ongoing attention as any of our other business activities. The difference is that without sound relationships, everything else sooner or later fails."

CONCLUSION

It is essential for all relationships to be participative if an organization is ever to be its customers' preferred supplier. For a true customer focus can be achieved only through the independent and interdependent relationships that underlie participation. Authoritarian relationships are incapable of sustaining the will or the spontaneous dedication that customer-focused quality requires. Authoritarian relationships also waste immense amounts of energy and attention on various kinds of coercive and dysfunctional behavior.

Effective relationships require all stakeholders to want to change. They blend independence and interdependence. They require everyone to assume responsibility for his or her own behavior in relationships, and they must have the support of formal processes and structures.

The relationships that are at the heart of participative governance occur in the context of mutual values and goals. Increasingly, in today's complex work environment, they take the form of collaborative decisions and actions. Complex work makes it difficult or impossible to separate the contribution of any one individual from the accomplishments of the group to which he or she belongs. Many attempts to highlight individual work are more likely to cause problems and to suboptimize the group's performance than they are to add value.

This may sound complicated, but in some ways it is one of the simpler challenges of participative governance. We have had the opportunity of working in some of the world's most complex and polarized situations. Even in South Africa, with its sad history of extreme racism and group separation, people from the most varying backgrounds have been able to establish resilient, mutual trust and respect. The core principle for the establishment of these relationships is both simple and profound. In meetings between extraordinarily diverse people—affluent and poor, well-educated and illiterate, managers and workers, Black and white, young and old, men and women—the vast majority of participants have rapidly and permanently transformed their relationships into truly participative interactions.

This transformation takes place when the conditions of truth, nonviolence, and trustworthiness exist. These conditions exist when everyone agrees to live by two statements: First, every person whom I meet has a contribution to make at which he or she is better than I am. Second, I will treat others as they would want to be treated, as long as it is within the constraints of the values to which we have agreed.

It is impossible to believe these statements and at the same time feel the superiority or the inferiority that are innate to authoritarian systems. It is impossible to believe these statements and to subordinate one person to another. Nor is it possible to live these statements and at the same time behave in self-determined ways that deny other people the right or the responsibility to influence their own life space. These beliefs dignify the presence and the contribution of every individual and make real participative governance possible.

Think about the relationships within your organization. Figure 10.1 contains five pairs of items. Allocate ten points between the two items in each pair. The points awarded reflect the extent to which each statement is true. Allocate five or more points to an item only if you can say that at least 75 percent of the people in your organization would agree that the statement closely reflects their views and experiences. Nine or ten points indicate that your organization is really a case study example of the statement. The points that you award to each pair of items must total ten. When you have finished rating the statements, add up the numbers in the A column and the B column, and record them on the RELATIONSHIPS row of the Governance Assessment Score Sheet in Appendix I.

Figure 10.1 Assess the Relationships in Your Organization

26A. People address and talk to each other in ways that reflect relatively fixed superior-subordinate relationships.

26B. People work together productively and respectfully regardless of levels and functions and without inappropriate use of formal power or position.

27A. People are often taken by surprise by decisions that affect their work lives directly.

27B. People are involved in decisions that affect their work life.

28A. People who do the work (including workers, union leaders, and suppliers) pursue their own agendas regardless of the needs of customers or of the other stakeholders in the business.

28B. People who do the work fully appreciate and take responsibility for the role that their work plays in the organization's success.

29A. People do not face their own dissatisfaction or abuses of their relationships, or they deal with them in indirect ways that do not resolve issues constructively.

29B. People raise relationship issues and deal with them openly so that these issues can be resolved constructively.

30A. People compete with each other in the belief that appearing to know more than others is important.

30B. People learn openly from one another, regardless of level or status.

CHAPTER 11

Competencies: A New Baseline

ROLES AND RELATIONSHIPS among all stakeholder groups change quite dramatically as the organization makes the shift from authoritarianism to participation. This dramatic change means that everyone develops new competencies.

Some of these competencies apply to everyone. These core competencies—self-management, broad business understanding, knowledge of business finance and economics, critical thinking, integrative communication skills, mutual learning capability, and flexible decision making—are the prerequisites for successful participation. Everyone needs them—chief executive officer of a large corporation, receptionist in a five-person firm, union steward in a manufacturing plant, or independent consultant to small or large companies. Obviously, the core competencies must be complemented by the technical, operational, and managerial competencies that each individual needs for doing the day-to-day work.

SELF-MANAGEMENT

Participative people are capable of independent action, and they have a mental toughness to take charge and defend unpopular stands. In a participative organization, this self-management capability means that everyone seeks out information about the larger context for his or her work. Individuals from all stakeholder groups set goals and prioritize, and they negotiate their own priorities. They manage the inevitable tensions between short-term pressures and long-term commitments. They get feedback and use it to improve. Under participative governance, every stakeholder also keeps his or her own personal energy and commitment high in spite of the immediate conditions at work—in spite even of barriers that he or she may encounter.

The core competency that underlies all these personal acts of initiative is the ability and the desire to take charge of one's life—to manage oneself. Self-management means that one accepts and nurtures the self-awareness, self-esteem, and self-control that are at the heart of independence. This independent capacity is a key personal foundation for true and empowered participation. As Stephen Covey (1989, pp. 186-187) notes, "interdependence is a choice only independent people can make. Unless we are willing to achieve real independence, it's foolish to try to develop human relations skills. We might try. We might even have some degree of success when the sun is shining. But when the difficult times come—and they will—we won't have the foundation to keep things together."

Competence in self-management is competence in independence. Authoritarian organizations do not need it or want it—except from those at the very top or those in key staff positions. But participative organizations cannot survive without it. It helps if the organization installs management processes that require self-management (Chapter Eight). It also helps if managers and seasoned players support others in developing independent and interdependent capacity. Restructuring the organization into value-adding work streams and ridding the organization of dependency-inducing hierarchies (Chapter Six) also boost self-management, as do discussing and debating empowerment and learning time management and assertive communication. Managing meetings to ensure that diverse views are expressed and to encourage conflict are other ways of building self-management muscle.

Self-management is the first key participation competency. It brings a tenacious and effective form of control into the institution: self-control.

BUSINESS AND INDUSTRY UNDERSTANDING

Successful participation requires everyone to have a basic understanding of the business and industry, the organization's paying customers, the key forces shaping the organization, and the general functions of the groups that work in and with it. Such a broad business and cross-functional understanding helps people, no matter what their role, to see themselves in the larger context and subject to the interdependencies of the business. It gives them the meaning and perspective that enable them to make good decisions about what to do and whom to involve, whatever the problem or situation.

As an organization's structures change (Chapter Six), people naturally find themselves in multifunctional and multilevel situations that stretch their knowledge of the business. They naturally take on responsibilities that require big-picture knowledge. Thus, the new structures automatically help people to develop their understanding of the business and the industry. Involving people in management processes (Chapter Eight) and providing all stakeholders with business information (Chapter Nine) are other ways of developing this knowledge base. Expanding the range of relationships that an individual or a team experiences—for example, to suppliers, customers, labor leaders, regulators, competitors, stockholders—also builds this important competency.

Broad business and industry knowledge creates a powerful context for ad hoc decisions and problem solving. Increased knowledge in these areas enables people in and around the organization to become more conscious, more knowledgeable, and more creative players. Because their knowledge of the business context sets a natural boundary for behavior and decisions, their need for hand-holding and external control diminishes. This is as true of labor leaders, customers, and suppliers as it is of managers and employees.

People who do not understand the business or the larger industry make up their own context. Since these contexts are not reliable, decisions based on them can be naive, and as such they call out for authoritarian control. Increased business and industry understanding among all parties thus eliminates one rationale for authoritarianism.

And it is one of the major conditions that make decisions at the lowest operational level—that is, participation—possible.

KNOWLEDGE OF BUSINESS FINANCE AND ECONOMICS

Business organizations make profits and suffer losses. They create—or at least they intend to create—economic value. They have income, and they spend it. They have key areas of operations that influence productivity and quality. Businesses must also strike an appropriate balance between investment and expenditure. And they are affected in various ways by events in the economic environment at large.

When the key stakeholders in a firm understand its basic financial indicators and what they mean, they can be conscious partners for economic success. Such an understanding also makes them more likely to understand the rationale for decisions that others might make to improve the organization's overall economic well-being. Of course, they are also more likely to challenge decisions that do not make economic sense.

People in and around authoritarian organizations are very naive about business financial data. They usually know little about their organization's financial goals or about its performance. They cannot interpret its financial statements, nor can they act effectively when revenues do not meet expectations or costs exceed budgets. In fact, many people—including employees, customers, and suppliers—can misinterpret financial data because they do not have the necessary knowledge about financial issues. For example, they see profits and wonder why wages do not rise. Or they hear that the firm has cost problems and act to cut their own expenditures, but then they wonder why other departments buy new equipment or expand staff.

Many financial actions cannot be defended—they are bad decisions. But many decisions that seem to be inappropriate can actually be in the firm's best interests. Stakeholders who do not understand business financial statements or their own effects on them cannot know the difference. It does not help for managers to keep financial data secret, because the grapevine view of a firm's financial health is usually worse than warranted.

The answer is to make everyone smart about the organization as a financial entity. Everyone needs to see him- or herself and his or her teams as little business units that use inputs and produce outputs. Everyone needs to know what the cost of doing his or her business is and how that cost affects revenues. The authoritarian organization focuses only on what the individual or the team produces and rewards them only for their immediate output. Such a system almost always causes units to optimize themselves at the expense of the organization as a whole. In contrast, the only way in which the participative enterprise can think about costs and value added is by keeping the larger business in mind. People must ask two questions: What do we add to the total value stream? and What do we cost? People must see themselves as part of the business as a whole. This means that they must understand the financial situation both of the business as a whole and of their own units. This necessity has implications for the reward system that we discuss in Chapter Thirteen.

The new structures discussed in Chapter Six help to bring financial accountability to people at all levels. This accountability means that people have to learn on the job. And the redesigned management processes reviewed in Chapter Eight mean that everyone has to understand and influence budgets. Chapter Nine argues that participative organizations provide everyone with financial information—in some cases, even with salary information. All these elements mean that people in and around the participative organization learn about the business as an economic enterprise. Business financial education is a priority. Chapter Ten suggests that such education can be reinforced in company newsletters and by the coaching that financial staff deliver during their regular interactions with those whom they serve.

Production employees in an oil refinery worked in their own little areas for years with little knowledge of anything but their own jobs. But automated system monitoring and new performance standards changed all that. The introduction of increasingly sophisticated monitoring equipment meant that employee teams were responsible for increasingly large areas within the plant. But they had no real context for solving the broader problems that they faced as a result. And they did not know how to think about budgets for the areas that they had come to control. In fact, they had worse than no context: Their assumptions about the uses that the business made of its resources were startlingly false.

These assumptions came out during a discussion with a training specialist at lunch one day. Several workers wondered aloud what management did with all the money that the workers earned. When the training specialist asked what they meant, they responded, "Well, every day, the managers come to work with their empty briefcases. They talk in their offices and have long lunches, where they can drink. At the end of the day, they put the money we made in their briefcases and leave. Then there is no money to fix the problems we see. And there is not enough money to pay us what we want."

"What a naive view," thought the training specialist, until she realized that there was no real reason why the workers' perceptions should be any different than they were. The company had done nothing to help them learn about where money went within the organization. Absent the facts, the workers had made up a context of their own. It included the story about financial operations just reported.

Within two months, the organization had implemented a new training program for all plant workers. The program taught about the financial dynamics of a modern business and about the financial dynamics of their organization in particular. The workers learned what happened to every sales dollar, why plant investments were important, where profits went, and how to think about their own financial role.

As the program moved across the organization, a surprising thing happened. Supervisors and managers began to drop in— ostensibly to observe the course. After a while, it became clear that they, too, had little understanding of the refinery as a financial and economic entity. They did not know how to analyze or interpret the financial data that crossed their desks every month. They had no clear picture of the economic and financial key indicators. So, they "dropped in on" and "observed" the course for production workers.

Hiding financial information and leaving financial decisions to senior people and financial staff are common ways of dealing with the financial naïveté that haunts most organizations. But these practices slow down the decision process and make productive participation—and therefore improvements in quality and customer focus—impossible. The answer is to develop the business financial and economic understanding of every employee, union representative, supplier, and even customer. Increased overall competence in this area is good for the business, and it is a more effective check on spending than anything else.

CRITICAL THINKING SKILLS

One sad legacy of authoritarianism is the underdeveloped thinking skills at all levels within the organization. People in authority under the old rules are not often challenged. Instead of exploring and debating issues deeply and looking at them from a variety of perspectives, many formal leaders instruct others to carry out their own autocratic decisions. At the same time, people lower in the organization, accustomed to fragmented jobs and limited decision-making authority, either follow orders or complain and criticize.

Stephen Brookfield (1987) identifies four key components of critical thinking: identifying and challenging assumptions behind ideas and actions; recognizing the influence of such things as history and culture on beliefs and actions; imagining and exploring alternatives—going beyond the obvious solutions; and being appropriately skeptical about solutions that claim to be the only truth or alternative. He adds that democracy is the form of governance that creates the best conditions for critical thinking.

When people take part in decision processes and when they have the power, rights, and responsibilities needed for effective action, the quality of thinking must be high. People must be able to defend their ideas, look for ways of integrating their own views with those of others, and seek solutions that are both technically sound and that others can commit to. Authoritarian decisions do not require or encourage such complex thought. People with power need only to mandate. Those without power can only implement, oppose, or subvert.

We can develop critical thinking by involving people in problem solving and decision making, by having them examine and dissect successes and failures, and by engaging them in discussions about the differences between such things as facts, assumptions, values, and goals. Even if we do not consciously examine and guide the quality of thinking throughout the organization, participation both requires critical thinking and helps to foster it. Participating is one of the best ways of spreading the capacity for critical thinking throughout the organization. Conversely, as capacity for critical thinking develops, it becomes increasingly difficult to prevent people from stating their views and needs openly.

In institutions that have a long history of punitive autocracy, it can take some time to build the trust that makes it safe to think critically. But there is no other way of beginning to develop that trust or the skills of critical thinking than beginning to get people involved. Participation initiates a self-enhancing spiral of intellectual development that eventually embraces everyone.

INTEGRATIVE COMMUNICATION SKILLS

Participation requires interaction. Interaction requires two kinds of communication: responsive and listening on the one hand, expressive and influential on the other. As many people soon discover, participation requires increasingly direct dealing with other people.

Effective participation is a hard option. It allows and encourages conflict, differences of opinion, confusion, and time-consuming exchanges. If people do not have well-developed communication skills, participation can disintegrate into hostility, unbridled conflict, submerged aggression, or surface agreement and inappropriate compromise.

Integrative communication skills can help to prevent the organization from falling into any of these traps and thereby proving that democracy can run wild. Everyone in the participative organization must be adept at expressing his or her own views, exploring the views of others, arguing for specific options, and finding integrative, high-quality solutions. Participative people are also skilled at telling the truth as they see it, with respect and with a willingness to share responsibility.

These communication challenges are not small ones, nor are they easy to meet. As most people discover, developing a capacity for integrative communication is a lifetime's work for anyone who takes participation seriously.

SKILL IN MUTUAL LEARNING

Today's organizations require continuous improvement and innovation as well as a capacity for high quality. Meeting these requirements is impossible unless everyone becomes both a continuous learner and a continuous supporter of others' learning. Authoritarian organizations are often slow to change because learning is not an entrenched value, and learning behaviors—admitting mistakes, admitting that one lacks knowledge, sharing ideas with others—are actually discouraged. Authoritarian organizations value perfection, being better than others, and being the one who has the best ideas. Participative people learn the new skills needed to create a learning organization.

Some of these skills relate to personal learning and change: reading, finding, and extracting key ideas from information; learning in a classroom; remembering things; applying theory to practice; and discovering theory in practice. People need skills in experiential learning—that is, in learning from experience—and they also need action learning—that is, learning by trying out new things and adjusting their actions until they become highly effective.

Other skills relate to supporting others in their learning. A participative business is, by definition, a learning community in which everyone is both a teacher and a learner. One key assumption of participation is that each one of us has areas of skill or capability that he or she can teach to others. Some of these transferrable skills are technical or business related. But it is also the job of each of us to help colleagues to increase their ability to act independently and interdependently. Thus, we all must be able to support others in the development both of special skills and of the skills that promote independence and interdependence. These *others* can be colleagues, managers, team members, customers, suppliers, or union leaders, and they can occupy positions that have more or less authority than ours.

Unfortunately, very few people know how to be coaches, facilitators, or teachers. Everyone in a participative organization must develop at least a basic level of skills in these helping functions. If they do not, they cannot pass their knowledge capital on to others, and they cannot help others to grow.

FLEXIBLE DECISION MAKING

Since everyone makes decisions, everyone needs to know how to make them. Participation can be successful only if people at all levels understand when and how to involve others in the process of making decisions and solving problems. We argue in Chapter Eight that not every decision requires involvement by others. Some decisions are best when they are made independently. Others require consultation before they can be made. Still others demand consensus or are best delegated.

In authoritarian organizations, many decisions are made independently or consultatively—whether or not this is the best way of ensuring that they will be implemented effectively. In all fairness, many autocratic decisions are made by people—managers or others—who are not even aware that they are making a decision. If they were, it would have been obvious that they needed to involve others.

Decision making is a very important process for the participative organization. People must learn to recognize that they are about to make a decision. They must be able to decide how to decide—whom to involve, what role to play—and they must be able to make the various decision processes—independent, consultative, consensual, and delegative—work. Participative people also know how to be involved, and they respect that it is sometimes important not to be involved. People who are new to participation after years of dependency and autocracy find it hard to know what the appropriate boundaries are. They may at first demand to be involved in everything and view exclusion for any reason as a sign of bad faith. Managers who are new to participation have the same uncertainties. They often overinvolve people or involve them at the wrong time. Sometimes, they involve others who have yet to develop the skills needed to make such involvement constructive.

Competence in flexible decision making develops over time. It develops because the new structures require it (Chapter Six). It develops as people expand their knowledge of the larger business issues (Chapter Nine). It develops as everyone gets increasingly involved in the formal management processes of the firm (Chapter Eight). But it also must develop through training, reflection on what in recent decisions has and has not worked, and real experience of decision making at all levels. The goal is disciplined, effective decision making that draws on relevant knowledge, that leads to committed action, and that requires everyone to have high-level skills, no matter what his or her status.

COMPETENCE MUST BE PERVASIVE

The right to participate and the right to influence decisions are not based on mere presence. Of course, participation does require presence and inclusion. But no one has an automatic right to question merely because he or she is ignorant or to reject something merely because he or she does not like it. Compromise on these principles can quickly lead to mobocracy—collective autocracy.

People need to develop the competencies that they need for legitimate participation. In the workplace, both management and workers share the responsibility for developing these competencies. Individuals and teams must work to develop the knowledge and awareness needed for informed and constructive contributions. For its part, management must provide the remedial support that people everywhere need in order to develop the seven participation skills described in this chapter. And management must continue to saturate the workplace with information and development resources and support that give those who need them the context for informed participation.

In practical terms, this means that everyone needs to seek out and try to understand up-to-date information related to decisions. They must learn from their successful and unsuccessful experiences. They must try new things, and they must work continuously to improve. People who do not accept responsibility for this kind of learning do not have a right to the same weight in decision making as those who have or who are developing the knowledge relevant to the decision at hand. This is not an elitist or hierarchic sentiment. The truck driver will invariably be more competent in matters related to truck driving than the middle manager who only has the M.B.A.

People everywhere must always test their views against their actual competence in a given area. It is speculative arrogance to step out beyond one's own level of expertise and claim the right to influence decisions. Such arrogance can cause serious backlash when the organization's performance begins to suffer. But it is immoral to suppress or deny someone's competence, and it is immoral to refuse to provide access to experiences and formal learning that can develop competence. Both practices are authoritarian, and they have no place in a participative system.

We realize that this chapter has advanced some dangerous positions, especially the idea that competence is a key factor in the ability to participate. That idea may seem to give a loophole to the few that they can use to justify imposing their own thinking on the many. However, if the values and relationships of participation are adhered to and if the competencies of self-management, critical thinking, integrative communication, and the rest are developed and respected, this potential for abuse will be contained. In many companies, several, perhaps many, years of such adherence, development, and respect will be needed to make up for the restricted communication and development practices of the past.

CONCLUSION

Seven capabilities—self-management, broad business understanding, knowledge of business finance and economics, critical thinking skills, integrative communication skills, mutual learning skill, and flexible decision making—are vital for the participative organization. In order to play an ongoing productive and meaningful role in the tasks of sustaining interdependence and participation, every stakeholder needs to possess these skills, along with the specific skills that he or she needs for his or her own work.

Leaders and change agents who must manage the change from autocratic to participative governance need the additional capabilities discussed in Chapters Seven and Eighteen. For the moment, it should suffice to think about the performance possibilities in an organization in which everyone either already has or is now developing the seven key capabilities for participation. It is not hard to imagine ongoing success under such conditions.

Think about the participation competencies within your organization. Figure 11.1 contains five pairs of items. Allocate ten points between the two items in each pair. The points awarded reflect the extent to which each statement is true. Allocate five or more points to an item only if you can say that at least 75 percent of the people in your organization would agree that the statement closely reflects their views and experiences. Nine or ten points indicate that your organization is really a case study example of the statement. The points that you award to each pair of items must total ten. When you have finished rating the statements, add up the numbers in the A column and the B column, and record them on the COMPETENCIES row of the Governance Assessment Score Sheet in Appendix I.

Figure 11.1 Assess the Participation Competencies
in Your Organization

☐ **31A.** *Only managers are expected to be competent in business and financial matters.*

☐ **31B.** *All stakeholders—employees, managers, union officials, suppliers, customers—have the business and financial knowledge that they need in order to be effective business partners.*

☐ **32A.** *Self-management actions are often seen as insubordination.*

☐ **32B.** *The development of self-management capacity and the ability to act responsibly are key and visible goals in the organization.*

☐ **33A.** *Only managers receive development in interpersonal skills and decision making so that they can give feedback, communicate, and control conflict.*

☐ **33B.** *People everywhere in the organization actively develop key interpersonal abilities for communication, learning, and decision making.*

☐ **34A.** *Disagreement and critical thinking rarely happen or are not encouraged.*

☐ **34B.** *People throughout the organization are actively developing their ability to recognize, explore, and solve problems, and they discuss and appreciate issues from a variety of points of view.*

☐ **35A.** *People's learning focuses on the tasks of their specific job.*

☐ **35B.** *People's learning deliberately goes beyond their specific job so that they can understand larger customer and business issues and see their work in context.*

CHAPTER 12

Controls:
A Different
View

ONE OF THE BIGGEST FEARS that managers have when their organization moves into participation is that they will lose control. But, we may ask them, exactly what is *control*? People describe it in a variety of ways. Here are some examples: Nothing happens that management does not want to happen. Plans are carried out to the letter, exactly as planned. People do not waste resources, including time. People contain their innate laziness and rebelliousness. All or most decisions are good and support what leaders have decided to do. People follow orders. People live up to their commitments. There are no surprises. There are no defects.

Any of these descriptions of control can be valid, depending on the situation. But however it is described, control must always be viewed as a means to the ends of high performance and customer satisfaction. In highly authoritarian institutions, controls are often ends in themselves.

Strict boss rule dominated one platinum mine since it opened in the early 1980s. After all, the reasoning went, mining is dangerous work, and the miners generally had no more than two or three years of primary school education. There were eight hundred employees and eight levels of management. The mine super-

intendent was at the top of the heap. Policies and procedures were clear. The mine workers were expected to do exactly as the shift boss commanded. There had been no serious accidents since the mine's opening.

In 1990, one of the most expensive pieces of new mining equipment began to have problems. Technical experts were flown in from great distances. Millions of dollars worth of production time were lost. Supervisors caucused, and problem-solving teams from the head office joined the fray. Yet every solution proved short-lived. The primary problem seemed insoluble. One day, a supervisor newly arrived from a rather progressive coal mine happened to be watching the production process. He noticed an older man making some adjustments on the machine that had been having problems. The man's concentration and seeming competence impressed him. He walked over to the man and addressed him in his own language. "Do you know what is happening to this machine, my friend—the one that we can't seem to fix?" The old man replied, "Well, yes, sir. The drill bit isn't at the right angle, and this causes breakage way down in the shaft. I could tell by the sound." "But why didn't you tell anyone?" asked the supervisor. "Sir, no one asked me. We only speak when addressed."

Later that day in the mine superintendent's office, a frantic clerk interrupted a meeting of senior managers. "Please, Mr. Superintendent, will you sign this requisition so that I can get the sales quotes out on time?" The requisition was for a $10 stapler.

The platinum mine was very highly controlled. But was it under control?

Here is another example:

A credit company decided to become participative. Two years after the decision to become a high-involvement organization, the company was gridlocked. People demanded to be involved in virtually every decision. At the same time, some important but highly technical decisions, such as those regarding the interest rates to charge, slowed to a halt as people from all parts of the organization attempted to get involved. No one liked the situation, and some dropped out in order to get on with their own work.

Decision processes broke down, and anarchy ruled. The change to participative governance was blamed for these problems, and the company spent a fortune getting unstuck.

The credit company equated participation with lack of good sense and discipline. Are controls incompatible with involvement? Is anarchy the only alternative?

Controls in a coercive or paternalistic authoritarian organization often rely on fear, control of information, close supervision, and carrots and sticks. Authoritarian controls are also very rational. Detailed plans, organization charts, clear hierarchies and reporting relationships, procedures, job descriptions, and imposed values and goals keep the authoritarian organization on its trajectory as it heads into the future.

Again, we must ask, What is control? Why do we need it? And why do we fear losing it? Only by answering these questions can we decide what kind of control is needed and appropriate for organizations today.

CONTROL IN PARTICIPATIVE ORGANIZATIONS

Today's organizations have two seemingly contradictory needs: On the one hand, they must be stable and focused enough to hold together and create synergy. On the other, they must be sufficiently flexible and changing that they can adapt to the very complex and dynamic environment around them and take advantage of it.

Control in a participative organization is control that is appropriate for a complex system in a dynamic environment. Controls have a dual role: They must ensure that focused and directed action occurs throughout the organization—that is, they must help to hold the organization together. And they must also enable the organization to learn, adapt, and change—that is, they must allow it to stretch in new directions. These roles may seem contradictory. In reality, both are necessary, and the tension between them is essential if the organization is to survive and thrive. Good control is the ability to manage the tension between the forces of freedom and constraint.

Today's organizations must attend to at least four facets of the control issue. First, they must stop perpetuating authoritarian controls as ends in themselves. This means that rebellion and "irresponsibility" must be viewed as products of authoritarianism, not as innate human traits that require constant control. Second, they must put appropriate stabilizing forces into place. Third, they must encourage organizational learning. Last, they must put into place "controls" that maintain the tension between the stabilizing forces and the learning forces.

■ *Stop Perpetuating the Authoritarian Control Cycle*

Authoritarian organizations leave a pernicious legacy of fear, distrust, counterdependence, subordination, and submission. As we argue in Chapter Eighteen, this is not an easy legacy to transcend. Coercive, secretive, paternalistic, and bureaucratic management of the past caused submission, and it minimized risk taking and self-esteem in the workforce. These results often led to sabotage, which then encouraged management to increase its controls. These controls took the form of excessive checking, removal of authority to think and act, multiple levels of approvals, and fragmentation of work.

One sad but inevitable consequence of years of dependency is that, when organizations increase freedom and introduce "permissive" management, many people cannot immediately act with commitment and responsibility. Employees who are given opportunities to be more involved may at first not want to take up the flag.

It is a mistake to see any initial reluctance as a sign that people cannot or will not participate responsibly. Just as management needs to be reeducated and reskilled when an organization wants to become participative, employees also need support if they are to change their assumptions and behaviors. Years of coercion and autocracy have created a need among managers to control and to enforce compliance. Suspicion, distrust, abuse, and control together form a vicious circle that must be broken. The new organization cannot afford to spend its precious energy in these negative ways.

In the participative organization, control is a by-product of everything that the organization does. Control comes from structures that integrate thinking and doing and that place people in accountable relationships with the teams that come before them and after them in the value-adding work stream. Control results when people commit to common values. Control also occurs when savvy leaders operate as stewards who provide appropriate levels of support and occasional discipline, not as autocrats whose behavior triggers counterdependence and sabotage.

Control occurs as a by-product of participative management processes (Chapter Eight): Involvement in the setting of goals for individuals and teams, managing goals, and giving feedback to individuals and teams all keep people aligned with the larger performance mandates. Involvement in goal setting is especially important for control. Helping to set their goals commits people to accomplishing them. Continuing research in industrial psychology confirms that participative goals are powerful motivators and therefore natural controls.

Real-time and open information also operates as a control, because it helps people to see how their performance measures up. Information operates like the gauges on a dashboard that provide instant feedback. The feedback enables the driver to make decisions and take action. When information is not punitive, it helps to activate the motives that lead people to increasingly high standards. Everyone likes to see the trend lines on their performance rise, but most people do not know what those trend lines are or what influences them.

On another note, participative relationships create social pressure to be a strong and contributing part of a team. And new competencies make it possible to perform and to intervene if the system is not supporting productivity and quality.

In the participative organization, pay systems (Chapter Thirteen) also reinforce performance that supports the good of the organization as a whole.

The bottom line is that the participative organization has built-in controls. In contrast, the authoritarian organization creates control problems, which it is then obliged to handle by autocratic methods. Autocracy creates its own self-supporting cycle of controls.

Many leaders use their position for personal power and gain, not for the larger good, which means that the organization needs external controls to ensure that decisions—even those made at the top—are good for the organization, not just for those who make them.

People who are overcontrolled often become rebellious and counterdependent. They stop thinking, just follow the rules, absent themselves mentally or physically, and often resort to strikes and sabotage.

These behaviors force the organization to clamp down, punish, and supervise closely.

People in authoritarian systems often do not have enough information to handle exceptions gracefully or effectively. When problems and surprises occur, they often do their best, but they can also make major mistakes because they are not familiar with the big picture or because they do not have the access needed to solve the problem once and for all. The result can be the view that "people don't care" and that they have to be lured with carrots and prodded with sticks.

Authoritarian institutions thus create a great deal of the need for external control. But control, we argue, is better built in. No imposed procedures, rules, pay systems, or reward policies can beat the control that results from having the organization's values, structure, and processes really require high performance.

■ *Put Appropriate Stabilizing Controls into Place*

A participative organization is not an anarchy. It has levels of authority. It has plans and responsibilities, power differentials and decision authorities. There are policies, reviews and approvals, and disciplinary systems. A participative organization also has common values and goals that operate as inviolate agreements and that help to determine whether people are and can be members of the organization.

An organization needs such binding forces to keep it together and to help it create more energy than it absorbs. But the stabilizing forces just reviewed have some important differences in participative organizations and in authoritarian organizations. For one thing, stakeholder groups help to develop the plans, policies, values, goals, and disciplinary systems in participative organizations. In authoritarian organizations, these plans, policies, values, goals, and disciplinary systems are imposed.

Participative organizations differ from authoritarian organizations in another important way: In participative organizations, power differentials, decision authorities, and reviews and approvals exist to add value, not—as in authoritarian organizations—to coerce or to create persistent dependency. They exist to ensure appropriate levels of thought and debate and the best use of resources. Authoritarian uses of power, approvals, and authority to make decisions are all too often the result of individual power trips.

In a participative organization, levels of authority are often a function of the type of decision that has to be made. Every group has sign-off power in its own work domain. For example, executives will have final authority in such areas as strategies, mission, and broad goals. Managers will be the final arbiters of decisions about medium-term issues, such as operational plans and policies on suppliers. Production and service people will have overall responsibility for day-to-day work decisions within the framework of their goals and agreements. In authoritarian organizations like the platinum mine described at the beginning of this chapter, people at the top dominate the decision making at all levels.

One major airline is approaching the issue of participation and control by reviewing all approval requirements. Its goal is to identify the critical decision areas that have far-reaching implications for safety, cost, or service. The airline wants to specify the decision process that uses the best expertise. And it wants to limit approval and review activities to those that clearly add value. The airline's leaders plan to focus their policies and procedures on these core decision areas and to devolve all other decision-making authority to as low in the organization as it can be.

■ Allow Organizational Learning

Learning is the main dynamic that keeps an organization relevant in a changing environment. Generally, the learning process requires a loosening of controls so that diverse viewpoints can be heard, new assumptions can be made, and plans and strategies can be challenged and questioned.

Two trends have emerged in the past few decades that are helping the learning process along. First, the expressions *action learning, being a learning organization,* and *encouraging risk taking* are becoming part of the language of many progressive institutions. As learning becomes increasingly legitimate, people improve their techniques for making it pay off. This conscious use of learning is both a force for change and a way of keeping mistakes—which are now viewed as a major source of learning—from being hidden, which means that it prevents them from becoming destructive. In authoritarian organizations, people are afraid to admit mistakes. This fear prevents them from learning, and it allows small errors to turn into major problems.

Second, self-organizing networks—whether they take the form of task forces, ad hoc work teams, or informal meeting groups—are becoming increasingly common in companies today. Knowing that they must build political and resource support in order to get things done, they often evolve their own informal communication and alignment processes. This communication, alliance building, and informal alignment of activities are often the only way of coordinating complicated and emerging activities. Attempts to put them into a rigid and defined hierarchy can kill them. Attempts to use rational and hierarchical controls prevent an organization from creating new capabilities and adapting to new conditions. Old controls can actually diminish an organization's ability to adapt.

> A very large telecommunications organization had a long history of authoritarian governance. Years of regulation had allowed many layers of management and large staff groups to expand procedures, checkpoints, and control. But, as the competitive environment heated up, it became clear that things needed to change, although business and profits were still good. Management began to retrench the workforce. Employee satisfaction and morale plummeted, especially as worker cutbacks increased.
>
> As the need for fundamental change became increasingly pressing, old decision and control methods were unable to respond. However, various projects began to emerge. Some were initiated by staff groups; others, by department heads. They included projects to develop new management skills, to act on the findings of surveys of employee morale, to change management processes, to develop new career systems, and to improve quality and service. There were many others. All projects were run by teams of people from across the organization. Some teams even included outsiders.
>
> "This is out of control," moaned a senior executive. "These projects should be part of one project plan." He did not realize that project teams were contacting one another, coordinating many of their activities and language, getting into useful debates, and competing usefully for resources and time. The methods of informal

control and integration were far more effective and direct than the executive could have ordered them to be. In fact, mandating controls and managing the changes within the organization's rigid hierarchy would probably have disabled the change process. Moreover, because the culture changes that were beginning to take place were very complex, the overlaps and conflicts between teams helped to identify and test the best ways of doing things.

Some control is inherent in participation. Politics, networking, and the building of internal support can be positive ways of ensuring that workable and responsive decisions emerge and that they are owned by a broad base of the people who must implement them.

■ *Manage the Tension between Stability and Learning*

Management is itself an important control in a participative organization. But, to be effective, management control must focus on maintaining the tension between control and stability. Perhaps the biggest change in attitude required here is that tension must be viewed both as a positive condition and as a form of control. In authoritarian institutions, tensions must be resolved, overcome, or submerged. In participative companies, they are often welcome, or at least they are tolerated.

There are many ways of managing the tension between stability and learning. This section reviews six: structural checks and balances, slack and redundant resources, politics, feedback loops, conscious use of power, and skilled management.

STRUCTURAL CHECKS AND BALANCES. Bringing stakeholder groups or representatives into formal decision-making bodies allows conflicting views and needs to be addressed in legitimate forums and thus reduces destructive behavior by outsiders. Labor union representatives can have seats on the board or take part in strategy-making sessions. Suppliers can participate in product development activities. Customers can be involved in quality assessment. Employees can take part in certain aspects of strategy development and business problem solving.

SLACK AND REDUNDANT RESOURCES. When the organization faces new problems and the best solutions are not clear, it is often useful to have several teams work on solutions for the future. As the example of the telecommunications firm shows, it can help to have redundant or overlapping activities, each of which approaches the same issues in a different way. As long as the teams learn from one another and integrate where possible, the cost of overlap and conflict may well be worth the organizational learning that occurs.

POLITICS. Politics involves selling ideas, building alliances, and influencing people who have different amounts and sources of power. All this activity can be very important in sorting out ideas and ensuring that decisions have the support that they need in order to be effective. In the participative organization, political activity focuses on all levels and groups, not just the top.

FEEDBACK LOOPS. Once an organization has decided to become participative, it is vital for it to conduct continuous assessments of progress. Surveys and focus groups as well as personal assessments help to remind people of the rights and responsibilities that are theirs in a participative institution. Formal feedback that is energetic and focused on action can help to prevent participation from degenerating either into a new kind of bureaucracy or into anarchy. It keeps the tension clear and dynamic.

CONSCIOUS USE OF POWER. Power comes from many sources: position, expertise, personality, trustworthiness. Nevertheless, there are costs whenever people use their power to move decisions in a direction in which others do not want to go. These costs include those associated with maintaining compliance and those related to rebuilding the team's desire and capacity to manage itself. In authoritarian systems, people at the top often use mandates and the power that comes with their position. In many cases, this use of power is unconscious, and followers collude in it. Participative leaders are always aware of their power and of the consequences of using it. They see any use of their formal power as a responsibility. When they use mandates, they do so with care and in full awareness of the consequences.

SKILLED MANAGEMENT. Management must nurture a view that defines *control* as maintaining a balance between stability and change. Control is a day-to-day, dynamic process that cannot be legislated, proceduralized, or delegated to pay and reward systems. For real control, skilled management is the key. Skilled management is management that consciously ensures involvement and accountability, management that provides information and support while constantly nudging the organization and the people in it toward the highest standards. Skilled managers work to help people to control and manage themselves, and they use mandates only when absolutely necessary—as a last resort.

The Age of Participation is a new era for management. It requires managers both to reject the coercive and paternalistic methods of authoritarianism and to avoid the abdication that can occur when participation is viewed only as a touchy-feely governance system. In this new age, every staff member, in the knowledge that the most powerful control is the control that comes from within, must also become a skilled self-manager.

The wise manager keeps the organization balanced on the knife edge between stability and change. For this reason, the participative organization requires a high level of expertise and discipline—and a much more thoughtful view of management control than one finds in authoritarian institutions.

CONCLUSION

In spite of what many fear and believe, control is a very important feature of the participative organization. But control in the participative context does not limit power and information to the few. Rather, control is the balance between stability and change that enables the organization both to perform and to endure.

This balance occurs when at least four things happen. First, the organization must break out of the dysfunctional cycles of control that are the hallmarks of authoritarianism. In these cycles, leaders coerce and parent, while workers rebel and wait for orders. These patterns increase distrust and dependency, which in turn increase authoritarianism and paternalism. While it takes time to break out of these cycles and create new patterns of behavior, it is vital to make the break.

Second, participative organizations use levels of authority and other constraints as value-adding activities to ensure broad debate and to get the best use of resources.

Third, participative organizations also use learning and informal networking to achieve levels of high control. Each has powerful built-in checks and balances that help the organization to adapt rapidly and experiment in new and complex areas. By old standards, such forms of control seem out of control, since the authorities must let them operate informally. But no prior mandates can determine the discovery of Post-It Notes, Xerox machines, or the best way for management and unions to relate. Only learning and informal networks are fluid and responsive enough to make such new and complex discoveries.

Fourth, control occurs when management actively keeps the organization on the razor edge of stability and change. Both management and people who manage themselves must be able to let learning occur, but they must also intervene and set limits where they seem necessary. Organizations also need structures that guarantee conflict and diversity. They need to allow activities and resources to overlap and conflict so that the best solutions can be found. And they must encourage politics and careful and conscious use of power. Surveys and focus groups can operate as feedback loops that test the balance between stability and learning within the organization.

Authoritarian institutions used procedures, sanctions, secrecy, threat, and authority to keep on course. Excessive submission and even sabotage led authoritarian organizations to great losses of energy. They created a compliance-based control system that seemed to keep things together but that was very costly and even created the need for more controls. The participative organization seeks functional and value-adding controls.

Think about the controls within your organization. Figure 12.1 contains five pairs of items. Allocate ten points between the two items in each pair. The points awarded reflect the extent to which each statement is true. Allocate five or more points to an item only if you can say that at least 75 percent of the people in your organization would agree that the statement closely reflects their views and experiences. Nine or ten points indicate that your organization is really a case study example of the statement. The points that you award to each pair of items must total ten. When you have finished rating the statements, add up the numbers in the A column and the B column, and record them on the CONTROLS row of the Governance Assessment Score Sheet in Appendix I.

Figure 12.1 Assess the Controls in Your Organization

36A. *Management develops and implements the organization's measures, policies, rules, and other controls.*

36B. *People at all levels, or their legitimate representatives, help to develop the organization's measures, policies, rules, and other controls.*

37A. *Managers control and oversee the work of task forces and teams and require them to be highly coordinated.*

37B. *Managers encourage ad hoc groups to form around important problems. They expect informal coordination and politics to occur, and they are reluctant to impose unnecessary constraints while the groups learn and build support for new directions.*

38A. *Management control focuses on maintaining predictability and eliminating surprises.*

38B. *Management control focuses on keeping the appropriate tensions between stability (doing things as planned) and learning (experimenting and deviating from plans). Managers see the tension as an important form of control.*

39A. *People in the organization often break the spirit of the rules while observing the letter of the law.*

39B. *People respect the rules and controls because they understand and accept the need for them. They may consciously decide to break the letter of the law in order to preserve its spirit.*

40A. *People behave in different ways when management is watching and when they are working on their own.*

40B. *People treat their goals and job responsibilities as commitments whether or not authorities are watching.*

CHAPTER 13

Pay:
A Focusing
Force

*"Can you help us? We're a really big team that's only been work-
ing together for six months. Actually, we should have been working
as a real team for years, but we were organized into functional
departments. We worked together in the past, but all that really
mattered was our functional work. As individuals, we still report
to engineering, or distribution, or credit, or manufacturing management, but it's our team goals that really matter.*

*"We need help, you see, because we've just heard that the
company is introducing a pay-for-performance system. We've had
an incentive system before, but this one has more bells and whis-
tles. It asks us to take lower base pay in return for higher rewards
at the end. That isn't the issue. Our big concern is that the main
reward focus is the individual. And the bonus pay will be related
to how well we do on our goals.*

*"This will be catastrophic for us. We have been working hard
to become a team. We've been skilling each other up in our technical areas. We have a lot more skill flexibility now. This new pay
system will tear us apart. We've had things like this before, and
they only lead to individualistic behavior and competitiveness.
Our team doesn't need that. We don't want it.*

172

"Beyond that, we have only just learned how to use goals to help us reach for quality and keep us focused on the customer. Today, our goals have greater stretch, and they build in the subjective things that are so important to our customers—our service attitude, how we handle surprise problems. Already, some members of our team are talking about how the pay system will neutralize these goals. They're saying, 'From now on, our goals are going to have to be very concrete and measurable. We've got to be sure that we can meet and exceed them and that there will be absolutely no doubt that we have done so.'

"The fact is that our goals are better now than they ever were before. They drive our performance, and they challenge us. We intend to meet them, of course, but the new pay system will force us to have motives other than performance, quality, and challenge. We will have to work toward our goals knowing that the bonus check plays by other rules.

"Can you help us? Can you talk with the designers of this system? We've tried, and it hasn't gotten us anywhere."

LIKE THE OTHER EXAMPLES in this book, this case is one that we encountered in our own work. It illustrates the point that, like every other element of organizational design, pay systems are caught in the cusp of change. But pay is perhaps the hottest issue of all. Deliberations about pay are like a lightning rod in a room filled with electricity. Once the topic comes up, the energy becomes visible, and it is difficult to discuss anything else.

For this reason, many change agents recommend that pay be one of the last design elements to change. When it is first to be changed, people are quick to focus on how to maximize their own gain from the new system. They do not put their energy into real participation or into the behavioral changes that are needed to create a robust, high-performing, participative system. This argument has merit. We have often made it ourselves. But the recommendation to change pay later in the change process makes sense mainly if individual incentive pay is likely to be part of the solution. If not, there may be considerable value in altering at least some aspects of the pay system early in the change process in order to reinforce the core value that participation has for improved organizational performance.

However the pay shift is timed, participation requires a substantial change in pay systems and in how most people view the role of pay. It also requires reeducation as well as a change in the ways in which the organization develops approaches to pay and communicates them to stakeholders.

OLD ILLUSIONS AND NEW ASSUMPTIONS

Pay in most organizations today is positioned as a motivator. We say that it rewards performance and that it attracts and retains people. These views of pay are the products of an authoritarian approach to management. Authoritarian organizations remove many intrinsic motivators from the work that people do. They put the thinking and the planning in the hands of a few, they fragment and specialize work, and they equate esteem with titles and levels of authority. The limited intrinsic rewards that an authoritarian organization makes available to both managers and employees cannot "motivate" them to superior and creative performance. So the organization tries to fill the gap with carrots and sticks.

Debates about the motivating effects of pay have gone on for years. Most experts now conclude that pay is more likely to be a "dissatisfier" than a motivator. Debate will doubtless continue to rage. But, even as it does, most of the experts on pay and organizational change are looking closely at the controversial issue of pay for individual performance—a name for individual incentive pay. It is very important to examine this area, because most managers believe that individual incentive pay is the best way of getting performance results (Mitchell, Lewin, and Lawler, 1990). However, research does not support this belief, except when the work is simple, stable, and relatively independent, like some sales work.

This discrepancy between what managers believe to be true—namely, that individual incentive pay motivates—and research findings creates real problems if we want to change the pay system. Fortunately, many distinguished voices are uniting in the call for change. For example, the late W. Edwards Deming (Walton, 1986) often chided organizations for giving individual performance rewards. Like the other proponents of quality, he claimed that the main causes of productivity and quality are business processes and management decisions, not individual performance. Besides, he argued, individualistic rewards destroy teamwork, foster mediocre performance, and focus people on the short term. Moreover, the comparisons, ranking, and competition among people that they promote diminish self-esteem, build fear, and ultimately demotivate many people in the institution.

Others echo these concerns. They say that individualistic rewards reduce information sharing, increase conflict within and between groups, and exert downward pressure on risk and goals (Mitchell, Lewin, and Lawler, 1990; Kohn, 1993).

The evidence is overwhelming that individualistic schemes have a more negative than positive impact on people and their performance. Yet managers continue to believe the contrary. And the people who have to work under such systems themselves continue to pay them lip service. When they have the opportunity to participate and help to create a participative enterprise, many employees will say, "Only if there's more money in it for us."

The authoritarian institution has taught its people well. Everyone has been conditioned to view extrinsic rewards as the main reason for working. However, as people become involved in an increasingly participative enterprise, they begin to see the intrinsic rewards, and the heat associated with the pay factor begins to cool. The intrinsic rewards start to become visible when jobs become increasingly whole and when people begin to be involved in the business of the organization as respected partners.

Eventually, of course, people must share in the wealth that they help to create, or the positive effects that participation has on productivity wear off. However, this sharing is better if it is on a group rather than on an individual basis. David I. Levine and Laura D'Andrea Tyson (1990, p. 209) conclude from research reviews and case research that "one can imagine profit sharing without participation and vice versa, but in fact the two are likely to go together in successful participatory systems. In the short run, participation may be its own reward for many employees. In the long run, however, sustained, effective participation requires that employees be rewarded for the extra effort which such participation entails and that they receive a share of any increased productivity or profits."

Increasing intrinsic rewards may seem like a pipedream. But intrinsic motivation is a common condition in the participative organization. The story recounted at the beginning of this chapter gives a glimpse of what the words *intrinsic rewards* mean and of the problems that inappropriate approaches to pay can cause. It represents the human side of the study results that we cited in Chapter Three when we discussed the relationship between participation and business performance. It may help to recall a key point from that chapter. International pay experts assembled by the Brookings Institution in 1990 for a conference dedicated to discovering the system best qualified for improving productivity discovered that pay was not the real key to productivity. The real key was participation, which can in turn be supported by pay: "It appears that changing the way workers are treated may boost productivity more than changing the way they are paid, although profit sharing or employee stock ownership combined with worker participation may be the best system of all" (Blinder, 1990, p. 13).

Pay is thus only part of any performance and management system. And it certainly does not have the major motivating effects that some people would like it to have. Managers and workers alike must change their views and expectations of pay and begin to do the hard work that will establish participation—and its intrinsic motivators. Pay can support. It can be the icing on the cake. But it will not drive performance. We must give up the belief that pay systems can manage people. They cannot.

DESIGNING PAY FOR SUCCESS

There are many approaches to pay. Some can be used over the short term to accelerate a key change. Others can become more enduring because they are at the heart of how the organization wants to govern itself. Some are approaches to deciding the fixed part of pay—the base—the amount of money that people get no matter how they perform. Other approaches focus on the variable part of pay—the amount related to performance. Fixed pay schemes include pay based on job evaluation and skill-based pay. Variable methods include bonuses for individual and team performance; gain sharing, which passes cost improvements on to employees; win sharing, which focuses on achieving company goals; profit sharing; and stock-type options.

Whatever the alternatives chosen, seven success factors are emerging for the pay systems of the future: First, they support the business strategies. Second, they do not attempt to manage people. Third, they give everyone a piece of the cake that they help to bake. Fourth, their "dark sides" are managed aggressively. Fifth, people at all levels and from all areas help to design them. Sixth, people know the what and the why of their pay. Seventh, they distinguish pay for the job, rewards for performance, and feedback on performance.

■ *Support Business Strategies*

In their search for the perfect pay system, organizations have often missed an important point: Pay should work with the organization's strategies, not against them. This means that, if quality, globalization, changes in customer retention rates, and change in the business culture are key strategies, the pay system must reflect these priorities. And if the work that people in the organization do is highly interdependent and if people's jobs change constantly as they move between project and task teams, then the pay system cannot be like a pay system for repetitive work.

As Chapters Six (on structures), Eight (on management processes) and Ten (on relationships) show, work automatically becomes increasingly interdependent when an organization shifts to the participative mode. The focus of performance also shifts to the organization as a whole: People do their own work in the context and in the interest of the bigger picture. But, as an organization becomes increasingly participative, the unique needs and issues in parts of the system also become more important. In some cases, parts of the organization need to restructure their costs or change their products and services. In other cases, parts of the organization need to show a dramatic increase in their impacts on revenue. Pay can play a focusing role here. The experts on so-called new pay call the focus on pay for strategies *win sharing* (Schuster and Zingheim, 1992). Win sharing means that the organization must define the end state sufficiently well to trigger financial "shares" in a win. We will undoubtedly be hearing more about this new area in the future.

For the moment, it is important to note that pay in the participative organization should relate to and support the organization's business strategies. It should not be a me-too approach copied from other companies.

■ Do Not Use Pay to Manage People

In the participative organization, pay is not expected to manage people and their motivation. Rather, people find motivation by doing whole jobs, by having meaningful influence, and by being involved. Performance is managed through good management and self-management, not by carrots and sticks, which in any case cannot manage people. In an effective participative system, pay reinforces the organization's major management processes (Chapter Eight). It does not replace, override, or discredit them.

■ Give Everyone a Piece of the Cake

In a participative organization, a relatively large proportion of an individual's pay is variable and related to the organization's performance. Moreover, this variable pay extends to all levels and all parts of the organization. The trend toward entitlement, which makes this year's performance bonus part of next year's salary, is clearly at an end. It is being replaced by a partnership ethic. Between 1988 and 1993, bonuses in the United States rose from 3.9 to 5.9 percent of payroll, while raises fell from 5.5 to 4.3 percent (Tully, 1993). And while few companies today involve unionized employees in variable pay plans like profit sharing, the trend is in that direction (Schuster and Zingheim, 1992). "Put simply, the company's earnings are your earnings" (Tully, 1993, p. 84), wherever you are in the organization. It is up to management to make sure that the formulas that the organization uses to share the wealth focus on making employees dedicated stakeholders as much as they do on stockholders.

■ Manage the Dark Sides Aggressively

Pay is not and will never be a purely rational part of organizational life. Money sends too many direct and indirect signals to people. Thus, no organization is likely to develop the perfect pay system, and any system that it chooses will have dark sides that need to be managed. An organization must select the approaches that are best for its strategy and then anticipate and manage the problems that they will create. For example, profit sharing relates variable pay to the performance of a large unit or the whole business, but in so doing it creates a line-of-sight problem for people whose work seems far removed from the bottom line. They cannot see clearly what difference their performance makes in a firm that turns over, say, $100 million a year. The way of handling such problems is to teach people about their economic impact, to educate them about the financial dynamics of the firm as a whole, and to communicate continuously about business issues and solve them at the local level. Anyone whose job adds value is in the line of sight of the organization's overall performance. The problem is to help every individual and team to feel and see this connection personally.

Profit sharing thus has its positive and negative sides. So also do team-based pay, skill-based pay, gain sharing, and all the other approaches to pay. There are no perfect answers to the pay question, just answers that are more strategically appropriate than others and whose dark sides can be managed.

■ *Involve Everyone in the Design*

In the participative organization, employees or representatives of employees are involved in the design of pay systems. This makes sense when we consider the rules of effective decision making in the participative institution. Decisions require participation when the formal decision maker does not have all the information that he or she needs in order to make a quality decision. Decisions also require participation when the people affected must be committed to implementation and it is not likely that such commitment will occur without involvement. Commitment is a major issue in the success of any pay approach. But as pay expert Ed Lawler (1990) has noted, it is important to get people involved for another reason: Involvement helps people at all levels to get smarter about the difficulties inherent in creating and implementing pay systems.

■ *Help People Know the What and Why*

People in a participative organization understand their pay and their other compensation. They know the value of their total package: pay and benefits. They may perhaps even be receiving a simple, personal total-pay report every year. The contrast between the participative organization and the authoritarian organization in this regard is dramatic. Few people in authoritarian organizations really know the difference between fixed pay and variable pay. They do not know the value of their total pay and benefits package. Worse, they often feel removed from the bigger picture, and thus they never really understand why their variable pay fluctuates as it does. They do not understand what the organization does with its money, and thus they cannot accept pay decisions that make sense on business grounds. When people do not understand the business as a financial entity (Chapter Eleven underscores the importance of such understanding) and when they do not understand the pay system itself, pay is a target of continuing criticism. Under these conditions, profit sharing and other variable options that are meant to create a partnership become entitlements. And the cycle of dependency continues.

Jay R. Schuster and Patricia K. Zingheim (Schuster and Zingheim, 1992) summarize the changes that must occur. Having studied pay practices in major corporations for more than ten years, they note that the so-called new pay is pay that has a significant variable portion; that focuses on group, not individual, performance; and that treats employees as partners in the successes and failures of the business. A study of sixty Fortune 500 organizations led them to conclude that the new-pay companies significantly outperformed companies that used more traditional approaches. If we take a closer look at the new pay in these more successful companies, we see that it is, first and foremost, participative pay. The participation ethic is woven into the fabric of the new pay system as well into the way in which the new pay plans are developed.

■ *Separate Pay from Reward and Feedback*

Authoritarian organizations lump pay for the job together with reward for performance and feedback on performance. They do so in the belief—erroneous—that money can motivate sustained performance. Participative organizations treat each of these three issues on its own.

First, participative organizations pay people a fixed amount for their competencies and/or for the outputs that they are expected to deliver. This is partly a market issue: For pay purposes, competencies and outputs that have long-term and systemic impact (for example, business strategy) and competencies and outputs that are shorter-term and more localized have a different value. All competencies and outputs are important, but some are worth more money than others.

Second, participative organizations base people's variable pay on the performance of the organization. Pay for competencies and outputs is individual. Pay based on the organization's performance (the piece of the cake) is a group matter. It must be so in an age in which customer delight has become a concern of the organization as a whole. It must also be so if the organization is to nurture a culture of mutual accountability, teamwork, and unity amid the diversity of activities.

Third, feedback on performance needs to be separated both from individual pay and from the variable pay based on the organization's performance. Feedback is vital to quality, continuous improvement, and personal and team learning. When it is connected with pay, it is hard to muster the openness and objectivity that are necessary if feedback is to have these benefits for performance. Feedback should be used only to support performance. If performance is poor and the problems are the fault of the individual, then there should be developmental and disciplinary action. The pay system should operate independently of feedback about the quality of an individual's performance.

OTHER HUMAN RESOURCE PRACTICES

We have focused on pay in this chapter because people attribute a great deal of power to it, and if pay issues are not addressed satisfactorily, the energy for change diminishes, and resistance develops. But, as the research reviewed in Chapter Three underscores, a broad array of people management practices helps to create the participative and high-performing organization.

The preceding chapters have dealt with many human resource practices under other governance headings: structure, leadership, management processes, relationships, values, competencies. In authoritarian systems, these areas are often considered to be personnel matters, and thus the related activities are relegated to administrative functions or to functions that are not in the mainstream of business performance and management. We believe that they are mainstream governance issues.

Three other human resource practices—selection and staffing; career paths and career development; and learning, training, and development—deserve at least a passing mention, and they receive it in this section.

■ *Selection and Staffing*

In the authoritarian organization, staffing decisions are often biased and discriminatory. Criteria for appointments are usually hidden, and they reinforce the personality preferences and comfort zones of current leaders. In the participative organization, the criteria are clear. Competency models are often available to guide the selection processes. Individuals participate in decisions about their career. The selection process is open, and it involves a broad range of stakeholders, who include the candidate's future colleagues, direct reports, and customers as well as the candidate's manager. As the research consistently shows, participative organizations are willing to invest time and resources in ensuring that they appoint the best people. They know that the quality of the people who do the work and the fit between them make a big difference in productivity and quality, and they treat selection and succession as important processes.

■ *Career Paths and Career Development*

In authoritarian organizations, the only career that matters is a career in management. Succession planning is usually a very secretive process that focuses only on top management. Executives spend a great deal of time identifying the best candidates for key positions. They create backup charts and plan how to move their high-potential people. Many authoritarian organizations also consider people to be infinitely replaceable: They hire when times are good, and they fire when times are tough.

In the participative organization, there are many career paths, and each one is considered to be important. They can focus on technical expertise, broad competence, or managerial or leadership directions. In the participative organization, people are aware of the variety of core competencies that are critical to the organization's success. They know that these competencies are both technical and managerial. They are aware that employment cannot be guaranteed for life and that future work with their company will depend on the fit between their skills and competencies and the organization's needs. People know these things, but they also trust that any decisions that displace people will occur participatively and that they will be made in full awareness of their seriousness and of the impact that they have. People in the participative institution can be confident that the organization will keep them up-to-date on its emerging competency requirements and on the skills that are becoming obsolete. They can trust the company to help them to develop career management skills and to be responsible in any decisions that affect employment.

■ *Learning, Training, and Development*

In authoritarian organizations, learning equals training. But few people have access to training programs or have learning plans. Training is also often disconnected from the job, which makes it one of the first investments to be cut in a downturn. In these organizations, it is more important to complete a course than it is to develop a competency.

In the participative institution, learning and development are an entirely different matter. Everyone has his or her own development goals and plans. People have the skills of self-managed learning described in Chapter Twelve. The goal in learning is to increase one's competence, not to complete a course. And learning is a key by-product of many things that occur on the job. Managers and more-experienced staff are expected to be coaches, and managers are evaluated on the increased self-management and skill capacity of the people whom they support.

CONCLUSION

Pay is an emotional issue that is surrounded by many myths. The prevailing beliefs about pay are understandable. They fit the authoritarian world view. In authoritarian organizations, people think that extrinsic factors are the best motivators, that individualistic rewards cause productivity, and that pay decisions should be made in secret and kept secret. The facts do not support these beliefs.

This does not mean that everyone should be paid the same or that an individual's pay should be shouted from the corporate rooftops. It does mean that people must think their pay is fair when it is compared with the pay that prevails in the market. Participation does not require everyone to be paid the same. Base pay should be higher for people who have higher levels of expertise and responsibility: Formal leaders and highly skilled specialists who shape long-term business strategy should be paid more than people whose activities have less impact on the final results.

Nevertheless, the participative organization is a partnership organization that values the contributions of all its stakeholders. It is also an organization in which individual performance cannot easily be separated from the performance of the organization as a whole. People in a participative operation are more clearly interdependent than their peers in a rigidly hierarchical organization. They work together as a total company work stream to ensure that the organization is efficient and effective and that it endures. If the company does well, it is clearly the result of a total team effort. If it does poorly, everyone must share in the results. Variable pay options like profit sharing and win sharing should thus extend to everyone—not necessarily in the same amounts but in proportions that make sense to everyone concerned.

Pay in a participative organization is relatively open pay. It assumes that everyone's contribution is valuable, no matter how small or short-term it may be. One characteristic of the pay systems that are emerging in participative organizations is that they apply to everyone: Pay supports business strategies. It is not used to manage people. Everyone gets a piece of the cake that he or she helps to bake. The inevitable dark side of the pay methods selected are managed aggressively. People at all levels help to design the pay approach. People know the what and the why of their pay. And pay for work, reward for performance, and feedback on performance are kept separate.

Pay, a sensitive issue, is still experimental for the participative organization, and managers and human resource staff are sometimes afraid to act. Yet, because they are used to using pay to drive change, many managers are reluctant to move on participation without first changing the pay system. Such a move creates unnecessary complications for the change process.

The reality is that managers do not need to be so anxious about pay if they are really serious about creating a participative enterprise. The pay system must change. But it is more important at the outset to work on the other eight areas that have the greatest leverage for change and perhaps to implement new practices in such other human resource areas as selection, career management, and development. Once people experience the motivating power of involvement, the lightning rod effect of pay will diminish, and people will begin to see the best pay route for themselves, as did the team whose experience we recounted at the beginning of this chapter.

Think about the pay system in your organization. Figure 13.1 contains five pairs of items. Allocate ten points between the two items in each pair. The points awarded reflect the extent to which each statement is true. Allocate five or more points to an item only if you can say that at least 75 percent of the people in your organization would agree that the statement closely reflects their views and experiences. Nine or ten points indicate that your organization is really a case study example of the statement. The points that you award to each pair of items must total ten. When you have finished rating the statements, add up the numbers in the A column and the B column, and record them on the PAY row of the Governance Assessment Score Sheet in Appendix I.

Figure 13.1 Assess the Pay System in Your Organization

41A. *Pay and extrinsic rewards are used as motivators and to shape and influence performance.*

41B. *The work itself and opportunities to be involved and to influence are key motivators.*

42A. *Bonuses are based on individual achievement. The amount of extra pay is determined by formulas and ranking systems.*

42B. *Through profit sharing and other group and team processes, people throughout the organization share in the wealth that they help to create.*

43A. *A punitive and blaming climate prevails in the organization. People try to win and to look good at the expense of others.*

43B. *An appreciative climate prevails in the organization. People feel acknowledged and acknowledge each other for their contributions.*

44A. *The pay system is designed by specialists. Much about how it works and applies to individuals is secret.*

44B. *The pay system was developed with input from all key stakeholders. It is an open system that everyone understands.*

45A. *More people are dissatisfied with the pay system than are satisfied that it is fair.*

45B. *People feel that the pay system is fair and that it is applied fairly.*

PART III

Life in the Participative World

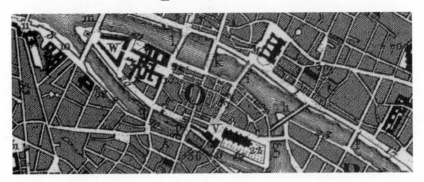

*M*aps were perhaps one of the first real inventions and tools of the information era. The only way to perfect them was through tireless use, dedicated exploration, and continuous improvement. Even in the twentieth century, we are still refining our maps. Committed researchers and users continue to collect and consolidate information and experience. But we still have not mapped all the world. We probably never will. For as we continue to explore the world, we have new insights, uncover new complexity, and deepen our appreciation of its integrity.

The wonders revealed by the new sciences have displaced the fears of the early mariners. In the same way, the Age of Participation will be established only with time and committed study and application.

CHAPTER 14

Five Levels
of Involvement

MOST PEOPLE CAN IMAGINE an authoritarian organization. It involves mandates, fear, restrictions on access to big-picture information, procedures, second-guessing, and so on. The picture of the participative workplace is much less clear, partly because experiments in participation are relatively recent and fragmented, partly because the images of participation that we do have have often been idealized.

What is life in a participative organization really like? We propose to look at it in two major ways. First, involvement in the participative organization occurs across a broad spectrum of activities ranging from tactical to strategic. Second, the participative organization meaningfully involves the full array of stakeholders.

A BROAD SPECTRUM OF ACTIVITIES

Participation occurs on at least five major levels, ranging from prescribed action—obeying rules and following procedures—to influencing or defining the mission, values, and strategies of the business. In this section, we describe how the participative organization involves people on these five levels.

■ *Level I: Prescribed Action*

On level I, people follow procedures and do as they are told. Prescribed action can apply to activities ranging from sweeping the floor to developing strategy for the business as a whole. In very authoritarian companies, even executives have very little freedom of action.

Prescribed action is important even in participative organizations. The difference is that decisions about the actions prescribed are often made participatively. However, once staff have committed to prescribed action, they persist in that action until there is an agreement or understanding that the action required must change. The fact that an organization is participative does not mean that everyone does his or her own thing.

Level I activities are anything that follows routine or procedures— such things as housekeeping, safety practices, machine-paced work, and routine management work like salary administration or budget reconciliation. Everyone in an organization has at least some level I activities to perform.

■ *Level II: Activity Participation*

On level II, people participate by influencing how the work that is part of their immediate job is done. That is, they decide on the tools and techniques to use and on how to sequence their actions. This is the first level on which we can look for real and meaningful participation.

Working in quality circles, setting requirements for the quality of work, job enrichment, gain sharing, and multiskilling to increase task flexibility are typical level II activities.

■ *Level III: Role Participation*

On level III, people participate by determining what they or their teams will accomplish. Participation on this level requires broad knowledge about customers and the organization's operations. In order to make wise decisions and recommendations about the organization's products or services, people need to have big-picture information.

Typical level III activities include setting production and activity goals, identifying the needs of customers, determining how to respond to them, setting goals for suppliers, and hiring team members.

- ## *Level IV: Context Participation*

On level IV, people participate by moving outside the boundaries of their own or their team's job to influence the processes and structures around and beyond them. On their own discretion, people go beyond their immediate job authority to resolve crises or solve immediate problems with customers.

Selecting or advising on the selection of leaders, choosing suppliers, influencing the size of budgets and budget trade-offs, deciding equipment and work technology, providing supervisors with performance feedback, and reengineering processes that involve others beyond the immediate team are some typical level IV activities.

- ## *Level V: Vision Participation*

On level V, people participate by shaping or influencing the most fundamental assumptions that guide their organization. Activities on this level help to determine the values, goals, strategies, and other frameworks that determine what the organization is and will be. Individuals and teams work together to determine the organization's broad direction. Their experiences and insights become part of the strategic and planning data that shape goals and strategies, and they are meaningfully involved in determining priorities and direction.

Helping to determine the values, principles, and mission of the organization is one typical level V activity. Involvement at this level also extends to decisions about how the core management processes, such as strategic planning, will occur and who will be involved.

THE FULL ARRAY OF STAKEHOLDERS

Broadly speaking, activity on levels I, II, and III relates to task issues, while activity on levels IV and V relates to power issues. Because the goal of the participative age is to make high involvement and empowerment the cornerstones of performance, it is impossible to restrict participation only to task issues or only to power issues. In an authoritarian organization, your level in the organization determines your level of participation and the extent of your influence. The interdependence promoted by participative governance and its relative seamlessness blur these boundaries.

In a participative organization, everyone is involved at every level. Formal leaders concentrate on levels IV and V—context and vision—while people involved directly in the work stream focus mainly on levels II and III—activity and role—although they can also participate at level IV. As everyone soon discovers, such multifaceted participation requires broad knowledge and commitment to the institution's goals and values. It also requires people to understand the customer and the impact that each and every job has on the business. That is why poor communication and lack of education are real enemies to successful participation.

THE SUBTLETIES OF MEANINGFUL INVOLVEMENT

Organizations that are trying to involve people in meaningful ways often fall into one or the other of two traps: Either they try to move sequentially from one level of participation to the next, or else they try beforehand to set the maximum level of participation for specific groups. Neither is possible.

First, a shift in governance is an organizationwide transformation, not a step-by-step adaptation. It is impossible to get to the moon by car or to the New World by horse. At some point, one must board an entirely different vehicle that is suitable for space or ocean travel. In much the same way, the shift to participative governance requires a leap into new ways of operating and relating at work. These new practices spill into many areas.

Second, participation, like authoritarianism, permeates all facets of organizational governance. It is impossible to be neatly selective about it. When the main goal is meaningful influence, all groups must be able to be involved at any level on which meaningful influence is possible and on which it will add value or raise commitment. Figure 14.1 shows the pattern of involvement in a healthy, participative enterprise.

There are two major transitions that any group of people goes through on its journey toward full participation. The first happens when people who are used only to following orders and taking prescribed action (level I) begin to get involved in determining either

Figure 14.1 The Spectrum of Involvement in a
Highly Participative Organization

Involvement Level	Executives Managers Staff	Typical Activities
V **Vision** **Participation**		Decisions/influence on - values - strategies - mission Decisions about organization structure Decisions about management process and culture
IV **Context** **Participation**		Selecting/advising on selection of leaders Choosing suppliers Influencing size of budgets Deciding equipment and work technology Performance feedback to leaders Reengineering work processes beyond the immediate teams
III **Role** **Participation**		Setting production/work goals and standards Production scheduling Determining customers' needs and responses to the needs Setting supplier goals Hiring/firing team members
II **Activity** **Participation**		Quality circles Statistical process controls Determining methods for the work Multiskilling across tasks Gain sharing
I **Prescriptive** **Action**		Housekeeping Safety Machine-paced work Some management processes

their activities (level II) or their own roles (level III). Both developments require levels of initiative and knowledge that change the relationship between people and their work in fundamental ways. The second key transition occurs when people begin to influence decisions at the context level beyond the realm of their own job (level IV).

Because activity and role participation entail very little challenge to management prerogative, authorities tend not to find them very threatening at the outset. For example, when South Africa legalized Black trade unions in the 1970s, it unleashed activity and role participation (levels II and III), but companies generally blocked involvement beyond those levels. Thus, South African institutions liberalized, but they did not democratize. That is, they brought a form of controlled involvement that initially helped to defuse workers' frustration and moderate their demands. But that involvement also helped to develop the skills and power bases that increased the workers' expectations for involvement beyond level III. As a consequence, labor legislation in that country is moving into areas that support power participation by the people who do the work.

A taste of involvement often creates an appetite for participation. At some point, either a critical mass of people begins to require a greater say in the affairs in which they engage, or the external forces driving the organization toward participation are just too strong. More positively, activity and role participation can begin to build the competencies and produce the productivity results that encourage management and employees to want to go further. Such encouragement launches people into context participation (level IV) and vision participation (level V). This is the first real opportunity for power sharing in institutional governance.

The fundamental transformation of an organization really takes off when people in every part of the organization begin to get involved at the context and vision levels. For participation at these levels to be successful, most employees need access to financial and strategic information. Only with such information can they become responsible and value-adding voices in the key power arenas of budgets, promotions, selection of customers and suppliers, and ultimately the organization's direction. To be sure, managers are still in charge of most of these activities, but policy is no longer determined by small groups of individuals behind closed doors or in smoke-filled rooms.

The movement toward participation on multiple levels should not be chronological—starting with the lowest level and proceeding toward the highest. The most significant gains are made by introducing aspects of all five levels at once. This is not to say that you should try to achieve everything at once. Rather, the needed change can happen as the consequence of "waves" of participative practice that wash across all five levels. Such a way of introducing change makes it clear to people that participation requires some dreary prescriptive actions as well as the more complex and potentially exciting activities associated with vision.

A PEEK AT ONE EXPERIENCE

At the end of the day, participation is both a personal and an organizational matter. Let's look at how one person experiences the journey.

Jackie is in her fifteenth year of work in a bottling plant. She used to run the machine that washes the glass containers before they are loaded into the filler, but her job has changed significantly. Two years ago, her plant began to re-create itself as a high-involvement workplace. Jackie found the initial stages quite exciting, especially after years of being ignored and just following orders. She and her colleagues got more attention than they had ever received before. They reorganized into total process management teams. For the first time in her career, others were expecting her to think about her work and to come up with ideas for ways of doing it better. That is how the change process started for Jackie (level II). Then the company provided Jackie and her teammates with courses on how the business makes money. She had never really thought about her work in terms of its costs and benefits to the business, and she had never known the real cost of one dirty bottle. But as soon as she and her colleagues understood it, they began to think for the business. Before they knew it, they had recommended that the washing and bottling teams merge (level III)—and their recommendation was accepted. The result was that everyone's job changed. Even the pay levels were raised.

Before long, with the aid of some team self-management processes, Jackie and her work colleagues detected problems related to their machines that they thought the equipment suppliers should address. Looking into the options and the associated problems, team members had several ideas that would require the business to change policy and operate in some dramatically differ-ent ways. At about this time, the senior management team became increasingly aware of the creative work and increased productivity that was now coming out of the old packaging area. They invited representatives of the team, including Jackie, to meet with them as part of their preliminary strategic planning work (level V). Management told team representatives that some of the best strategies would come from discoveries that workers made. Management wanted continuously to tap the ideas of frontline workers. Were they willing to play such a role?

Over the years, the packaging team's involvement came to extend beyond the immediate jobs of team members (levels I, II, and III). Teams began to play a significant role in the selection of supervisors and suppliers. They hired and managed their own team members, and they took responsibility as a group for achieving increasingly rigorous performance goals. Team members who were used to following orders and did not want increased responsibility dropped away. So did suppliers on whom the team could not rely. Meanwhile, the team's activities spread across the spectrum of the levels of involvement in ways that could benefit the business, not in ways that preempted executive decisions by the management team. The packaging team's main focus was on doing the work well. All its other activities helped to ensure that it met this goal.

CONCLUSION

Regardless of their job, individuals in a fully participative organi-zation are involved in many types of activities, wherever they can have meaningful influence. There are five possible levels of involvement, ranging from prescribed action (level I), activity participation (level II), and role participation (level III) to context participation (level IV) and vision participation (level V).

In authoritarian organizations, frontline staff work mainly at level I, although they sometimes proceed to level II. In participative organi-zations, senior managers and people with special expertise have primary responsibility for the levels on which participation is highest, but there is a great deal of collaboration at levels IV and V. People everywhere have a major say in what their work will be—that is, in determining the products and services that they will provide (level III).

Broad involvement is possible in a participative organization because it has been designed to make real use of the contributions that people make. Its structure, values, leadership, management processes, information, relationships, competencies, controls, and pay systems both support and demand high involvement and high performance.

CHAPTER 15

New Roles
for Everyone

Now I know that I can say to my manager, "I have an idea," and he
has to listen to me. It is my right to think about better ways of doing
my job. This has changed everything for me in my work.

— A young Black female production worker

THIS YOUNG WOMAN expresses one basic truth about participation: It
transforms life for everyone in and around the organization—
executives, middle managers, work teams and individual performers,
support staff, customers, suppliers, and union representatives. Thus, it
requires a new integration of thinking and doing.

The participative organization is a connected organization that
involves everyone on all levels of participation—deciding and acting,
formulating and implementing. Of course, executives still bear the
weight of strategy and vision, and the workers shoulder the responsibility for assuring the quality of products and services and for innovating. But, if someone in a participative organization has something
to contribute, there is a good chance that his or her contribution will
be considered and debated, and—if it has merit—that it will be acted
on.

But everyone has to assume new roles, because in today's dynamic
environment vision and action are in constant tension. That may be

the primary reason why the old habit of separating thinking (at the top) from doing (at the bottom) cannot work. Action and experience inform vision, and vision guides action. The process is unfolding and interconnected.

A lovely story suggests how this occurs: Legend tells us that Michelangelo was rolling a big block of marble down the village road when a friend shouted, "Where are you going with that rock, Michelangelo?" The sculptor is reported to have said, "I am going to free the angel that is locked up inside." He made his way with the stone to his workshop, where he chipped away at the marble, constantly reshaping his vision of the form that the angel could take. Some time later, the friend walked into Michelangelo's workshop. Before him stood an exquisite angel of marble. "How did you carve such a masterpiece?" exclaimed the visitor. "It was always there in the rock," replied Michelangelo. "All I did was take away the parts that didn't look like an angel."

If Michelangelo had not been pulled by a vision that drew him on and guided his action, he would have ended up with a pile of useless chips. And if he had refused to deal with the special features of the stone when he had the chisel in his hand, the rock would have ended up formless. The masterpiece that he produced was a result of the interaction between vision and action.

This story shows how responsive strategy works. A responsive strategy requires the continuous integration of three forces: the vision pull that gives us a gripping picture of the desired future embedded in the rock of organizational options, the practical action of realizing where we are and using tools and skills to release the vision within, and the tension in the interplay between the vision and the discoveries that each of our actions produces.

In any organization, the vision that we have of what we want—the equivalent of the angel that Michelangelo had in his head—responds to the constantly shifting circumstances that surround us. To make things more complicated, every person in the organization is a sculptor chipping away at the rock with different tools and different skills. It should be no wonder that the authoritarian solution is failing. There is simply no way of planning, coordinating, or controlling the interplay of vision and action among so many people. Only participation has any hope of harnessing and channeling the tensions between them.

The story about Michelangelo has several lessons that relate to life in the participative organization: It is impossible to create something if the people who must "chip away" do not have a personal vision of what they are creating or if they are not committed to it. The vision is constantly modified as those who must implement it learn more about the qualities and the potential of the "rock" that they are carving. Anyone who works to turn a collective vision into reality must be constantly aware of any changes in what is possible and desirable. Personal involvement in making the vision come alive is a key to success. Touching the rock and watching how it responds to the chisel help to shape the vision that guides the next stroke. If many people must work together to give the vision life, then there must be some way of creating and maintaining a collective and unfolding vision.

All this requires participation. The organization's achievements are the collective product of the integrated thoughts and actions of many stakeholders. The remainder of this chapter reviews how each group of stakeholders—customers, work teams and individual performers, executives, functional and specialist staff, union officials and employee representatives, suppliers—helps to make the final product great by optimizing its own participation in the process.

CUSTOMERS

The watchword in the 1980s was that the customer must be king or queen. Unfortunately, many interpreted this dictum as meaning that customers replaced top management as the new autocrats. Autocratic customer demands, one-sided service agreements, and various forms of supplier abuse became accepted practices. The participative customer-focused organization does not invite the customer to be abusive or to don the despot's robe. In fact, our own experience as customers tells us that we get much better quality if we treat our suppliers with respect. As customers, we know that we share the responsibility for our own satisfaction, even as we expect higher and better quality and delight.

As Figure 15.1 shows, in a fully participative organization, customers become partners in the process of meeting their own needs.
They communicate their requirements, they are willing to learn from
their suppliers, and they make strategic alliances when they can be of
mutual benefit. Customers help to educate suppliers, they respect the
demands on their time and their requirements, and they give them
direct feedback about their satisfaction with products, services, and
the relationship itself. Customers take time to be appreciative as well
as critical.

Customers are part of the participative organization, and they may
even participate in the planning and design of products and services.
Today, many customers—for example, those of American Hospital
Supply—can access information about their supplier's inventory from
their own computer system. In effect, customers sell to themselves. At
the very least, they write their own orders and create their own
invoices. The customers of GE Medical Systems create their own
invoices. That company's new organization chart has customers inside
the organization's boundaries, not outside. Customers are part of
teams, and they play a key part in the organization's vision of itself.
Sometimes this interaction happens face-to-face. Sometimes it happens through technology. In any event, the customer is progressively
moving into the company as if the company's walls were permeable—
or as if the company had no walls.

Does such inclusiveness work? The Ford Taurus was designed by
teams that combined customers with company people. These teams
identified more than ninety key requirements and worked together to
devise ways of meeting them. The result of these efforts has proved to
be one of the biggest automotive success stories in this decade. But the
experts had to run the risk of bringing in customers and having them
participate in the organization's activities.

Is it impossible to involve customers who are spread geographi-
cally over a large area? Not for a large U.S. shipbuilder: Ship's captains
are often interviewed on videotape. The company's employees then
review the tapes and discuss their implications. This practice brings
customers from all over face-to-face with employees. Their work sud-
denly has flesh and blood users, and it gets a real boost in meaning.

Figure 15.1 summarizes the relationship between the participative organization and its customer.

Figure 15.1 The Customer and the Participative Organization

Vision Level (V)

Specify quality requirements for the relationship.

Enter into special partnerships (for example, technology sharing, resource sharing, long-term guarantees) where appropriate.

Commit to a win-win relationship.

Help to envision dramatically new ways of being seamless with suppliers.

Context Level (IV)

Be willing to link systems and staff where mutually beneficial (for example, computer linkups).

Include key workers and teams in relevant customer events and correspondence.

Action Level (III, II, I)

Articulate quality requirements and standards for products and services clearly.

Educate teams and individual performers regarding how products and services are and will be used.

Appreciate and acknowledge quality in products, services, and the relationship.

WORK TEAMS AND INDIVIDUAL PERFORMERS

In a participative organization, the entire company's first order of business must be to support frontline workers as individual contributors and as teams. The goal is to ensure that there are no barriers between the people who make and distribute the product and who serve customers, and being the best.

One discovery about today's most successful organizations is clear: The people who do the work have knowledge, they think, and they have power. They know the big picture. They know their jobs. They know their customers and suppliers. They think about the best way of doing their jobs. They think about unique ways of meeting specific customer needs. They think about things to do that can support the business's direction.

Individuals and teams have power to act in crises, power to stop the line if quality is poor, power to pull product from shelves if something is wrong. They have power of ideas, which they make known for vision and strategies.

Over time, as individuals working alone and in teams develop skills, perspective, and trust, they develop budget power, too. Jack Welch (1991, p. 4), CEO of the General Electric Company (GE), reported to shareholders: "In the critical steam turbine bucket machinery center, teams of hourly employees now run, without supervision, $20 million worth of new milling machines that they specified, tested, and approved for purchase. The cycle time for the operation has dropped 80 percent. It is embarrassing to reflect that for probably eighty or ninety years, we've been dictating equipment needs and managing people who knew how to do things much better and faster than we did."

It is becoming commonplace in many new plants to assume that individual performers and teams will participate at levels V (vision), IV (context), and III (role) as well as at levels II (activity) and I (prescribed). It is not uncommon for one of GE's new plants to have ratios like these: one manager, fifteen salaried "advisers," and one hundred seventy-five hourly workers. In such a configuration, the workers have to operate at all levels of participation. Job rotation, cross-department teamwork, and skill- and business-performance-based pay ensure that such participation works for the people and the business.

Management theorist Henry Mintzberg (1994, p. 30), perhaps one of the best thinkers on business strategy today, gives an example that highlights the role of frontline staff in what used to be the exclusive domain of top executives: "Out in the field, a salesman visits a customer. The product isn't quite right, and together they work out some modifications. The salesman returns to the company and puts the changes through; after two or three more rounds, they finally get it right. A new product emerges, which eventually opens up a new market. The company has changed strategic course."

The Minnesota Mining and Manufacturing Company (3M) has known the power of vision participation (level V) for people on the line. Since its founding, people with ideas have been able to nurture their products until they become big business. Scotch Tape and Post-It Notes are two products of that system. Of course, many ideas do not make it to the top. But without the nurturing environment and the belief that everyone can contribute to the future vision, 3M would not be the phenomenal and enduring company that it has become during this century.

Unfortunately, many companies do not welcome strategic ideas from their people. And their people have been conditioned to accept this as one of the ground rules. Consider this abbreviated version of a dialogue that one of the authors had with a communications specialist at a large international transportation company:

> Communication specialist: I can't understand why you are suggesting that we have a more interdependent work style here. My boss gets paid to tell me what to do.
>
> Pat: What does that mean, exactly?
>
> Communication specialist: Well, he's supposed to find out what the corporate priorities are and then distribute the work. And it's his job to tell me what he thinks of my work at performance review time.
>
> Pat: Let me ask you something. How long have you been a communication specialist, and what does that mean?
>
> Communication specialist: For five years. I've been trained in it. I've got a university degree in mass communications.
>
> Pat: Have you ever had any ideas that you thought would be worth acting on that were "better" than what your boss wanted you to do?
>
> Communication specialist: Well, sure. Lots of times.
>
> Pat: What did you do?
>
> Communication specialist: Now that you mention it—nothing.
>
> Pat: What if you had been able to act on your own good idea rather than just following the decision that came down?
>
> Communication specialist: I get your point. I've been making some assumptions . . .

Hard to believe? This is a true story about a very competent and articulate person.

As Figure 15.2 underlines, strategy interacts with action at all levels. In a participative organization, individual performers and teams are involved across the spectrum. They do not assume that thinking occurs somewhere else.

Figure 15.2 Work Teams and Individual Performers and the
Participative Organization

Vision Level (V)

> Help to create the values of the business.
>
> Contribute ideas and experiences for vision and strategy.
>
> Find out about the big picture.
>
> Redirect own work to carry out the organization's larger goals.

Context Level (IV)

> Aggressively pursue the information needed for meaningful participation.
>
> Make decisions to purchase equipment and major work tools or influence them meaningfully.
>
> Develop the business knowledge needed to understand and influence larger business processes.
>
> Help to select supervisors who can be trusted to support and add high value to the team.
>
> Clarify the expectations of internal and external suppliers. Provide them with honest and respectful feedback.
>
> Expect and require that systems, processes, and procedures add value to the work.

Action Level (III, II, and I)

> Evaluate, improve, and innovate continuously in work.
>
> Control the quality of own work.
>
> Monitor the expectations and perceptions of customers and users regarding own work.
>
> Provide feedback, appreciation, discipline, and development support to others on team.

EXECUTIVES

Faster, more positive change in governance may or may not depend on the speed of executive action. But it does seem to be true that decisions and dedication from senior management at the beginning of the move to participation can be valuable. People who are used to being told what to do may not be able to move unless an external, authoritative force ignites them.

Once the participative organization has been launched and has acquired some momentum of its own, executives can focus on keeping it moving. The role of the organization's executives is very much one of taking a broad and long view. Executives must see the organization as a system of relationships, processes, core competencies, shared visions and values, and energy—lots of real and potential energy. Participative executives encourage questioning and diverse views. They develop deliberate strategies and capture strategies that emerge from the field. They are present with the people—workers, customers, suppliers—listening and gently channeling energy toward common goals.

In 1984, two rather unlikely transformational leaders took charge as chairman and chief executive officer of South Africa's electrical utility. The chairman, a conservative businessman newly recruited from the armaments industry, started out with a national mandate to rid the company of financial scandal and inefficiency. He was joined by a new chief executive, an operating manager who had started as an artisan and worked his way up through the ranks. Together they started an odyssey of change that would spread out to most of the nation's labor unions and into all communities.

Within eight years, they had earned the utility a reputation as one of the most enlightened companies in their country. In the early days, there was experimentation. At monthly education sessions, the senior leaders explored the world's latest business and leadership theories and practices. Strategy sessions began to reach out and involve representatives from special-interest groups. These were followed by goal-setting and participative performance feedback sessions that reached all 55,000 members of the company's staff.

In any week, you could find the chief executive, with tie loosened or no tie at all, talking with people in the plants and the communities. What did they talk about? Well, the chief executive did a lot of listening. And somehow—one often did not know how it happened—the discussion always moved to the company's three visions: to be a world-class utility, to provide electricity to all, and to create an electricity grid that could serve an entire trade block.

*In the course of these discussions, the vision came alive for every-
one. They talked about what it meant to the work, how employees
could help to make it come true, and what it would mean to the
community. They discussed what the chief executive could and
should do. People sparked with energy about energy.*

*Then, over time, the change processes gathered momentum—
helped, no doubt, by political developments then taking place in
the nation. Representatives of eleven trade unions, whose views
ranged across the entire philosophical spectrum, met with fifty top
managers. Task groups reached out to others in and around the
organization as very diverse stakeholders began to work their way
toward profound new agreements about the utility's governance.
Today, trade union and community leaders sit on the Electricity
Council, the utility's governing body. And their discussions have a
foundation in shared values and agreements about goals.*

*What role did the leaders play in these developments? They
provided the air cover and the institutional framework, and they
took the personal risks that allowed new relationships and visions
to grow and ultimately take off.*

*The organization has much more to do, but its new chief
executive, who only took on his leadership role as the nation
inaugurated its first democratic government, inherits a powerful
legacy. The progress that the company made toward becoming a
participative enterprise before the nation itself changed its mode of
governance is almost miraculous, given the many powerful forces
that could have destroyed these efforts. But its experience illustrates the point of this section: Change could not have occurred
without a new kind of participation by executives. With such participation, the organization itself changed forever. Figure 15.3
summarizes the role of executives in participative organizations.*

Figure 15.3 Executives in the Participative Organization

Vision Level (V)

Scan the environment constantly.

Ensure that internal and external stakeholders have a broad
involvement in strategy.

Be prepared to lead change even if the organization is doing well today.

Get nontraditional data for insights.

Anticipate and recognize discontinuities and surprises. Do not rationalize them away.

Buffer environmental upheavals. Keep the organization focused on important longer-range priorities.

Communicate and interact with people around larger vision and strategies. Help these to become meaningful for the people who must make them work.

Context Level (IV)

Be sure that stakeholders have the information they need in order to carry out their roles.

Assess key organizational processes and competencies continuously. Support and drive revitalization when it will deliver value.

Ensure that information is available and accessible for work, not used merely to support personal power.

Action Level (III, II, and I)

Stay aware of and be able to identify with the real work that people do.

Have a personal presence with all stakeholders. Press the flesh.

Encourage the direct access and contact that people need in order to get work done. Disable bureaucracy and unnecessary controls.

Ensure that required approvals and levels of authority add value.

Be stewards who support people in their work. Do not expect to be served and adulated.

MANAGERS

At this writing, the role of managers—those between the executives and the people who do the work that makes the product or serves the customer—is just emerging. Clearly, their past roles—filtering and channeling information, and controlling—are disappearing. And the practice of creating levels and titles in order to advance careers and increase pay is also being challenged. It must cease.

It is possible that many supervisory and middle management positions will disappear. Sophisticated information systems that simplify complex things for frontline workers, coupled with new expectations that workers and teams will manage themselves, will make many layers of management unnecessary. Already, organizations are beginning to extend their so-called spans of control. Recall the fifteen advisers for one hundred seventy-five workers at the General Electric plant mentioned earlier. Those numbers mean that the ratio of management to staff is one to eleven. In the past, the common pattern was something like six executives, eighteen managers, and perhaps eight shift supervisors, which means one manager for every five frontline workers. In very large organizations that have as many as ten levels top to bottom, the ratios often approach or even exceed one to one.

Participative organizations seem to be developing roles for middle people as connective tissue and as facilitators. In these roles, middle managers help to connect larger strategies and actions. They look after broad customer and supplier connections that extend across functional synapses within the organization. They help to connect people and developmental resources. Middle-level people must also remain alert to catch the issues and problems that fall between the cracks and detect the patterns in day-to-day operations that have implications for larger strategic action. They must notice where processes break down and where there are opportunities for improvement, and they must help teams to work together smoothly.

The role of the middle-level people is difficult to define today because so many organizations are unsure about their governance philosophy. Old governance practices coexist with new ones. Structures retain a lot of unnecessary hierarchy while people in the workplace reorganize into full-service teams. Systems in formation take away some of middle management's work, while the increased demands to manage organizational change seem to require management to be there for support. Through all this, others in the organization often see middle management as the major obstacle to change. Middle management's role is unclear, but there will certainly be fewer middle managers in the institutions that we are constructing. Figure 15.4 summarizes the role of managers in the participative organization.

Figure 15.4 Managers in a Participative Organization

Vision Level (V)

>   Continuously clarify and tell the truth about the organization's internal capacity and core competencies.

>   Bridge from strategies to action in ways that add value, build commitment, and encourage creative ways of accomplishing larger goals.

Context Level (IV)

>   Ensure that relationships with customers and suppliers are high quality.

>   Help to develop efficient and effective information systems that promote the speed and quality of work.

>   Move the capacity for day-to-day personnel management— recruitment, development, feedback, staffing—to the front line.

>   Help to specify the competency requirements for future work.

>   Be sure that any management job adds real value.

Action Level (III, II, and I)

>   Expect decisions to be made and problems to be resolved at the levels closest to the information and the problems.

>   Help to remove bottlenecks and barriers to performance.

>   Create a positive and developmental climate.

>   Coach and support skill development.

>   Help to develop the self-management and teamwork capacities of all staff.

FUNCTIONAL AND SPECIALIST STAFF

In authoritarian organizations, the relationships between staff and line people are often adversarial and dependent. Especially in big bureaucracies, staff—human resource specialists, finance and accounting people, lawyers, information specialists, technical advisers, communication staff, and so forth—make policy and strategy, and line management and employees implement them. In fact, in many fully developed bureaucratic autocracies, even senior executives wield little power. Finance people control financial decisions. Human resource people make the major people decisions. Information systems people decide what information will be provided and how it will be presented. And marketing people make policy on pricing and customer relations. In many companies, the idea that executives have much power and control has been a useful fiction. Functional staff have wielded the real power.

As an organization shifts into participative gear, staff can become marginalized unless they are willing to re-create their role in the context of participative governance.

One key effect of participation is that it increases the number of generalists: People at all levels must acquire many basic skills that in authoritarian organizations belong to staff. Eventually, every employee acquires more power and responsibility for his or her budget and for the team's budgets and for personnel actions like the development, feedback, coaching, and selection of fellow workers. Employees everywhere also become more involved in decisions about information and reporting, customer satisfaction and retention, and even product planning and development.

What, then, happens to central staff? Do they become redundant and irrelevant? Do they lose control of the decisions that they are uniquely qualified by their expertise to make? Does the organization risk becoming mediocre in functional areas where competitive advantage requires stellar performance? How can an organization retain its functional excellence and at the same time devolve basic functional decisions to the workforce as a whole?

The participative organization requires staff people to change their role. They must both ensure that functional excellence is pervasive in the organization and put as many functional decisions as they can into the line, down to the level at which the work is done. Achieving this aim usually means that central staff groups shrink and that functional experts move into the line organizations. Functional experts become educators, system designers, coaches, standard setters, and gatherers of information about functional quality. It is not unusual for the finance specialists in a participative organization to develop and teach line people how to budget and identify the financial implications of projects and decisions. The new role is not to do the work oneself but to help others to do it. It means helping others to develop a deeper, contextual understanding of excellence in one's functional area.

Human resource people no longer solve personnel problems for managers. Instead, they coach managers to work together with employees to solve the problems. Marketing people do not develop product and pricing plans in a vacuum. Instead, they lead cross-functional and customer groups that make the decisions themselves. Functional groups can still do some of the proceduralized work—process payroll, write computer programs, track market statistics. And they can also do the high-end thinking about how to extend functional excellence throughout the organization. However, the doing of much of the functional work moves to the line people.

At first, this is a hard transition for staff specialists to make. Many are used to working in a vacuum, telling the rest of the organization what to do and being the organization's specialist thinkers. The dichotomy between thinking and doing that this pattern creates is often as dysfunctional as the dichotomy between thinking and doing for managers and workers. Staff groups are entering a new age in which they must help to reunite the thinking and doing of functional work and reintegrate functional thinking into the mainstream work of the company.

When staff take on this educational and support role and shed the isolation and power that they had in the past, the organization has put another pin into place that will help it to sustain participation. If the staff role is not redesigned and if those who perform it do not accept the new role at an emotional level, it is hard for true participation to be self-sustaining. Figure 15.5 reviews the roles of functional and specialist staff in the participative organization.

Figure 15.5 Functional and Specialist Staff in the Participative Organization

---

Vision Level (V)

> Ensure access to world-class functional practices, ideas, and expertise.
>
> Benchmark the organization against the best standards in the functional area.
>
> Align functional tasks and operations with the organization's overall business vision.

Context Level (IV)

> Ensure that functional systems support the empowerment of teams and individuals.

> Develop the basic functional knowledge and skills of people on line.

Action Level (III, II, and I)

> Coach and support teams and individuals toward day-to-day functional excellence.

UNION OFFICIALS AND EMPLOYEE REPRESENTATIVES

Traditionally, the relationships between labor and management and within labor unions themselves are characterized by authoritarian practices and assumptions. The use of win-lose negotiations, threats, distributive bargaining, and power plays is typical of low trust and authoritarian relationships. However, this, too, changes when organizations adopt participative principles.

Under the banner of participation, labor officials and management sit on the same side of the table, working together to ensure that both the business and its stakeholders prosper. Both parties recognize that the unions have a right to represent the collective interests of the employee groups that have chosen them. That employee groups, via pension funds, now own more than half of the share capital of U.S. business underlines the fact that the interests of worker collectives and companies are becoming increasingly mutual. Authoritarian gamesmanship can only endanger everyone's interests. Indeed, it could trigger an employee-owner-driven run on an organization's own management!

Within industries that are changing rapidly, unions can also help with the tasks of developing workers' skills and of retraining and deploying workers—tasks that are difficult for a company to manage by itself.

The need for new relationships and roles is there no matter what the country.

"We are in a new era of labor-management relations."
(R. Hartshorn, associate director of the Ford Executive
Development Center)

"Our problems and issues are bigger than either of us. Working
together, the pie is bigger. We do not have time to waste."
(Gwedi Mantash, general secretary of the National Union of Mine
Workers of South Africa)

The new relationships between labor and management are only now emerging. The shape of national politics determines some of the form. For example, in Germany, unions have statutory roles. Employee representatives sit on the boards of all publicly held institutions. In the United States, they do not. South Africa, where Black trade unions played a major role in the final stages of political struggle, is hungrily learning from other nations and developing a hybrid model of its own. Whatever form these relationships take, participation must forever change the role of unions in institutional governance. Figure 15.6 summarizes the role of unions in participative organizations.

Figure 15.6 Unions in Participative Organizations

Vision Level (V)

> Represent the long-term collective interests of employees.
>
> Balance the interests of employee and other stakeholder groups, and resolve any conflicts between them.
>
> Improve own ability to be long-term representatives.
>
> Redefine own role.

Context Level (IV)

> Evaluate and recommend improvements in day-to-day business processes from the perspective of all employees.
>
> Put into place collective representation processes that ensure justice and meaningful influence.

Action Levels (III, II, and I)

> Educate and support workers to trust legitimate change.
>
> Encourage participation, self-management, and innovation.
>
> Support individual and group rights and expressions of needs.
>
> Manage and work participatively within the union itself.

Represent workers in grievance procedures and in other appropriate ways while encouraging them to work out their issues responsibly, on their own, and face-to-face.

Work with supervisors and teams to help the organization become and remain world-class.

SUPPLIERS

Not too many years ago, vendors were outcasts. They set their prices high, knowing that customer buyers specially equipped with distributive negotiating tactics would expect large price breaks. These win-lose relationships were yet another expression of authoritarianism at work. But, as we know today, such hostile or at best protective relationships increased costs and eroded quality.

Today, suppliers are very important partners in any organization's drive to achieve success. This is true whether they supply raw materials, components, whole systems, packaging, services, or technical expertise. Organizations that receive high-quality products and services from their suppliers have less costly failures with their customers. The cost of fixing a failure that originates with a supplier can be significant if it is not detected before the customer has the final product. One major appliance producer discovered this the hard way when it had to recall thousands of refrigerators due to a poor-quality door fastener. What a buyer had negotiated as the cheapest deal became a nightmare involving costly repairs and damage to the company's image. The increasing popularity of total quality measures has made the so-called ten-by-ten-by-ten rule familiar to purchasing people. That is, errors made early in the production process have exponentially increasing implications for the eventual cost.

This rule means that the smart organization communicates with and involves its suppliers as the true partners that they are. It treats them with respect and helps them to be winners. Today's world-class organization provides long-term business guarantees that enable a supplier to gear up for special services, such as just-in-time delivery and codevelopment of products. As *Fortune* magazine (Magnet, 1994, p. 60) reported, "close customer-supplier relationships help trim costs in today's predatory world economy. They improve quality by disseminating quality-enhancing management techniques across company boundaries and by enlisting each supplier's technological expertise in helping to design and make parts. Moreover, interdependency boosts speed, essential in a world of ever faster product cycles."

Close customer-supplier relationships have a long history in Japan, where so-called partnership sourcing between large and small companies is common. The partners develop designs together, and the supplier is guaranteed levels of customer support.

The point is that suppliers and customers today must interact at all levels of vision, context, and action. Suppliers may even be on internal mailing lists and connected by computer to an organization's information systems. Such developments are simply other examples of the boundaryless organization that Jack Welch (1991, p. 1) has been trying to create for General Electric.

If an organization as diverse as his can do it—it conducts more than 40 percent of its business outside the United States, and GE's products can be found in most major categories of U.S. industrial and service output—then it should be possible to change the old fear of foxes in the henhouse. The participative supplier is a key factor in the success of an organization, no matter how we look at it. Figure 15.7 reviews the role of suppliers in the participative organization.

Figure 15.7 Suppliers in a Participative Organization

Vision Level (V)

> Provide perspective, expertise, and insight for strategies and plans.

> Commit to relevant agreements and alliances. Be willing to look for breakthrough ways of serving customers.

Context Level (IV)

> Help to educate and work with customer teams and individuals to ensure win-win relationships.

> Give customers access to information systems; give them the information they need—even cost data.

> Advise customers to use processes and systems that will support higher-quality supplier performance (for example, bar codes on consumer goods).

> Seek to get involved early in the customer's planning process in order to help to ensure high-quality and low-cost supply of goods and services to the customer.

Action Level (III, II, and I)

> Clarify the needs and requirements of customers. Ask for feedback.
>
> Work constantly to reduce costs and increase quality.
>
> Be absolutely trustworthy and reliable. Do what you say you will do.
>
> Give feedback that will help a customer to become a better customer.

CONCLUSION

An organization can be truly participative only when all stakeholders are actively involved in creating the vision, interdependencies, and systems of the enterprise and when their day-to-day actions are appropriately participative.

Participative behavior extends beyond an organization's traditional boundaries. The truly participative organization involves customers, suppliers, and union representatives as well as employees, managers, and functional staff members. Since members of all these groups help to create the quality of the organization's products and services and of the business relationships that unite them, participation must extend to all these groups. No one group can use its position in an authoritarian manner over other groups.

Perhaps no organization has yet experienced a total mutual dependency, service, and respect of the kind just envisioned. But the trends are clear: Participation is a way of being and interacting that knows no boundaries. In these complicated and interdependent times, there is no real alternative.

CHAPTER 16

What Have We Committed To?

PARTICIPATION IS A WORLDVIEW. This means that each person, whatever his or her role, comes face-to-face with what philosophers call *existential issues*, that is, with issues of the role of the self in the world and the world of work and ultimately of governance itself.

Many people demand participation or decide to bring participative governance to their organization without recognizing the existential implications. They treat the shift as they would the move to another office or the purchase of a new car. However, the change is far more profound than either of these two events. By accepting participation, we accept the right and responsibility to choose, to influence, and to be activists. We also accept diversity as a constructive and necessary force in our own and our institution's evolution. These commitments are relevant to everyone, no matter where he or she is within the institution.

PARTICIPATION IS CHOICE

Participation is a choice, and it requires choice. Everyone must take responsibility for the choices that he or she makes. Stephen Hawking (1993), one of our greatest theoretical physicists, makes an important observation about the rising importance of choice and free will in the world today. His observation relates to the tension between instinctive aggression and personal responsibility. Aggression, he says, is a genetic human trait, bred into us over centuries by the fact that our ancestors had to fight or flee in order to survive. Today, survival does not depend on aggression. But the tendency toward aggression remains. We can only counteract violent and aggressive tendencies by choosing to do so. Thus, choice is the antidote to an instinct that has outlived its usefulness. As Hawking (1993, p. 135) writes, "there is also a Darwinian reason that we believe in free will: A society in which the individual feels responsible for his or her actions is more likely to work together and survive to spread its values. Of course, ants work well together. But such a society is static. It cannot respond to unfamiliar challenges or develop new opportunities. A collection of free individuals who share certain mutual aims, however, can collaborate on their common objectives and yet have the flexibility to make innovations. Thus, such a society is more likely to prosper and to spread its system of values."

When we accept the idea of choice, we must accept the conditions that go with it. We must accept our own right—and therefore the right of others—to choose. And we must accept responsibility for our actions. This acceptance necessarily drives us into independent and interdependent relationships with others, because it is only in such relationships that choice and its related rights and responsibilities are respected.

Choice requires consciousness. We must be aware of our environment, decisions, and personal impact in order to choose responsibly how to respond. But constant consciousness and acceptance of the right and responsibility to choose are difficult. And aggressive instincts are automatic. It is easier to maintain a coercive or dependent relationship in which aggression is expected than it is to be part of the participative world. At first, many people do not want to make the shift.

Psychology and philosophy in the last few centuries have not provided compelling reasons why individuals should accept responsibility for their own choices. Western theories since the seventeenth century have been dominated by subject-object, we-they thinking. The underlying reasoning has been something like this: We are forever separated from the world, because we can know it only through our own distorting lenses. Because we are forever separate, we must choose whether to exploit the universe for our own gain, to avoid dealing with our isolation (for example, by using drugs or by joining a group or cause), to be a victim and accept purposelessness, or to become hostile and alienated. We find ourselves choosing between apathy and self-importance. We objectify things in an attempt to move beyond our own perceptions so that we can study and predict events around us.

When the prevailing worldview in psychology and philosophy encourages isolation, there is no real reason to participate. Coercion and unhealthy dependency are the most likely behaviors. These behaviors do not require people to control their aggressions, and they allow people to abdicate to others the hard work of personal responsibility.

Fortunately, new psychological and philosophical perspectives that seem more relevant to our age are emerging. In this century, psychologists Sigmund Freud, Carl Jung, and Stanislav Grof (Tarnas, 1991) discovered new connections between us and the universe. This discovery corresponds with the discovery in the hard sciences of the creative connection between the observer and the observed. The major conclusion today is that human beings both interpret and help actively to create the universe. Philosopher-psychologist Richard Tarnas (1991, p. 434) makes this important point: "It is only when the human mind actively brings forth from within itself the full powers of a disciplined imagination and saturates its empirical observation with archetypal insight that the deeper reality of the world emerges. . . . The human imagination is itself part of the world's intrinsic truth; without it the world is in some sense incomplete."

Addressing the current shift to participation as a dominant world-view, Tarnas (1991, p. 440) asks, "And why is there evident now such a widespread and constantly growing collective impetus in the Western mind to articulate a holistic and participatory worldview, visible in virtually every field? The collective psyche seems to be in the grip of a powerful archetypal dynamic in which the long-alienated modern mind is breaking through, out of the contractions of its birth process . . . to rediscover its intimate relationship with nature and the larger cosmos."

For modern-day philosophers and psychologists, participation grounded in choice and free will is a key dynamic, for we take our real place in a universe that requires our participation only when we fully and consciously choose to focus energy, observe, and imagine. It is then that we become fully human.

PARTICIPATION IS MEANINGFUL INFLUENCE

In the first decade after World War II, W. Edwards Deming (Walton, 1986) and Joseph Juran (Garvin, 1988) introduced the principles of total quality management to Japanese industry. These principles did not receive the same attention and status in their own United States. Why did the quality revolution, spearheaded as it was by two Americans, take off in Japan and flounder in the United States?

One possible answer is that the more rational and material methodologies of total quality management succeeded in Japan because Japan had a two-thousand-year-old social and cultural foundation of participation and meaningful influence. When Deming (Walton, 1986) and Juran (Garvin, 1988) arrived in Japan, they sowed their ideas in the deep and fertile soil of a culture that could nurture them.

Shuji Hayashi's (1988) story about rice farming in Japan illustrates this point. For centuries, the Japanese peasant farmers have had to work cooperatively in order to produce rice. Cooperation is key because, although each farmer must periodically flood his paddies, he cannot do so without also flooding and draining his neighbors' fields. Consequently, communities of rice farmers have needed to work together to make flooding and drainage decisions that would meet group as well as individual needs. The interests, capacities, and schedules of all participants need to be synchronized if the flooding and draining is to succeed. The failure of individual farmers to participate in and influence these decisions could destroy crops and cause debilitating conflict among farmers.

Traditional Western organizations do not have the cooperative base that makes Japanese interdependence possible. Many have tried to transplant the cooperative techniques of total quality management (for example, quality circles, statistical process controls, built-in quality, continuous improvement) into their hierarchical and internally competitive businesses. Not surprisingly, many attempts of this sort have failed. The West is learning that quality cannot take root if real participation and meaningful influence are absent.

Richard Semler (1993), president of Semco/SA, describes what happens when the members at all levels of an organization take an active part in influencing decisions at work. Ralph Stayer (Belasco and Stayer, 1993), the former philosopher-president of Johnsonville Foods, describes very similar examples of meaningful influence. David Nadler (Kearns and Nadler, 1992) details how Xerox eventually managed to engineer a turnaround by, among other things, giving people the right and responsibility to influence their workplace. The research and stories cited in the preceding chapters of this book underline the effects of broadening influence.

Meaningful influence is essential to productivity and quality. People throw up their hands in exasperation and despair when management asks them to produce quality and improve continuously but prevents them from doing what they need to do in order to influence the environment in ways that enable them to deliver tangible results.

Meaningful influence requires some uncomfortable shifts in behavior by everyone in and around an institution. People who used to control from the top fear loss of power. The rest often view their own greater power with skepticism, wondering when it will once again be snatched away from them or how severely they will be censured if something goes wrong.

But success in participation requires an unwavering commitment to meaningful influence. Here are some of the more powerful actions that can entrench such commitment: direct involvement of team members in all decisions that affect team membership (recruitment, selection, discipline, development, work allocation); multidirectional feedback among team leaders, managers, team peers, customers, suppliers, and the people whom they themselves lead; open communication and access to information relating to the performance of teams and the organization as a whole; intense involvement in traditionally difficult but high-impact decisions, such as those required in restructuring and downsizing; interactive involvement in the redesign of jobs and work processes; team goal-setting practices and involvement in the development and setting of continuous improvement targets; and direct involvement of internal and external suppliers and customers in determination of quality requirements and in evaluations of performance.

PARTICIPATION IS ACTIVISM

It has been said that, for evil to prevail, all that needs to occur is for a few good people to do nothing. This statement is particularly relevant to participation. To make the same point in a different way: For authoritarianism to prevail, all that needs to occur is for members of the organization to remain passive.

The participative way of life requires everyone to shed the automatic behaviors of the past and to become real activists. Real activism goes beyond meaningful influence. The participative organization invites all its stakeholders to think deeply and passionately about what they believe in and what they think the organization can and should accomplish. It invites them to develop ideas and opinions and to defend them without fear of reprisal.

Thus, participative organizations are active organizations. People speak up. They disagree. They debate. And they work to build active networks of support leading to formal agreements and funding for their ideas. All these activities require senior managers to loosen the controls. They must allow and encourage the personal lobbying and politics that go with activism—as long as the lobbying focuses on ideas and does not turn into pandering aimed at getting preferential treatment from people in power.

Dependence and reactiveness have been bred into institutions over hundreds of years. They are part of the authoritarian covenant between leaders and led. The members of both groups must take steps to break out of this straitjacket and to assume the activist stance that is so important for sustained participation.

According to Amitai Etzioni (1991), only about 10 percent of the resources available in any social system are used for conscious action and change at any one time—not because there is an upper limit on the ability of a community to use its own resources but, more likely, because of inbred passivity and dependence. Participation requires people everywhere in the system to put energy into creating the organization and redirecting it when necessary. Only such activism can meet the demands of continuous improvement, rapid response time, creative thinking, and other challenges that the modern organization must face.

PARTICIPATION IS DIVERSITY

The more we participate, the more we interact with people who do not share our views and approaches. This fact has important survival value, for variety—often referred to as *diversity*—is a major source of innovation and responsiveness—survival—in a complex system. We could argue that diverse people from around the world are beginning to mingle just at the time when we need an increased supply of new ideas to help us succeed in today's volatile world. Unfortunately, in many economic institutions, homogeneity is inbred. White male executives select and promote white male managers, which ensures that those who occupy tomorrow's leadership positions will also be white males. Such continuity is only another form of the ethnic group rule that characterizes many nations today.

There are many sources of diversity, including the obvious: race, gender, ethnicity, and culture. There are good historical reasons for addressing these areas. Racism, gender discrimination, and ethnic or cultural differentiation have all been closely associated with authoritarianism. However, in remedying the discrimination of the past, we must be careful not to endorse another form of separatism, one that pigeonholes and categorizes people.

We do not resolve diversity issues by getting to know one another's culture or differences. It is true that we do have differences, but it is unlikely that people can teach their culture and differences to others. A more useful approach is to accept that everyone brings his or her own uniqueness to a situation and to adopt a nonjudgmental and childlike curiosity to the challenge of learning. Each situation gives us an opportunity to explore different perspectives and points of view. This attitude of exploration and learning is much more important than knowing someone's culture or understanding his or her past experiences.

It is not easy to accept and treasure diversity. Each of us over time develops views and values that become his or her own personal "truths." Opening up to challenge and new perspectives takes a lot of self-confidence. It is probably also difficult because accepting the differences in others means that we must acknowledge and accept the diversity within ourselves. Carl Jung suggested that the enemy we fear is in us (Tarnas, 1991). We project the parts of ourselves that we do not accept or own onto other people. If I myself am the enemy who must be loved—what then?

The acceptance of diversity extends beyond the obvious issues. People in a participative institution must work across functional boundaries and across levels. Some of the most daunting challenges involved in managing diversity occur when the finance and marketing people or a vice president and an operator try to work together.

The same is true of relationships between customers and suppliers. The two groups seldom have the same requirements and work processes. Yet increasing the interdependence and participation within a workplace inevitably brings very diverse work cultures into contact. The best solution is not to create one culture but to understand, value, and benefit from the differences of individual cultures, even if it means working through and with the attendant conflict. "At the University of North Texas last year, ethnically diverse teams of business students were pitted without their knowledge against all-white teams for seventeen weeks. At first the homogeneous teams sprinted ahead, but by the study's end the heterogeneous groups were viewing situations from a broader range of perspectives and producing more innovative solutions to problems" (Rice, 1994, p. 79).

As we move into the participative world, the capacity to respect the situation, views, and contributions of others will become increasingly important. This capacity means learning to value diversity. But it also calls on us to look beyond differences and to see the wholeness that is possible. Computer-generated art provides a useful comparison. When we look at one of the new three-dimensional drawings—the kind that requires us to look into and beyond the surface of the picture to see the 3-D image within—we experience the essence of valuing diversity. We can see the 3-D image only if we do not try to figure it out consciously and only if we do not try to connect the hundreds of little parts that compose the drawing. The whole picture lies within the complexity, but it is not only greater than the sum of its parts, it is also different from its parts. Yet without the parts, the whole could neither exist nor be seen.

CONCLUSION

Participation requires people to adopt a new worldview and to take several very mature life positions.

First, everyone must accept the responsibility of choice. In order to be contributing and involved decision makers and organizational citizens, we must take responsibility for and exercise free will.

Second, participation calls for meaningful influence. People everywhere have both the ability and the right to put their views forward and to shape the dialogue and decisions that affect them.

Third, participation demands activism. People must act if they are to break out of the assumptions of the old world. They must stand up boldly and lobby passionately for their beliefs and ideas—without fear of abuse.

Fourth, participation requires that diversity be valued deeply. The synergies of participation are possible only with diverse perspectives. Committing to participation requires us to open our minds and emotions to views and practices that are different from our own. Such commitment takes more than just "understanding" how others differ from us. It requires that we make a commitment to move with and through our differences to solutions that no one could have foreseen on his or her own.

These four requirements challenge every member of the organization to be fully and responsibly human. As the next chapter shows, meeting this challenge can require us to confront some very tough issues and misperceptions about participation. At the very least, it requires us to take responsibility for our behavior and choices, no matter what the price.

PART IV

Leading the Transformation

*P*reparing for the adventure, telling one another
stories, and studying the experiences of others
are essential when we make new settlements
and establish new ways of living. But no amount of intellectual preparation and understanding can replace the
sweat and effort of action and the reality of being there.
No matter how comfortable we are with our maps and our
preparations, we have to plunge into the operational and
technical realities: crossing new boundaries, scaling steep
heights, plunging into the icy cold ocean. Sudden gusts blow
us off course. Blizzards leave huge drifts that we must plow
through. Moments of exhilaration when we reach the peak
of a new mountain are followed by the laborious descent.
And all the while we have to maintain our commitment to
developing the tools and techniques that our environment
demands, even as we are discovering and covering new
ground.

Some of the pioneer's tools and techniques, like the maps of early settlers, are quite general and not always accurate. They do not apply with the same force in every situation. Yet they provide frameworks that help to guide action as we move into uncharted territory. More specialized tools and techniques need to be designed for specific uses: ships for the seas, vehicles for the prairies and plains. But they are all essential if we are to explore and appreciate the new world that we are entering.

CHAPTER 17

Tough Issues
in Participation

IT IS HARD TO BE AGAINST PARTICIPATION. It is socially acceptable governance. It is moral, it fits the prevailing democratic mood of the times, and research shows that it can work. It just makes sense. Yet few organizations operate participatively. Some have made some tentative steps in this direction. They have involved people in quality circles and teams and even in some key business decisions. But, as a system of governance, participation is still more an idea than a reality. Why is this true?

Perhaps it is because we are now only in the early stages of a new governance paradigm. In twenty years, we will know much more about participation and about the practices that really work. In the meantime, there are many roadblocks to success. The rational dream of participation must be reconciled with its emotional and human reality: People are not perfect. Many people are not fully developed emotionally, nor are they fully responsible. Some long for the protective cocoon of dependent and even coercive management, while others will abuse any power that comes their way, even in a participative system.

These and other legitimate fears and concerns keep people from putting their full energies into the transformation from authoritarian to participative roles and ways of working and being together.

For the foreseeable future, we must take these fears and concerns into account. And we must confront them head on, for they contain truths that will probably haunt the emerging participative organization for many years to come—perhaps forever.

Eight concerns are especially worth a review: that control will be lost, that decision making will take too long, that groupthink will reduce quality, that individuality will be lost, that apathy will threaten the process, that rights and responsibilities will not be in balance, that the focus on performance will be lost, and that management will abdicate.

We must recognize these concerns and address them, or participation will not develop deep roots.

CONTROL WILL BE LOST

When a company starts its journey toward participation, there is often a fear that participation will run wild. Management in particular fears that people will not work in the best interests of the organization unless there are strong direction, close supervision, and clear consequences for noncompliance.

The fear has some justification. Control is indeed lost—but we are talking about the old style of autocratic control, which relies on patronage and fiat. Moreover, managers often do abdicate in the early stages of participation, and workers sometimes do use their new freedoms as an opportunity to rebel. It is quite possible that at the outset neither side will have the skills, the self-image, the trust, or the understanding that it needs if it is to do more than react in these standard ways. The fact is that years of autocratic rule have alienated the governed from those who govern. In the early stages of change, that alienation is often expressed in dysfunctional ways.

But this concern also involves some myths, which need to be exploded. For example, much of the control in autocratic organizations is illusory. Why do so many autocratically managed firms produce less than participative firms if their methods of control are so effective? One might well ask those who raise the issue, What makes you think you have control now?

Businesses and other institutions need controls. Participative organizations need controls. Organizations that involve people have many controls, but they are not the same controls as those used in coercive and dependent organizations. The controls used in participative organizations include controls from a distance, like the shared values, goals, and commitments and the team norms examined in Chapter Twelve.

Every system must have controls. It is just that authoritarian and participative organizations have different kinds of controls.

DECISION MAKING
WILL TAKE TOO LONG

The charges that participation takes too long, that it slows down decision making, and that the decisions made under such conditions will almost inevitably be obsolete are serious, and, like the charge involving loss of control, they have a kernel of truth. It can indeed take longer to make a participative decision. Involving people and dealing with the resulting conflict take time. One or two people can often reach a conclusion in a fraction of the time required by a group. And in the early stages of participation, managers often go overboard in involving people. It is also possible for people to have inappropriate expectations for involvement. As one of our clients told us after about eighteen months of struggle with the change process, "When we started to involve people, they wanted to be involved in everything. I guess we went a bit too far with participation then. Today, now that everyone knows we are serious about appropriate involvement, the people are the first to question if their time will be well spent in any meeting. We're all setting our own limits."

Regardless of the dynamics involved in transition, it is not fair to judge the efficiency of a decision-making process by the time that it takes just to make the decision. After all, the full decision-making cycle has two major parts: The decision not only has to be made, it also has to be implemented. Honest measures of effectiveness consider both parts.

So we can restate the key question in the following way: How long does it take to make and to implement a decision? Is it better to decide quickly and then implement slowly—the authoritarian way—or is it better to decide slowly, then implement quickly—the participative way?

Some decisions should be made independently. This is clearly the case when people will accept and want to implement an independent decision and when the decider has the information needed to make a good decision. But decisions that require understanding and commitment from many people benefit from being made slowly. This is true also when the people who must implement a decision have important knowledge bearing on it.

To make good decisions, people need skills and understandings of the decision-making process that are impossible to acquire in authoritarian systems. In the early stages of participation, people need time to acquire these skills and understandings. They need time to work out their confusion and mistrust of one another. Meeting these needs can lengthen the time it takes them to make decisions.

However, as people become increasingly skilled in participation, this concern begins to dissipate. People begin to value the benefits of an approach that decides slowly and implements quickly. They also become better able to decide which decisions require involvement and which do not.

GROUPTHINK WILL REDUCE QUALITY AND EFFICIENCY

Participation requires people to work together. Yet few people have really learned how to work in groups. Most of us come out of schools that encouraged individualism and competition. For many of us, our work experiences have been the same. Thus, when people get together in groups, they often underperform. People drop out, they are reluctant to confront, or they use the group as a platform from which to air their personal agenda. Pressure can build to perform in a mediocre way or to be a hero at the expense of the group.

These tendencies have the effect of reducing quality. We must acknowledge this. The concern that participation will not be able to deliver high performance in the long run is thus not entirely unfounded. But it is important to see that the problem is in part a consequence of authoritarian governance.

Groups must function effectively if participation is to deliver on its promise. But the problems that occur are not the fault of participation. Years of authoritarian values and practices have retarded the development of group skills. These skills must be developed and legitimized for participation to realize its promise.

INDIVIDUALITY WILL BE LOST

Participation seems to be especially threatening to individuality in Western society. Some people fear that they will get lost in the group. Others wonder what to do about the star performers. Still others are adamant: They do not want a workplace in which everyone is treated the same. Even young Japanese workers are now echoing such concerns. And, in the last fifteen years, Chinese entrepreneurs have challenged the individual anonymity that is part of their closed culture.

These concerns about the individual are real, and they reflect a fundamental human tension: the tension between individuals and the group. It is such a long-standing philosophical and psychological issue that we can draw only one conclusion: Neither the group nor the individual should prevail. The tension between individuals and groups is essential. Any system that puts one over the other will probably fail.

Cooperative education is a good case in point. Cooperative education makes groups the main learning unit. Individuals in the group are expected to ensure that each of its other members develops to the highest level that he or she can. The group is responsible for seeing that no one fails, but individuals are responsible for meeting their commitments to the group. The group must also confront individuals who are not performing. Individuals are expected to excel where they can and to help others who are not as gifted in those subjects.

Cooperative education produces high-performing individuals and high-performing groups. Individuals develop their own strengths, but they also assume responsibility for the group. These are two goals for the participative workplace.

This does not mean that people whose work is largely individualistic cannot work and excel alone. To require teamwork where there is no real need for it is silly and not the intent of participation. Likewise, individualism at the expense of the team is dysfunctional. The reward and promotion practices that encourage inappropriate individualism must be redesigned if participation is to succeed.

APATHY IS A THREAT

One of the comments about participation that we most often hear from managers and workers alike relates to the willingness of others to get really involved and take responsibility. Managers often say that workers are apathetic: "They want to look up at the deck of the ship and see a tough captain up there. They don't really care as much as we do about performance." And workers point to management and say, "They will never change. They're on a power trip."

These are legitimate concerns, because the behaviors pinpointed in these statements are indeed the behaviors of some people. Moreover, participation is difficult. It takes energy and a willingness to be accountable. It requires us to take an activist stance and overall to endorse personal responsibility. After many years of coercion, autocracy, and dependency, we can reasonably wonder whether participation really can work. People on both sides—manager and worker, customer and supplier, union and management—are well equipped with authoritarian mind-sets and skills. Why change? And is it even possible?

The jury is still out. Recent developments in Eastern Europe provide a mixed picture. The people there do not seem entirely ready to accept responsibility for themselves or for democratic government. And in companies that are trying to become more participative, the spotty participation in open meetings seems to support the fears centered on apathy.

Social scientists again point to the years of alienation that have accompanied authoritarian institutions. Hostility, cynicism, and apathy have been inbred, they argue. Leaders are afraid to let go because they do not trust people to approach participation responsibly. And people are afraid to take the initiative because they do not trust their leaders.

Apathy and alienation are among the most pernicious enemies of participation. Activism is the antidote. Meaningful and fulfilling influence is the antidote. But will a critical mass of people wake up long enough to realize the benefits of participation and involvement and make them self-sustaining? The question remains an open one.

RIGHTS AND RESPONSIBILITIES WILL NOT BE IN BALANCE

Traditional authoritarian institutions have not been very good at balancing rights and responsibilities. Their leaders often demand results without endorsing the rights to information, resources, and access that should accompany such demands. In such systems, managerial prerogative or the right of managers to manage has a firm foothold. Yet neither company nor constitutional law defines or protects this prerogative.

All over the world, pressure for managerial accountability is now emerging. Nevertheless, power-related rights have been generally reserved for managers. In more authoritarian systems, managers have a special right to everything from parking spaces to strategic information. And they should—as long as the organization remains authoritarian. For, under those circumstances, workers are not expected to think, or innovate, or challenge. But when the rules change, the rights question is inevitably raised. That is when the tough issues arise.

When people begin to have access to information, when they are drawn into decision making, and when they are empowered to exercise meaningful influence, they often demand rights without seeing that rights have related responsibilities. They want more money, they want to have what the boss has, they want to be involved in every key decision. They may test the new participative atmosphere by refusing to support the larger goals of the business, or they may reject feedback about their own poor performance as an abuse of their rights.

This problem can become particularly acute if the organization that is attempting to make the shift from authoritarian to participative governance has based its actions on naive humanistic assumptions. While participative governance praises and values the capacity of people to be respected, to grow, and to contribute meaningfully to performance, it does not suggest that respect, growth, and meaningful contribution occur in a vacuum. When people come together in an institution, they do so with a purpose. When they come together in an economic organization or a workplace, an effort must be made to ensure that the organization is productive, that it adds value, and that people work together toward a common purpose.

The right to be involved, to be respected, to grow, and to have information imposes certain responsibilities on the person who receives this right: thoughtful participation, mutual respect, dedicated performance, and responsible use of information. Unfortunately, people everywhere in organizations have been conditioned to expect rights and responsibilities to be out of balance. It is no wonder, then, that so many people misinterpret what participation means. Participation is about balancing rights and responsibilities—not about taking rights away from one group (for example, management) so they can be given to another group (for example, workers).

THE FOCUS ON PERFORMANCE WILL BE LOST

Perhaps the greatest fear raised by participation is that it will have an impact on performance. This fear can be expressed in a number of ways: *All they want is more money. People need constant pressure and management. The natural laziness will come through.* These are all ways of expressing concern about the possible effects of participation on performance.

Some of these fears are justified. The reasons vary. For some people, the accusations may be accurate: They may indeed be lazy, or they indeed may not care, or they indeed may have chosen passivity as their approach to work. Other people may not know how else to respond when the rules change. Past experiments that resulted in punishment may make others reluctant to take risks or assume the initiative. Or the move to participation may not actually be balanced. That is, it may be prompted by the same naive humanitarianism that emphasizes rights over responsibilities.

Participative governance is not an end in itself. It must focus on making an organization more robust and enduring than it has been in the past. Unfortunately, many organizations view participation as a miracle cure and see it as a panacea for all the people problems that authoritarian methods have created.

The reality is that authoritarian organizations have not proved capable of uncompromising performance. What they have excelled at is in exacting uncompromising adherence to rules and regulations. So when the old system of rules and procedures that places thinking at the top and doing at the bottom is dismantled, a vacuum results. The practices, disciplines, skills, and attitudes needed for quality performance are just not there.

Participation does not exist for its own sake—it is important because performance today requires it. In fact, one of the main challenges facing today's leaders is to rekindle the interest in performance for its own sake. But the rifts between managing and working on the one hand and between people and the organization on the other must be healed. If the healing process is not managed carefully, participation can trigger a drop in performance. Such a drop can in turn cause supportive managers to lose faith in participation, while those who resisted it in the first place will renew their efforts to undermine participation and wrest back control. If they do, employees may conclude that management's intentions were dishonest from the outset and claim that management never had any real commitment to change. Such a vicious cycle perpetuates old authoritarian styles and adversarial, dependent relationships.

MANAGEMENT WILL ABDICATE

Managers of many organizations have risen in the ranks because they have been able to survive in and squeeze results out of authoritarian systems. When confronted by loss of their traditional, preemptive managerial authority, they often do not know what to do. They may be confronted by new aspirations and demands from employees who want to be involved but, at the same time, do not yet fully understand what involvement means or what it requires from them.

Against this background, many managers give participation the benefit of the doubt. They delegate work aggressively. But they do not know what to do after they have delegated. If the managers do not have the skills needed to coach and support their people as they confront the uncertainties that come with their new rights and responsibilities, they abdicate.

When this abdication occurs, some good things can happen. People may take risks and welcome their new responsibilities. But others may make large and unnecessary mistakes. Without support and not knowing where to go for help, they may cause the company to lose customers or money. Still others, afraid to act and programmed for years to be passive, may do little or nothing. If the manager continues to abdicate, then nothing gets done.

It is important in the shift to participation not to lose the wisdom and skills of any manager or employee. To prevent such loss, several things must happen at once: Managers must take chances and increase people's responsibilities. At the same time, managers and employees must be helped to acquire the skills needed for effective delegation and decision making. And support must be provided without over-supervision or abdication.

CONCLUSION

The shift from authoritarianism to participation is not easy to make. And it is not easy to make participation work once it has started. Many tough issues accompany the change.

Although some of these tough issues may haunt participative enterprises forever, none is a potent enough reason not to change. However, these tough issues must also not be ignored or dismissed. Some, it is true, involve fears that it is easy for resisters to play on in hopes that they can derail participation before it has a chance to start moving. This is especially true of accusations involving the impact of participation on performance—the concerns about the length of time needed to make decisions, the effects of groupthink on quality, and the loss of focus on uncompromising performance. There are strong arguments regarding the positive impact that participation has on performance (Chapter Three).

Some of the issues reviewed in this chapter—loss of control, the effect of groupthink on quality, loss of individuality, apathy, abdicating managers—really are issues in authoritarian organizations, but their toxicity decreases dramatically under participation. The associated fears are legitimate in authoritarian systems. Under authoritarianism, managers do lose control when they turn their backs. Groupthink is inefficient because it gives people cover and provides opportunities for finger-pointing. People do often lose their individuality (*them* against *us*). Workers are often apathetic. And delegation often does become abdication. A whole system of changes must take place before these issues subside. And they will not subside until participation is firmly entrenched in the processes, structures, and assumptions of the enterprise.

Some issues probably reflect various aspects of human psychology: the existential fears, the good, and the potential for evil that are inherent in the human condition. Probably no system of governance can guarantee against abuses of power and rights. No one can guarantee that all decisions will be made in the least possible time, that group decisions will not sometimes be poor ones, or that some people will not feel lost in a participative process. Nor can we ensure that no one will be apathetic, that no one will reject his or her new responsibilities, that at least some managers will not abdicate, or that performance will be the driving force in every situation.

Authoritarian institutions are not perfect in these areas. Nor will participation cure all their defects. But once we eliminate the smoke and mirrors that these tough issues can introduce and once we establish a reasonably sound and systemic platform for the participative institution that we want to build, the negative influence of these issues will probably diminish. When they do arise, the organization will be able to handle them. And when it does, we will know that participation has arrived.

CHAPTER 18

Guiding the Transition

EVENTUALLY, EVERY ORGANIZATION will have to pay the price of becoming more participative. There are two key questions: When will the changes start? and What price will we pay in the future if we delay? Ford Motor Company began its participative journey years ago. General Motors did not. Today, the Taurus automobile, the product of Ford's participative effort, is one of the highest-quality and most successful motor cars in history. What has it cost General Motors to delay?

I.B.M. persisted for years in being a centrally controlled, hierarchical, and limited-prerogative organization. In the meantime, new companies in the computer industry established traditions of customer and user involvement and employee participation. The best technical talent and an increasing proportion of the customers flocked to the more flexible organizations. Big Blue's devastating financial losses of the early 1990s may be part of the price that it has paid for its slow response to the mandate for participation.

It is not just a matter of starting. We must learn how to accelerate the change process. We can by applying what others have learned and by dedicating resources and attention to transition and change leadership. The change leaders of the 1970s and 1980s worked as pioneers. They had no maps and very little support. They often look back today and say, "I learned by trial and error. If I knew then what I know now,

I would have done it faster." Ten years after he began to prepare his organization for the twenty-first century, General Electric's Jack Welch said that, if he could do it all over again, he would act with greater confidence and speed.

We can learn from other people's successes, failures, and insights. But we must base our conclusions and experiments on the sometimes partial or incomplete experiences that we have available.

There are two important focuses for those who must manage the shift from autocracy to participation. First, it is important to develop a deep understanding of and respect for how people and organizations change. If we understand that process, some of the strange events that occur during change have a context. We can see reaction and resistance as expressions of movement and change, not as threats. Second, there are specific actions that we can take in order to accelerate the move from autocracy to participation.

HOW PEOPLE AND ORGANIZATIONS CHANGE

Although change is a relatively new field of study, there are many emerging insights about how people and organizations change. These insights can be grouped under three heads: the psychological reactions to change, how change starts within an organization and then ultimately becomes the way things work, and the features unique to the shift from autocracy to participation.

■ *The Psychology of Change*

The psychology of change is ultimately the psychology of individuals' growth and adaptation. Several insights about people and behavior are particularly relevant to change. They relate to how people deal with loss, how people learn, and how being in groups affects behavior.

HOW PEOPLE DEAL WITH LOSS. In the 1960s, psychologist Elisabeth Kübler-Ross (1969) discovered that everyone who experiences the death of a person whom he or she loves goes through a series of similar reactions: At first, we deny the event. We say, "I refuse to accept this" or "I expect to see her tomorrow." Next, there is usually a period of intense anger and blaming. It is followed by a period of deep depression and then, for mentally healthy people, a period of accep-tance and readjustment.

In the early stages, it is virtually impossible to be positive, learn new skills, or move into different habits or lifestyles. We can make these changes only after the grieving—which takes the form of denial, anger and blaming, and depression—is done.

Any major shift in work, relationships, or life patterns can trigger the grief cycle. It can because such change involves a loss or the figu-rative death of old ways, relationships, and assumptions. Perhaps the human psyche needs time to say goodbye to the old, prepare the ground for the new, and plant the self in new soil.

Unfortunately, some of these natural and normal responses are frightening to people who are trying to guide change. We would like to think that denial, anger, blaming, and depression or disorientation have no place in the workplace. These reactions also seem to be per-sonal attacks on those who are driving the change. People at work are supposed to be rational, composed, and flexible. They are supposed to accept and respect new ideas that are good for them. Perhaps it was possible to expect these things of people in organizations in the past. But, as long as change is a key factor, reactions characteristic of the grief cycle will be there, too. Change processes take longer and create much more hardened resistance when these natural emotions are sup-pressed. Many organizations want to change, but their leaders do not want to tolerate emotional responses. That is one of the major reasons why change takes so long—if it happens at all.

HOW PEOPLE LEARN. Change requires learning as well as loss. This is certainly true of the shift from authoritarianism to participa-tion. Everyone must learn new skills and acquire new mind-sets.

But learning is another process that has its own strange dynamics. Some learning calls important personal values and assumptions into question and therefore causes reactions characteristic of the grief cycle. If people feel insecure about giving up their autocratic or submissive behavior, then learning will involve some painful and troubling moments.

There are also plateaus, times when we regress, and times when skills take a great leap forward, as anyone who has tried to learn how to play a sport knows. The learning process is not like a straight and smooth upward line. People make progress in increments or leaps. For long periods, there may be no visible progress at all. Bad old habits may even reappear. But this does not necessarily mean that learning is not taking place. We need to give and request space and time while we change. Leaders of change must take the big-picture view and not draw conclusions as if the process with which they were dealing was rational.

HOW BEING IN GROUPS AFFECTS BEHAVIOR. Participation is a compelling philosophy. It draws on very positive beliefs about human intentions and behavior. We want to think that, given an opportunity to be involved and to have influence, people will be open, trusting, and trustworthy and that they will act in the best interests of the larger cause. This positive view is usually confirmed when we ask people what their values are: Most people say that they value truth, open information, high performance, and so on. (See the list of participation values in Chapter Five.) Yet, when we work with others, we often withhold information, try to increase our own personal power, and act in other authoritarian ways. What is going on? Can people really make their behavior match the values that they profess?

A school of thought that its developers call *action science* (Argyris and Schon, 1974) is gaining adherents. Action science helps people to look at discrepancies between professed values and actual behaviors. The proponents of action science find that such motives as the desire to win, the desire to save face, and the desire to minimize threat and risk can keep us from doing as we say we should. This finding by itself should cause us to think twice about participation: Is participation really possible if it is grounded in values that people cannot live?

The fact is that authoritarianism has helped to deepen the fears that keep people from living the values that they desire. The change process must help people to confront the behaviors based on fears and see that it is possible to walk the talk of participation. At the same time, it is important to put into place the new controls (Chapter Twelve) that make clear exactly what behaviors are acceptable in the participative institution.

People will go through the grief cycle, make their way down the rocky road of learning, and battle to live the values that they profess. The best approaches to change both tolerate and guide these human processes. Change cannot be managed mechanistically as if people were totally rational. They are not.

■ How Change Starts and Then Becomes the Norm

Change for organizations is no more rational or linear than it is for individuals. The only times when change can be managed rationally in an organization are the times when it does not require anyone to give up anything and when it requires changes in only one or two aspects of the business. Some changes are not very disruptive: changes in furniture, changes from one software package to another. Even changes in structure can be managed rationally if they have relatively little effect on relationships. However, other, more fundamental changes require dramatic and extensive transformations in relationships, roles, and behavior. The shift from autocracy to participation is a transformation. It requires changes in many parts of the system, and it affects many roles and relationships within the organization.

Transformational changes move in waves. They often start with one person—the change maverick—who sometimes is not even part of the organization but brought in from outside. Then, a very small group of committed and visionary people—the creative minority—begins to build. Their job is to think about and introduce the changes to people whom they think will be favorable toward them and who can provide the resources and support that are needed if the process is to move ahead on a large scale. The creative minority is like the match that can start a bonfire.

The creative minority usually works alone for a while, perhaps without accomplishing much, until it can build a base of support among the people who have the power, connections, resources, and energy needed to bring the changes into the organization. This third group becomes the critical mass that can begin to bring the change process into the rest of the organization. The critical mass must decide where to put the resources and what to attend to during the early stages of the change process. In an organization that is trying to become participative, the critical mass must begin to involve representatives of all key constituencies in its efforts to create and implement the visions, values, and plans that will guide change in the organization at large.

There is some evidence that the phase in which the critical mass develops should also be the one in which new values (Chapter Five), new structures (Chapter Six), and new leadership practices (Chapter Seven) are developed and put into place. As these new structures, values, and practices begin to operate, they provide the institutional framework that is needed for making the truly extensive changes involved in the fourth phase of the process—the phase of the committed majority.

In this fourth phase, the masses of people within the organization begin to make the change, which includes the time-consuming process of their own grief and learning cycles. If the change is successful, the people who do not want to be part of a new kind of organization may leave it at this time.

Involving the broad constituency or its representatives in the shaping of leadership expectations, values, and structures can probably shorten the time required for this phase of implementation. However, such involvement means that the critical mass must involve a relatively broad group while its own members are going through the dark phase of their own personal change process. It means also that the critical mass must involve others before its members' own vision of the end state is clear. Meeting these two obligations takes a lot of courage and self-confidence.

At some point, as skills and confidence reach a stage that makes participation self-sustaining in the organization, we reach the point of the competent masses.

> *The change process in a large beverage-producing company was about four years old when an executive from a shipping company approached the lead internal consultant. "We'd like to see the forms you use in your various management processes, for we understand that you are making some significant changes." The internal consultant said, "I'll show you the forms, but that will not tell you much about our change. The real change is in the relationships among our people as they develop strategies and goals and as they give and receive feedback. Why don't you call on one of our managers in operations? Here are some names."*

Several days later, the executive called back. "Everyone I talk with gives me the same answer—it's in the relationships, not the forms. Sounds like something significant has happened there!"

What we want is to produce self-sustaining levels of competence at which people see no difference between theory and practice. Xerox reached this stage in some of its businesses about ten years after starting its total quality effort. The values and language of teamwork and quality were evident from one geographic area to another. Was it worthwhile? The company reversed the significant loss of market share that it had experienced in the 1980s. As a result, Xerox once again became competitive in plain-paper copiers.

In guiding change, it is important not to underestimate the intense learning that takes place as people move through their grief and learning cycles. Even leaders in the creative minority or the critical mass face their own personal resistance, anger, uncertainty, exploration, and discrepancies between behavior and values. In the change process, everyone accumulates valuable learning, but it is often at a subconscious level. If this learning can be made conscious, it can become very useful in helping others whose involvement and learning will come later.

However, the early proponents of change often underestimate or soon forget their own experiences of personal change. They become impatient when the large masses do not embrace the new ways. But latecomers to the change process, just like the leaders, need to go through their own personal learning. Rather than become frustrated or impatient, the change maverick, the creative minority, and the critical mass need to treasure and have compassion for the needs of others as they work through their own changes.

There are special requirements for the change mavericks and the people who make up the creative minority and the critical mass. At the very least, they must be deeply committed to the principles underlying the change. They often are gutsy and strong personalities who have a high tolerance for uncertainty and challenge. They must be psychologically robust, because they often become the targets of blame and anger as people throughout the organization struggle with their emotions and issues. The change maverick and the creative minority have to be especially hardy. They often bear the brunt of reactions to the change process for the critical mass as well as for the population at large. If the change process is like a rocket blasting through the atmosphere, they are like its nose cone. As individuals, they need extra toughness, guts, and will.

Successful change is like a bonfire. It starts with a match, which may have to be repeatedly struck (the change maverick). The flame then moves to the newspaper (the creative minority); the paper may have to be rekindled several times. If the newspaper burns, it ignites the kindling (the critical mass), which eventually sets fire to the logs (the committed majority), which then burn using their own resources for fuel and enabling everyone (the competent masses) to use and benefit from the resulting light and heat.

Another way of thinking about the change process is to see it as occurring in waves, which have troughs and swells. We can measure its progress only by looking at the volume of water that it carries over time. A snapshot can never tell us how far it has reached. A picture taken at ebb will look very different from one taken at flow. However, over time, successful change builds in increasingly large swells as the energy moves from change maverick, to creative minority, to critical mass, to everyone. Figure 18.1 represents this process.

Figure 18.1 The Waves of Change

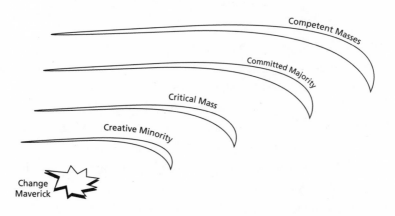

■ *How Organizations Shift from Autocracy to Participation*

The shift from autocracy to participation is a difficult transformation. People and organizations that make it undergo all the psychological dynamics of the change process. As a result, there are times when things in the organization actually seem worse than they had been before the process got under way. There are times when a great deal of productive energy is lost because it is being spent on the emotions and reactions necessitated by change. Some energy is also spent on regressing to the safety of old behaviors.

To illustrate, the following sequence of events is typical of the early and middle stages of un unsuccessful change to participation:

> *An autocratic manager, in good faith, delegates increased power and responsibility to a worker. The worker, who has lived for years as a dependent person in an autocratic system, becomes suspicious of the manager's motives. In the past, the manager allowed little freedom and acted punitively when employees failed. So the worker takes a wait-and-see attitude, expecting the manager to tell him what to do and how to do it. In the meantime, the manager, who has never trusted workers to have much initiative, sees the worker's hesitation as a sign of his laziness and dependency. Discouraged, the manager takes the power and project back, resolving not to take such risks again. The manager's reaction further reinforces the worker's reluctance to take responsibility, and the participation project is set back, perhaps forever.*

Shifting from autocratic to participative practices requires everyone to change at the same time. Workers and worker groups, managers and management groups often expect the other to be the first to change: "I will change when management begins to be participative." "I will change when I'm convinced that the people will really take on responsibility." The fact is that neither group can change unless both groups change. Participation is a dialectic, which means that it requires reciprocity. Both sides must manage power and accountability. Thus, each individual involved in the process has to deal with more than his or her own change. Everyone must also accept that others have imperfections and that they can regress while they undergo the ups and downs of change. It is unreasonable for workers to expect managers to become perfect participative leaders or for managers to expect workers to display initiative and take risks immediately. The legacy of mistrust from years of autocracy and dependency affects behavior and risk taking on both sides. Success in these changes takes mutual effort and a commitment to a longer-term vision of participation and trust.

Of course, the organization's formal leaders have the greatest responsibility for initiating changes in the relationship between autocracy and dependency. That is why it is crucial to work on the capacity for participative leadership early in the change spiral (Chapter Seven). It is also important to craft common values that can unite everyone behind one way of working and living in the organization (Chapter Five). Finally, structural changes (Chapter Six) that spread legitimate power and accountability broadly can help in making this crucial change in relationships. Organizations that do not address these three areas early face a long and probably futile battle to remove dependency and overcontrol. If these three areas are not addressed early, it is probably a sign that a critical mass has not formed or that the organization has not addressed the initial core challenges of the change to participation.

GUIDING THE CHANGE TO PARTICIPATION

We used to refer to the work of changing an organization deliberately as *managing change*. However, change in complex systems cannot be managed. There are too many variables and too many uncertainties. In order to be truly powerful change agents, we must give up our need for control. We can guide and accelerate the kind of change that transforms, but we can never manage it. The best we can do is to channel the flow of change toward participation. And we can work to shorten the time that it takes for the transition.

There are many powerful things that we can do to make participation a way of life in the organization. However, doing them does not guarantee success, nor will it eliminate surprises. It is still too early in our understanding of the change process, of institutions, and of participation itself to expect certainty of any kind. But our knowledge is growing, and we can begin to prescribe actions for success.

In this section, we make six recommendations about guiding the change process. Our experience suggests that they are particularly helpful when an institution seeks to become viable: First, go for leverage. Second, treat change as a learning process. Third, approach change as a discipline. Fourth, activate the hierarchy. Fifth, use ESP. Last, be in it for the long haul. The remainder of this section examines these recommendations.

■ *Go for Leverage*

An organization is a complex, dynamic system. A complex, dynamic system cannot be tightly controlled. It can be influenced—in the way in which a weak magnet can influence the nails in a cardboard box or paper bag. The question is, What is the best magnet?

We have suggested that nine organizational elements must change: values, structure, leadership, management processes, information, relationships, competencies, controls, and pay practices. No existing organization can afford to change all these elements at the same time. However, changes in single elements, one by one, will not give the organization the thrust that it needs to launch into a new, participative orbit. At least three or four areas must be actively changing at the same time for the organization to get the propulsion required. We think that values, structure, leadership, and management processes are good starting places. But, as any experienced change agent knows, any area that the critical mass wants to change is a good place to start. Energy for change is a great asset, even if it focuses on what should be a later change area. (For example, we think that human resource systems, especially pay, should change later. In the absence of a shift in values, things like pay have emotional connections that deflect people's energy way from participation toward such questions as, How do I win under the new rules?)

Moving actively from creative minority, to critical mass, to committed majority also creates leverage. It is important to continue to expand ownership and active personal involvement in the change. The creative minority must plot and act aggressively to get a critical mass on board. The critical mass must put resources and energy into creating a committed majority. Many change efforts get stuck and even die in the creative minority and the critical mass stages.

Finally, having all stakeholder groups involved creates leverage. This is a rule that companies often break. They focus only on managers, or only on workers, or only on suppliers. They ignore unions. But transformational change is a dialectic. It occurs inside relationships. It is a social phenomenon. All parties must change and participate in the change, or no one can change. This is a very important fact of transformation. It is the primary source of leverage.

■ Treat the Change as a Learning Process

Complex systems do not change according to a project plan. Plans are useful as unfolding visions of intent. They also help in aligning resources, and they provide benchmarks for continuous assessment. But the rational side is only one facet of change. Every organization is unique. The way in which an organization changes to participation will also be unique. As we learn more about the participative enterprise and how to make it work, we will be able to provide better and better guidelines for the change process. But participative governance is still in its infancy. Any organization that wants to become participative today is a pioneer. We are all still learning about participation as we implement it.

Within an organization, the shift to participation must be treated as an action learning project. That is, leaders apply principles and bring in processes like those described in this book. But they must periodically stop and ask, What is working? What problems are we having? Are the problems a sign that we are grappling with change constructively or a signal that it is time to intervene? What assumptions should we question? Is this a time for patience or for action and even sanctions? What is getting in the way of progress?

Periodic focus groups and in-depth reviews are essential. But the attitude must be one of learning and even of increased risk taking, not of fear or blame. Continuous feedback is essential, because no one can devise a perfect intervention. (Chapter Two argues that complex systems cannot be predicted perfectly or controlled.) A learning attitude is important, but it is often very difficult to get going in an authoritarian institution, no matter how much people want to change.

■ *Approach Change as a Discipline*

Before the 1960s, change was taken for granted—it was evolutionary. But, as the pace of change and global interdependence increased, people began to study change. How does it happen? What retards it, and what accelerates it? How do the new systems theories affect our view of institutional and societal change? What is the role of the change agent?

The body of knowledge and theory about change is growing. Any organization that undertakes a major change effort must consider the implications of this fact. It is foolish to try to guide change without tapping the expertise and theories of change that are already available. It is particularly important for the creative minority and the critical mass to become students of change dynamics. Their members need to learn about themselves as potential change agents, about the characteristics of successful organizations, about the dynamics of large-system change, and about how to assist change in individuals and groups.

Organizations must not be afraid to bring in outside people who have experience in major change efforts and in participative governance. Outside people should be part of the creative minority, and they may be involved for several years thereafter as guides and educators and as sources for additional perspectives and feedback. External support and education for change leaders have their costs, but the costs of naive change management are far greater. Many organizations simply cannot get out of the authoritarian cycle because they do not have the expertise in change that they need.

■ *Activate the Hierarchy*

Few change processes can last without institutional support. Moreover, years of dependency have immobilized the initiative of many people and conditioned them to look upward for permission and support. If people in authority do not support and get actively involved in the shift to participation, it will be an uphill battle all the way. The governance changes in South Africa were much less painful than they could have been because the ruling party participated in the transformation.

In the creative minority stage, it is helpful to involve one or two people who have formal authority. They can provide institutional air cover as the first change agents begin to develop vision and change skills. The idea of air cover is crucial. People who lead change often become the targets of blame and anger. While this is an occupational hazard that change agents must expect, someone powerful in the organization must be totally committed to sponsoring and standing with those who are in the line of fire. Organizational sponsors must also be prepared to play an active role in helping the creative minority to reenter the mainstream after their change duties are over.

Once the change has moved to critical mass, a majority of the institutional leaders should be on board and actively dealing with their own development issues, as discussed in Chapter Seven. This means that the creative minority must work with institutional leaders early in the change process to ensure that they will be prepared to enter the process actively as part of the critical mass.

Sad to say, few change processes succeed without the commitment and active involvement of institutional leaders. That is one reason why the most successful participative efforts are in new plants and start-up operations. Such organizations can be participative from the very beginning. Their leaders themselves design and guide the development of participative systems and attitudes. Once the participative systems are self-sustaining and many of the nine areas are operating participatively, the participative fibre is less likely to be destroyed if an authoritarian leader is appointed. But, early on, people at the top must change—either through learning or by being replaced.

■ *Use ESP*

ESP stands for *empathy, space,* and *pressure.* One of the questions that we most often field from change leaders is, How do we handle resistance to change? The answer is: with appropriate combinations of ESP.

But before we consider how to deal with resistance, we need again to recognize that resistance is a natural consequence of change. It may be due to the grief cycle, the learning process, or social defenses. It may occur because trust levels are so low that change is an excessive risk. Or it may be due to true disagreement and philosophical opposition. The best course of action depends on the stage that the resisting individual and the change effort as a whole are in.

There are many tactics that a change leader can use to deal with resistance. Some tactics concentrate on applying pressure. Mandates, rewards and sanctions, and persuasion are the most common pressure methods. At the other end of the spectrum of possible responses are actions that create space and time for people. Asking people themselves to design part of the participative process and listening to managers, workers, and union leaders and representatives express their issues before acting are two ways of creating space. Other methods have the effect of applying pressure and creating space at the same time. These methods include education, restructuring, and getting representatives of groups, such as union representatives, active as change leaders.

Generally, in the early stages of change, space-creating actions are the most successful. People need time and room in which to understand issues and come together as a productive and creative part of the change effort. Generally, people need to know that trial and error will be tolerated and that there is time for questions. They also need to know that mistakes—their own and others'—are welcome if they occur in the spirit of learning and growth. And they need to know that they will not have to make a final decision about whether participation is for them until they have had a chance to learn what it is all about.

A U.S. plant making brand-name photographic film was reorganized several years ago to eliminate three of five levels of management and to create a participative workplace in which the workers made virtually all the production decisions. The change included predictable wait-and-see behavior by managers as well as by workers. The direct workers at first resisted the invitation to speak out and assume new responsibilities. Managers, too, were very uncomfortable with the new levels of authority on the shop floor. But the plant manager wisely provided training and encouraged everyone to try out the new roles. It was only after several months of exposure to the new governance approach that the manager applied pressure. "Now that you know what this is about, if you do not want to be part of the new participative organization, you can move to one of the company's other, more traditional, plants."

About 15 percent of the direct workers and two of five managers took him up on the offer.

After people have had time to move through part of the grief cycle and are in a position to assess whether participation is for them, it becomes time to apply pressure. The message must be that people who want to be autocratic or dependent, who want rights without responsibilities or responsibilities without rights are not welcome in the new organization. If people have had a chance to learn and change but still reject participation, pressure is both fair and necessary.

The final general way of dealing with resistance is to use empathy. Change is difficult and involves a good deal of personal trauma. Think about the manager who, in the past, satisfied her need for appreciation by being the expert problem solver in times of crisis. She will now have to help the people whom she leads to do the problem solving. For another person, the change can mean having to conquer his shyness and introversion so that he can collaborate with others. Having a third party simply acknowledge the difficulty that such losses and changes entail helps to ease people through their change cycle. All it takes is a statement like, "This is a difficult change for you, isn't it? Take your time. We'll help you through it."

To summarize, empathy, space, and pressure are three broad ways of dealing with the predictable difficulties that everyone faces as we try to turn big ideas like participation into reality.

▪ Be in It for the Long Haul

The shift to participation takes time. How much time depends on the resources and the attention that the change receives. The organization, its leaders, and its people must be prepared for a process that extends over years. Too many realignments have to be made for it to happen any faster. This fact can become a real test of commitment: Most people get bored with participation or indeed with any long-cycle change long before it is established and running on its own. For senior managers and anyone else whose need for new stimulation is high, this presents a real challenge: Leaders must keep talking about, supporting actively, and living the change to participation years after they have decided that their organization will move to participative governance.

But this long-term view cannot be an excuse for slow action. Real change does not begin until people struggle with the real issues of change. They cannot struggle with these issues until everyone gets involved. In fact, the real change does not start until a critical number of the nine areas described in Chapters Five through Thirteen begin to change. And real change does not start until everyone begins to struggle with the new rights and responsibilities introduced by participation. In other words, change agents must apply enough consistent heat that the waters of change come to a boil and remain there. Early action across the board and across all levels gives change a better chance of happening fast. It limits the time that resistance has to build and finally block the effort.

CONCLUSION

The shift from autocracy to participation is always turbulent. It unleashes many nonrational reactions. Attempts to manage change of this kind by logical and mechanistic methods only harden the resistance and lengthen the time required.

Attempts to guide change of this type by honoring and moving with the many natural change forces are likely to be the most successful. We must use pressure, space, and empathy at appropriate times in the change cycle. There are other powerful actions that change leaders can take to help speed the change along, whatever their formal title or role. For example, it is vital to use leverage rather than try to manage all the details of change. Leverage comes from building waves of support for change, from changing several different organizational components at a time, and from having all stakeholder groups involved.

Success also depends on treating large-scale change as a learning process rather than as a project to prescribe and implement. And change is also a discipline that has its own theories and practices. Savvy leaders ask change experts to assist them in the transition. They also ensure that internal change leaders study change as a discipline. Both measures help to save time, money, and unnecessary aggravation because they make the world's accumulated wisdom about change available to the organization.

Change also needs to have organizational legitimacy. It needs resources, access to formal power, and sponsorship by people who can influence others. This usually means that people at the top must be actively involved. Finally, change leaders must take the long view—one involving perhaps five years or even more—while acting vigorously to keep the heat of change at the boiling point.

These are just a few of the actions that can guide and accelerate change. While they may be daunting, there are really no acceptable alternatives. Participation is emerging as the governance system that we need for institutions today. Although the forces that keep us from escaping authoritarianism are very powerful, we can use our emerging knowledge of change to accelerate organizations to escape velocity. We can launch any organization into the new age. But it does take guts, will, and understanding of the growing body of knowledge about how complex systems break loose from old patterns.

CHAPTER 19

Getting Started

HOW DOES A COMPANY BEGIN a fundamental change that will affect all facets of the organization and its relationships? Most companies have in fact begun such a change. They are involved in total quality efforts, reengineering, quality circles, customer-focus campaigns, training supervisors and managers in coaching skills, identifying the values that underpin participation, and so on. The problem in many organizations today is not that the change has not started but that it simmers along never quite reaching a boil. It simmers because we often fail to realize that being world-class requires a long-term commitment to transforming the workplace, to making all facets of the organization congruently participative. Change also simmers because people at all levels often do not have the courage and stamina they need to carry them through the inevitable dark hours of resistance and confusion that accompany fundamental change. And change cannot reach the point of transformation unless everyone involved sees him- or herself as the departure point for change.

If you stand at the foot of a tall mountain—or even a bit higher, at base camp—the climb looks daunting. So is the view of participation as we move into the new governance era. The best first step is to take a deep breath and acknowledge that, for large organizations with long histories of bureaucracy and autocracy, the shift may take more than five years. Leaders at Xerox talk about the ten-year process begun in the 1980s that then cycled into additional change processes. Jack Welch at General Electric sees the changes there extending beyond his total tenure as chief executive. Ralph Stayer (1990), who turned his little Johnsonville Foods Company into a world-class player, describes a ten-year journey of fundamental change that merely positioned the company for yet other changes.

When we choose to take charge of change, we thus enter a flowing river. And we build our raft while we ride the rapids. We build, train, read the terrain, develop leadership capacity in an attempt to propel ourselves faster and with fewer accidents than anyone else. And, all the time, we are in the river getting wet. As we navigate the rapids, we know that we are never fully in control but that our efforts really do make a difference in how well we perform and in whether we survive at all.

SOME GENERAL ADVICE

Many specific actions can launch and entrench systems of participative governance. We discuss them in the next section of this chapter. But it is important to realize from the beginning that success requires more than a project plan, a budget, and a well-articulated set of action steps. Plans are important, but so are intuition, guts, and a willingness to take advantage of the opportunities and surprises that occur.

This section relates some of the lessons that we have learned from experience, discussions with other change agents, and continuous reading and research in this area.

■ *Don't Expect to Find a Perfect Place or Time to Start a Change Process*

Some organizational elements—for example, structure, values, leadership—seem to be generally more powerful places to start if it is possible to take a textbook approach. But if there is energy for change in another area—say, management processes—then begin where the energy is, and move out from there.

And be aware that there never is a perfect time. Things will never settle down much more than they have today. There will always be competing priorities and financial trade-offs.

■ Work on Several Areas at a Time

There is simply not enough leverage from any one of the nine governance areas to move the organization to critical mass by itself. But no organization can afford to transform all nine areas at once. However, there must be enough heat to bring the organization to the boiling point, that is, to the point where transformation can occur. Plan to work actively on several of the nine areas at once in order to reach that point.

■ Move to Action As Quickly As You Can

Change only begins when there is action. Many change efforts fizzle, strangled by incessant debate and conceptualizing. This is a key resistance strategy that people often use successfully to kill the transformation process. Here is an example:

> A large European transportation company decided in 1991 to become a participative organization. It had strong future-oriented business reasons for doing so. But, at the time, the company was also one of the most successful in the industry. Initially, the plan was to involve all employees quickly and broadly in efforts to redesign the company's management processes and then to expand participation to other areas. However, various short-term issues repeatedly delayed action on the initial plans. A reorganization in the human resource department, various cost-cutting efforts, and attempts to streamline information at the management level continually pushed the governance change effort onto the back burner. Virtually every project that caused the delays preserved and supported the prevailing authoritarian governance system. In the meantime, various executives were appointed to short-term assignments as overseers of the company's change process. Pressured to deliver short-term results and seeing the appointments as a significant career step, the project executives chose to make the existing management processes more efficient rather

than to make them participative and go for possible major leaps in performance.

The old system simply co-opted the change process. The lack of committed and decisive action early on allowed the forces of resistance to take the initiative and gain unstoppable momentum. The company today remains fundamentally authoritarian. Many of its best people talk about leaving, and the results of climate analyses continue to be below world-class levels.

Just accept the fact that you will make mistakes, and get started. You cannot make something different happen if you do not do something different.

■ *Don't Try to Control Everything*

The change to participation is very complex. No one can orchestrate it perfectly. Because the values that underlie participative governance are attractive to most people, there will be some natural motivation for starting local change efforts. It is not necessary or even desirable to coordinate these initiatives under one project plan. It may even be good to have people try out different methods in their areas (for example, to provide information, to control, to design management processes, to lead). As long as the approaches support the values of participative governance (for example, commitment to performance; shared power, rights, and responsibilities; access; thinking close to doing; learning), encouraging local experimentation can be constructive for the overall change effort. The only requirement should be that people communicate across groups and learn from one another. Redundancy is costly at the front end, but it often leads to better insights for the organization as a whole in the long run.

■ *Get People Everywhere Involved As Soon As You Can*

The authoritarian way is for change to "cascade" down through the ranks and to focus most of the early energy on management. This makes sense in dependent, hierarchical systems, because in such systems management is responsible for the success of budgets, performance reviews—and change projects. But participation is an interdependent form of governance. It is as impossible for only the management side of the equation to be participative as it is for only the employee side to be participative. Participation exists in relationships. In order to develop it, everyone must be working on it at once. Many organizations have discovered the truth in this advice. Their leaders admit that not much happened until the employees themselves got truly involved.

■ *Expect to Balance Plans with Action Learning*

Plans and project calendars are important. But expect to revise them as the result of research and experience. That is, you must go into the change process expecting to make mistakes, to be surprised, and to learn as you go. Since authoritarian cultures discourage such a learning mind-set, this combination of flexibility and planfulness is often very difficult at first. But it is essential for success and sanity.

■ *Provide Early Change Initiatives with Nurturing Protection*

The first few of the nine areas that you attempt to change will face very strong resistance. Thus, they will need commitment and protection that exceed what you must provide in later stages of the change process. Give this protection by refusing to back off the process when it runs into trouble; by ensuring that key executives provide visible, personal support; and by publicizing early success stories. Remember that the first few changes will be transplants into a somewhat alien world—like jungle plants placed in the desert. They will need new soil, diligent watering, and personal attention.

The point is to approach the change process with a combination of deep commitment, courage, flexibility, and maturity. Know that you will learn as you go and that it will take time. These are very important insights for success.

THE FORMAL CHANGE PROCESS

We have learned that it is important to take five steps within the first year or two of change:

1. Senior management commits to the principles of participative governance.

2. Key stakeholders rigorously assess the current status of governance within the organization.

3. Key stakeholders create a shared governance vision and implementation plan.

4. The first changes occur in a few of the nine governance areas while the creative minority begins to develop.

5. A cycle of continuous learning and unfolding vision begins.

Each of these steps can be carried out in any one of many ways, and they are not the only way of getting started. But they do help significantly to accelerate the shift to participative governance and the improved performance that comes with it.

■ Step 1: Senior Management Commits to Participative Governance

Senior managers must commit to creating a new governance system. When they do, change can occur very quickly. In fact, it is very unlikely that significant change will occur without senior management's support. This step has six key outputs:

» A business reason for making the change

» A broad vision of the desired end state and of the values and principles that will guide governance in the new organization

» An understanding of the change process as a long-term commitment that requires even leaders to learn and make changes in roles and style

» A broad assessment of the organization's current capacity for change

» A list of the key stakeholders who should be involved in the planning stage

» An awareness among senior managers of their leadership role in the change process and their stated commitment to that role

The first item requires further comment. Unless there is an economic reason to adopt a participative governance mode, the company should not consider it. Purely moral reasons, sadly, will not be able to carry the day unless people at the top are deeply committed on principle.

There are many ways of developing the commitment needed from leaders. Generally, it is the result of many one-on-one discussions, team debates, and educational sessions led by experts on participative governance. Some amount of research through questionnaires and focus groups, and critical reviews of climate surveys and competitor best practices may help. Credible data are usually very helpful in developing support for the position that change is needed.

■ *Step 2: Key Stakeholders Assess Current Governance*

It is impossible to get to New York from Lima if you think that you are in Moscow. Successful change requires facing the truth about where the organization is. If all stakeholders meet to assess the current situation and its impact on performance, competitiveness, and stakeholder relationships honestly, then everyone can work together to move the organization forward.

This assessment has two major focuses: the organization's current levels of authoritarianism and participation within each of the nine governance areas, and its current level of skill in organizational change.

To assess the first, people from all stakeholder groups should use questions like the ones at the ends of Chapters Five through Thirteen to rate the organization in these nine areas. They can then compare notes and talk about why they see the organization as they do. At this point, it is not necessary to agree on numerical ratings. But it is important to understand thoroughly how each stakeholder sees the current situation and its impacts on future performance and organizational viability.

To assess the organization's capacity for change, ask who has played a meaningful and exposed role in any big change process that the organization has undergone in the past. Identify people who have been actively learning and changing—keeping themselves exposed to and challenged by new ideas and being active with groups in other organizations that are undergoing fundamental change. If there is little change capacity here, it will be vital to bring in one or two experienced and wise consultants to stimulate and accelerate the development of change capacity and skills.

■ *Step 3: Key Stakeholders Create a Vision and Implementation Plan*

The organization's key stakeholders must be part of the change process from the very beginning. It is especially important to involve labor leaders, other key employee representatives, and managers who lead large groups of people. Key suppliers and customer representatives can be involved in various ways. Stakeholders must work together to:

» create a broad and shared vision of the desired end state and the reasons for moving toward it;

» develop mutual clarity about the interests of each stakeholder group and the roles that each group will play in the change process;

» develop a shared understanding of the ways in which individual groups now view the organization's current governance;

» reach agreement regarding which of the nine governance areas will be the first to change;

» decide whether the process needs support from consultants and, if so, of what kind;

» decide how to coordinate the change process so that all stakeholders are represented and the effort has the resources and legitimacy that it needs for success;

» formulate clear and unambiguous statements for circulation within the organization regarding the intent to implement participative governance;

» decide how to signal that fundamental change is afoot.

This last point can benefit from a couple of examples.

The president of a large bank that had committed itself to becoming more participative set up a satellite communication to all bank staff. "From now on," he said, "each of you, whatever your job, may take one hour per week of company time for personal development of your choice. You do not need any approvals by anyone to exercise this option."

Ralph Stayer, executive, author, and spokesperson for organizational transformation, struggled to get the message of fundamental change into his sausage company. The message hit home

*the day he announced that the people who make the sausage must
do the quality tasting. Since that had been Ralph's job as owner
and president, delegating this important responsibility made it
clear to everyone that the organization was really operating under
new rules.*

Depending on the current relationships among stakeholders,
many one-on-one meetings may be needed to help overcome any
adversarial feelings and to build trust in others' intentions.
Management can have informal discussions with various stakeholders
to set the stage. Or a professional facilitator or change agent can conduct these discussions. The important thing is for key people to
develop a hope for and a confidence in the process before large groups
of stakeholders meet to explore and make decisions together.

Large meetings to educate stakeholders and help them develop
common visions and plans are the climax of this step.

■ Step 4: Make the First Changes and Develop the Creative Minority

The visible part of the change process begins in this step. It has five
important results: The governance areas selected in the preceding
step—for example, new organization structures, management
processes, values—are redesigned and implemented. The people who
will guide the change—they can include senior managers, line managers who are active in change projects, and human resource staff who
will act as internal consultants—experience intense development.
Local activities that are congruent with the envisioned end state and
that do not drain resources away from the primary change projects are
encouraged. Senior leaders are personally, meaningfully, and visibly
involved in the changes. And the change process is managed as a primary business commitment. This means that senior management and
stakeholders regularly review its short-term accomplishments and its
progress toward the longer-term vision.

Achieving these results requires continuous training and guided
on-the-job learning for all active change leaders. Usually, an outside
change expert plays a key role in facilitating this organizational learning. Task forces work and meet, the overall change coordination

groups meet and critically review progress and issues, and senior management and key stakeholder representatives are active and on call.

In this step, it is important not to overstructure but to have targets and get constant feedback. There must be no punishment, and leaders must encourage immediate discussion of mistakes and problems. People who are leading the change process must be supportive of each other—keeping the end states in mind—knowing that it is a long-term process that will have ups and downs.

■ *Step 5: Continuous Learning and Unfolding Vision Begin*

Feedback and learning play a vital role throughout the change process. They begin formally just after the initial changes are set in motion. For example, if values are one of the nine governance areas to be developed, then it is important to set feedback cycles in motion just as soon as the values have been identified. How are the values being lived? What are the major barriers? What support do people need? These questions can be discussed in focus groups, via E-mail, or as part of monthly team meetings. But follow-up is vital, and relevant information must go to the group that is coordinating the changes so that it can refine its strategies as determined by common needs in the organization.

We have found that action focus groups are very powerful ways of keeping feedback loops going and of getting continuous improvement. Every line manager and team leader—in fact, anyone—can be trained to lead a focus group. Focus groups identify issues and make action commitments on the spot. The change coordination group needs to provide training in the method and material used to guide the questions. The rest is up to local people to use for improvements and refinements in their area.

The coordinating group can take the feedback into account by creating and continuously updating a list of *Stops, Starts,* and *Continues* for the total change process. This list, along with any new ideas about the envisioned end state of participative governance for the organization, becomes an unfolding vision that evolves continuously as the result of new learnings and insights.

Once an organization reaches step five, its capacity for change and participative governance is building. The organization is firmly in the critical mass stage of change, and key stakeholders are ready to decide which of the remaining nine governance areas to tackle next. At this point, the organization has enough experience with change and the basics of participative governance to decide for itself, perhaps in collaboration with a good consultant, what must happen next. It is ready to move those of the nine governance areas still remaining into alignment with the participative vision and principles.

Now the organization is truly ready to free itself of the gravitational pull of the old authoritarian paradigm and launch into the Age of Participation.

PART V

Toward a New Global Consciousness

W hen the early Apollo astronauts returned from space, they gave the world a precious gift—the first photo ever of planet Earth. It is perhaps the single most influential photograph ever taken. One picture displayed the delicate and holistic beauty of our home and also revealed it to be finite and vulnerable. More than anything else, that photograph showed us that we are all fellow voyagers on Earth. Confined as we are to this small globe, we appreciate that humanity is interdependent, and we increasingly realize that we prosper or perish together. Our long-term destiny is a product of our collective actions.

The Age of Participation, whether realized within the microcosm of a company or local government or on the larger scale of a nation or trade bloc, is the response to these growing realizations and the challenges that go with them.

CHAPTER 20

Taking the Transformation beyond the Workplace

PARTICIPATION IN THE WORKPLACE is not an end in itself. Organizations pursue it because it helps them to endure and succeed. The evidence that participative governance systems deliver superior performance and customer focus is increasing. Virtually every story of world-class performance is a story of participation at work. From whatever angle we view it, it is not possible to introduce enduring and responsive competitive practices without threading participative governance through the system. Participation is the stitching that holds the organization of the future together. Without it, the organization soon falls apart.

But governance does not exist in the workplace in isolation. It is shaped by and it shapes all the governance structures in the environment around it. Every human institution is affected. For we are living at a time of massive change in human consciousness that is affecting all the institutions and expectations around us.

We propose to close this book by broadening the view of participation to global and national governance and to governance in key microsystems: schools, churches, local government, families, and business. Then, striking a more philosophical note, we suggest that participation is unavoidable: It lies at the heart of life itself.

GLOBAL AND NATIONAL GOVERNANCE

Few would disagree that national and international governance is in flux. Central-command socialism in Eastern Europe and the old Soviet Union has fallen. So has the authoritarian apartheid regime in South Africa. The paternalistic controls of China are beginning to crack. Nation-states are increasingly merging into trade blocs. Structural unemployment haunts most of the developed world and wreaks havoc on voter moods and election results. Cynicism about government is rampant. In the meantime, the poor, young billions of Africa, Asia, and the Middle East look with disgust at the lifestyles of the rich, old millions of the affluent industrialized world. One of South Africa's key entrepreneurs, Dr. Anton Rupert, has warned that no nation or person can sleep in comfort while his or her neighbors are hungry. This threat is very real. Weimar Germany proved that poverty is a dangerous breeding ground for demagogues.

We know that even the slightest increase in economic well-being increases the demand for self-governance. As knowledge and education increase, people expect to have a say in the decisions that affect their lives. So, as the world develops—or at least as it becomes more media aware—we can expect a new wave of political disruption. Current leaders and institutions, steeped as they are in authoritarian ways, are not likely to give up their privileges willingly. By then, the more-developed regions of the world are likely to find that their economies have become increasingly intertwined with the economies of regions less stable. It will not be easy to invade or bully these emerging nations, for they are the potential markets and suppliers that the developed world needs for its own continued growth and prosperity.

No one yet really understands the emerging new national alignments and relationships. All we can say with certainty is that it is not possible to wish away or ignore the problems of others as if they did not affect us. We are part of an increasingly interactive and interdependent world. The potential for the proliferation of nuclear arms in some of the less-stable environments of the globe is very real. Acid rain, pollution, and global warming do not respect national boundaries. The eradication of the rain forests touches each one of us—or our children. The complexities are simply too great for only a few individuals, some organizations, or isolated governments to address. Thus, participation is an international imperative. Participative governance, it appears, is a necessity for securing the long-term well-being of all the citizens of the world. It is the ultimate expression of John Donne's observation: "No man is an island entire of itself; every man is a piece of the continent, a part of the main; if a clod be washed away by the sea, Europe is the less. . . . Any man's death diminishes me, because I am involved in mankind; and therefore never send to know for whom the bell tolls; it tolls for thee" (Bartlett, 1992, p. 231).

The individual sits within this macroworld. The speed of developments over the past few decades has in many ways exceeded the expectations raised by Alvin Toffler (1970). The boundaries on which we once relied to define us have become increasingly blurred. People now in their seventies and eighties can tell personal stories about life in the village and in closely knit communities. In the meantime, many of the rest of us find ourselves lost in the massive urban sprawl, and we are not quite sure where we belong. We are in the twilight world between the comfort of the old ways and the seemingly insoluble issues of a very new world. We are not likely to recapture or replicate the good old days, if indeed they were. But we do need to ask ourselves seriously, How can we recapture the basic human urge for community with others, even as global issues place increasing demands on our attention? As one of the primary shapers of modern society, organizations in the productive sector will have to bear at least part of the burden.

GOVERNANCE IN KEY MICROSYSTEMS

Such microsystems as schools, churches, families, local governments, and business institutions themselves float on the immense ocean that is the changing world. However, they are not passive recipients of these changes. They interact with and help to shape emerging worldviews and approaches to life. Ironically, the increased complexity and interdependencies of today's world are making it increasingly important for small players to make a difference. Corporate giants live in fear of the small shareholder who raises an embarrassing issue at a shareholders' meeting.

In fact, the habits and worldviews of leaders and led are shaped by their experiences in the groups of which they are members. In most cases, the microsystems perpetuate authoritarianism. All too often, they develop and then release new generations of authoritarians and reactive dependents who are just looking for someone else to dominate or to blame for their misfortunes. The microsystems also help to sustain the culture of entitlement that permits people to insist on having rights without responsibility.

■ *Schools and Universities*

Primary and secondary schools need to adjust their methods of teaching so that participation can become the norm. Schools can play a much larger role than they now do in developing the critical competencies of participation: self-management, knowledge of how the economic and political sectors operate, integrative communication skills, skill in mutual learning, flexible decision making, and critical thinking, among others. Such an expanded role requires changes in teaching and learning methods as well as in subject matter emphases.

Universities and business schools can begin to break down the walls that divide the disciplines. The problems and issues of life in today's world are multidisciplinary. It is difficult to participate in solving them and creating a better tomorrow if people learn in subject matter silos. As *Fortune* notes, "The business world is ahead of the university in promoting teams, cross-functionality, and project groups that bring together disparate elements" (O'Reilly, 1994, p. 65). At the same time employers say that "MBAs must be inspiring leaders, capable also of applying know-how from a dozen different disciplines to unravel and solve the most convoluted problem" (O'Reilly, 1994, p. 64). This is a challenge that by and large is not being met.

■ *Churches*

Religious institutions have played an extraordinarily powerful role in society for centuries. Of all social institutions, they have the only history that can be traced farther back than that of universities. Not surprisingly, they often exhibit strong authoritarian worldviews, with the priest's or rabbi's word carrying significant weight. In most cases, places of worship are still dominated by men who often express strong paternalistic values. Saying this is in no way to deny the faith and beliefs that the various churches uphold. The question is whether they perpetuate the authoritarian practices of the past.

Father Matthew Fox (1988) suggests that the church in general, regardless of denomination, needs to reconcile itself with the interconnectedness and seamlessness of existence. In particular, he proposes a holistic view of the world and everything in it. Regardless of our own religious orientation, one thing is certain: The church has a significant role to play in developing the values and beliefs that support participation as a way of life. Certainly, it is unlikely that the millions of church members will be ready to embrace participative worldviews if their church happens to practice authoritarianism and bases its ideas of superiority on religious persuasion. As the primary guardians of spiritual life, the churches have a very important role to play in developing the competencies and attitudes needed for a participative world.

■ *Local Government*

The size of national governments and the large issues that they must address are often far removed from the person on the street. This fact makes it increasingly important for local government to become the vehicle that brings government close to the people. But local governments, too, must break out of their traditions of bureaucracy and hierarchy. In Wales, local governments have played a major role in the nation's economic recovery. Northern England is viewed as one of the world's best investment areas today because of the dynamism of its local governments.

The challenges that local governments face do not differ much from the challenges that big corporations face—with one exception: The role and the intentions of the elected politician are a complicating factor.

People who are elected to political positions are often hamstrung by the short-term view imposed by political expediency. Constant tensions between elected officials and the full-time people who run the local departments complicate matters. One key question is whether local governments can restructure themselves to focus on the citizen-customer. Such a development would require politicians to move from being the customer to representing the customer. New ways of integrating the fixed-term political agendas of elected representatives with the medium- to long-range concerns of full-time administrators must also be found. Participative governance at local levels will rise or fall with the ability of governments at these levels to resolve such issues.

One other issue about governance in the public sector is worth mentioning. It is absurd that politicians' interactions are still based on the adversarial and exclusive assumptions of authoritarian governance. The media are partly to blame, because they focus more attention on conflicts than on agreements. But the image of opposing political parties using parliamentary forums to score petty political points has not been fabricated by the media, nor have the ridicule, mudslinging, and half-truths that pour out of campaign headquarters at election time. If these are the examples that the supposedly great democracies set for the world, then we should not be surprised that emerging societies have been slow to adopt this ideal.

■ *Families*

The family is the smallest unit of interaction for most people. It is where we live out the majority of our moods, beliefs, and aspirations. Families are often the victims of decisions and forces in the macro-environment: economic forces, political issues, social problems. But in many ways the family is the most flexible institution of all. A decision by the few members of a family is all that is needed for it to relocate or change its immediate environment.

Inside the family, there is an extraordinarily rich mosaic of activities and interactions. Many of these activities and interactions provide a valuable nurturing ground for participation. Even in the most paternalistic home headed by a traditional authoritarian father, there is some opportunity for participation. No father to date has forever remained the strongest, the fastest, or the sole provider. And many families do accept their role in helping members to become competent community members.

It is easy to ignore the many kinds of development that can and do occur in the family. Many skills that would be valuable in other contexts are often unrecognized. Yet there is a wealth of untapped potential. We need only to name it and appreciate it. The following real-life experience shows how.

> *Peter is a semiliterate worker in a production plant that manufactures composite acrylic materials. Murray, the founder and CEO of the organization, has two postgraduate degrees. The two men came from totally different backgrounds, and they had virtually nothing in common. Yet together they helped to make the plant more participative.*
>
> *Both agreed in principle that operations at the plant had to change. But each was uncertain about the other's real willingness and ability to change. Murray felt that Peter would not be able to take on budget responsibility for the team that he coordinated. And Peter viewed Murray as aloof and without real problems in life.*
>
> *We explored family life as a context that they shared. After a bit of discussion about the mutual problems of keeping a family going, the discussion turned to household budgets. Peter lit up. "I know how to budget," he said. "Have you ever tried to make ends meet and look after the needs of a family of five on a machine operator's income? I have to count every cent three times before I spend it, and at the end of the month I must make sure that my expenses have not been more than my income. Would you call that budgeting?"*
>
> *Murray had to agree and asked Peter whether he wanted to take over the operational budgeting for his team. Peter agreed to do it but only if he could talk to Murray whenever he needed to. For the first two months he did, indeed, talk to Murray often, but then his budget competence reached a level from which he could handle most issues on his own.*

The family is a crucible for the development of participation skills. In it, we can learn about discipline; about how to develop values, resolve conflict, learn, and teach; and about responsibility and rights. This learning can take us down the authoritarian path to perpetual superiority or dependency or down the participative path toward high levels of self-esteem and mutual accountability. Unfortunately, for many today, the participative option is not fully developed.

■ *Business*

This book has been primarily about participation within companies. But business also has power to influence participation in the larger context. Many business leaders still claim that that is not their role. But whether or not business consciously accepts the role, business governance spills over into other institutions. People spend more of their productive time at work than they do anywhere else. How they work, how they are treated in the workplace, and how they choose to influence the workplace mold the character and attitudes that they carry to their family, their church, and their sociopolitical activities.

The tight link between cause and effect in the business world forces business organizations to make their subsystems congruent. This fact puts business in a unique position to shape people's worldviews. A business organization cannot survive if it is not reasonably consistent internally—it wastes too many resources, and things cannot get done. New employees know very quickly what is important in an organization, because its structure, leadership, management processes, controls, pay systems, and other components deliver clear messages about the organization's values. This conditioning can reinforce authoritarianism or participation. If it reinforces participation, participative skills and experiences become available for use in the wider world.

Business is also in a special position to influence society because the economic sector is vitally important to the well-being of society at large. As the following story shows, business can have real clout in national policy if it chooses to exercise it.

> By the 1980s, South Africa's policies of apartheid had nearly destroyed South Africa's society and economy. The National Party government was unwilling to accept that its policies were the major cause of the problems. Leaders like Nelson Mandela were in jail, and popular movements like the African National Congress (ANC) had been banned. South African society was severely polarized.
>
> In the mid 1980s, a small group of senior business leaders decided that they needed to play a more forceful role. The economy was grinding to a halt, and productivity was actually declining. Every day people were jailed without charge, and people

were held for months without trial. The rule of law had effectively been suspended. Although the business leaders in the group had no personal experience or contacts with the Black community, they worked to develop new relationships and new understanding.

Over a three-year period, they established a nationwide network of people who had never before worked together. In 1988, the Consultative Business Movement (CBM) was formed. The result of direct—although illegal—consultation between people who in the past had viewed each other as enemies, the CBM drew hundreds of people together into workshops at which issues ranging from politics, economics, and poverty to development and democracy were debated.

This business-led venture became a very powerful force for change in South Africa. The CBM was the facilitator in the negotiations that led to the first democratically elected government in South Africa. It also led to the creation of the National Economic Forum, where government, organized labor, and business meet regularly to share views on issues of common concern.

Business is involved whether or not it chooses to be. It shapes the values and develops the skills and attitudes that entrench authoritarianism or that make participation possible. Its economic role makes it one of the potentially most powerful voices to affect institutional governance today. If business worldwide rose to the challenge posed in this book, the world truly would change.

PARTICIPATION AS ART AND LIFE

Participation raises the likelihood that people will bring their full energy and capacity to what they do. In fact, participation demands that people accept their responsibility to choose, exercise meaningful influence, be activists, and be interdependent members of a diverse universe (Chapter Sixteen). When they do, the likelihood that more people will do work that they enjoy seems to increase.

There is no reason why we cannot or should not enjoy our work. It is possible to experience the worth and joy of even the most mundane task but only if we are conscious of its role in the whole and of the value that we add by doing it. The spirit of participation is this spirit.

> The Blue Train runs from Johannesburg in the center of South Africa to the beautiful coastal city of Cape Town. It has an international reputation for excellence. On a recent trip, we met the barman who had served on the Blue Train for almost twenty years. We asked him how he felt about working on the train. He responded by asking whether we would first like to order something. After he brought our drinks, he replied, "Please tell me whether you enjoy your drinks." We tasted them and thanked him for having prepared them so well. "I have made that drink perhaps a thousand times this year, but your smiles are new. It will now be a permanent part of your journey. That's why I like my work after all these years!"

When people associate themselves with the outcome of their work, work becomes art and loses its aura of labor.

> One of our sons, Roark, was in grade two. One day, Christo asked him what they had done that day in school. "We just played," Roark replied. Christo's sense of priorities told him that even a seven-year-old should not spend a whole day playing in the middle of the term. "What exactly were you playing?" he asked. "Oh, things like math and comprehension," Roark said. "Well, when do you work?" asked Christo, who was slightly bewildered by that response. Roark thought for a minute and said, "When we do things like gym and art, because then we sweat and get dirty." No amount of persuasion could get Roark to say what he liked best. "I like them all," he insisted.
>
> Another of our sons, Dan, the communication director for a U.S. senatorial campaign, said passionately in the final waning days before the election: "I don't want this to end. This is the best job, with the best people. I can't imagine doing anything else. And, no, I don't know what I'll be doing after election day."

People today are reassessing their relationship with work. Technology, downsizing, and the permanent loss of job security; new work structures; and tentative but inexorable shifts toward participative governance contribute to this reassessment. People expect a far greater say over their work and their work life.

At the same time, in a world where the only constant is change, interpersonal connections and interactivity are becoming the major point of reference. Participation is the governance form that provides this reference point. It is also a form of governance that delivers results: Virtually every organization that has a success story to tell in the 1990s tells a story of participation in action.

We are entering a new and exciting age. A megashift of governance in which the loop closes and the ages meet, it is a time when our children participate in helping us to cope. This development started centuries ago, and it has woven its way through ages and history, beginning with the first Greek experiments with democracy. Now, like the coming together of circumstances that caused humanity to look at the moon and say, "We will walk on it," we have the potential for an even greater convergence of forces as participation becomes the governance mode of the future. There will be many peaks and many valleys as we learn. But the ascendence of participative governance is somehow inevitable. Participation, like time, space, communication, and growth, is a self-sustaining spiral, for it is a central dynamic of life itself.

Governance Assessment Scoring and Interpretation Guide

THROUGHOUT THIS BOOK, you have had an opportunity to evaluate your organization against the emerging governance standards that have been presented. Return to your ratings now, and use the information in this document to guide you in interpreting what they mean.

Step 1: Record the totals of your ratings for the nine individual assessments of governance in Chapters Five through Thirteen on the Governance Assessment Score Sheet on the next page. You will create two scores for each of the nine areas: a score that reflects the extent of authoritarianism and a score that reflects the extent of participation. In each area, the highest score that either authoritarianism or participation can receive is fifty. The A and B scores for each area must total fifty. Thus, if authoritarianism receives fifty, the participation score is zero. Place two Xs on each row in the positions that correspond to the numerical scores for authoritarianism and participation.

After you have placed an X on each side of each bar, color in the space between the authoritarian and participative Xs. Use different colors on the authoritarian and the participative sides of the 0|0 point. You will have a bar graph that shows the distribution of authoritarian and participative governance in your organization.

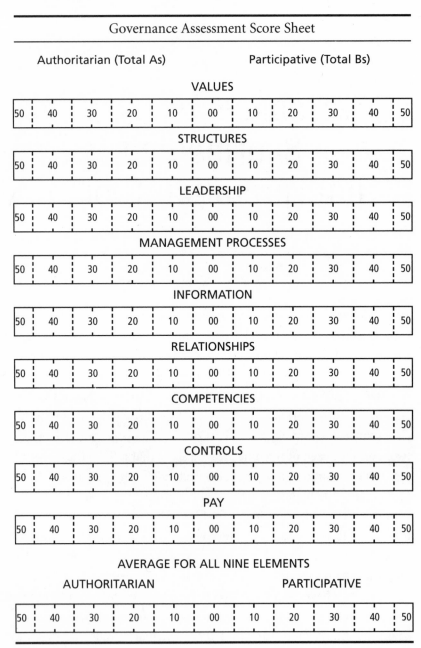

Governance Assessment Score Sheet

Authoritarian (Total As)   Participative (Total Bs)

VALUES
| 50 | 40 | 30 | 20 | 10 | 00 | 10 | 20 | 30 | 40 | 50 |

STRUCTURES
| 50 | 40 | 30 | 20 | 10 | 00 | 10 | 20 | 30 | 40 | 50 |

LEADERSHIP
| 50 | 40 | 30 | 20 | 10 | 00 | 10 | 20 | 30 | 40 | 50 |

MANAGEMENT PROCESSES
| 50 | 40 | 30 | 20 | 10 | 00 | 10 | 20 | 30 | 40 | 50 |

INFORMATION
| 50 | 40 | 30 | 20 | 10 | 00 | 10 | 20 | 30 | 40 | 50 |

RELATIONSHIPS
| 50 | 40 | 30 | 20 | 10 | 00 | 10 | 20 | 30 | 40 | 50 |

COMPETENCIES
| 50 | 40 | 30 | 20 | 10 | 00 | 10 | 20 | 30 | 40 | 50 |

CONTROLS
| 50 | 40 | 30 | 20 | 10 | 00 | 10 | 20 | 30 | 40 | 50 |

PAY
| 50 | 40 | 30 | 20 | 10 | 00 | 10 | 20 | 30 | 40 | 50 |

AVERAGE FOR ALL NINE ELEMENTS
AUTHORITARIAN   PARTICIPATIVE

| 50 | 40 | 30 | 20 | 10 | 00 | 10 | 20 | 30 | 40 | 50 |

Step 2: Create a total score for authoritarian governance and a total score for participative governance. Add up all the scores in column A and all the scores in column B. Subtract column A from column B. The result tells you how far your organization must go to adopt the new governance fully.

Total column A (authoritarian)   _____

Total column B (participative)   _____

Difference between A and B   _____

Step 3: Review your ratings at the end of each chapter. Select from the forty-five individual items the five to seven items that received the highest scores for authoritarianism and the five to seven items that received the highest scores for participation. List them here:

Highest Authoritarian Items   Highest Participation Items

Step 4: Interpret your results. Review the profiles and the list of highest authoritarian and highest participative items. What do these say to you about your organization? What appear to be the strengths relative to participative governance? Are they in one, a few, or a broad array of the nine governance areas? Why do you think they are stronger than other areas?

What are the major areas of autocracy? Why do you think they are as strong as they are?

Step 5: Identify the action implications. Use the following questions to help you identify what to do next:

a. How advanced is your organization's process of moving into participative governance? (Check one.)

___We are solidly in authoritarianism.

___We are waking up to the need for change.

___We have implemented or we are now in the process of implementing one or two new processes of the new governance.

___We have implemented or we are now in the process of implementing four or five of the new governance facets, and a critical mass of key players (Chapter Eighteen) is behaving supportively.

___We have implemented or we are now in the process of implementing key changes in six or more governance areas, and a majority of people have been through the early and mid stages of the transition process.

b. What do you think needs to happen in your organization to accelerate the change to participative governance? (Check as many as apply.)

____Educate senior management: Get their commitment and ownership.

____Rigorously assess the current state of governance in the organization and the costs and benefits associated with moving more aggressively into the Age of Participation.

____Work with key stakeholders (management, labor leaders, other key employee representatives, customers, and suppliers) to create a governance vision and implementation plan.

____Identify specific areas of governance to change and develop.

____Develop change agents and leaders so they have a deep appreciation and understanding of the new governance and how to help the organization adopt it.

____Other (see Chapters Eighteen and Nineteen for ideas).

Appendix II contains the complete list of assessment items found in Chapters Five through Thirteen. You can copy it and use it for your company's own self-analysis and action planning.

Authoritarian and Participative Practices

THIS APPENDIX CONTAINS the assessment items that you have seen at the ends of Chapters Five through Thirteen. These assessment items help you to examine specific actions and events in each of the nine critical areas of organizational governance described in this book. You can use this assessment to assist you in guiding your organization into the Age of Participation.

Instructions: For each of the nine critical areas of organizational governance, this appendix contains five pairs of items. Allocate ten points between the two items in each pair. The points awarded reflect the extent to which each statement is true. Allocate five or more points to an item only if you can say that at least 75 percent of the people in your organization would agree that the statement closely reflects their views and experiences. Nine or ten points indicate that your organization is really a case study example of the statement. The points that you award to each pair of items must total ten. When you have finished rating the statements, add up the numbers in the A column and the B column, and record them on the appropriate row of the Governance Assessment Score Sheet in Appendix I.

SECTION ONE: VALUES

1A. Values are not used in any explicit way in our human resource practices (for example, selection, recruitment, orientation / induction, performance review, and so on).

1B. Our human resource practices were (re)designed and are evaluated to reflect and reinforce our values.

2A. Our stated values were developed by people at the top of the organization and communicated to the people who must align their behavior with the values.

2B. Our values were developed participatively. All people and stakeholder groups were involved.

3A. We have no formal way of enforcing our values or evaluating day-to-day behaviors and decisions against values.

3B. People everywhere in the organization are evaluated against our values. They are part of our explicit employment contract.

4A. The values we say that we stand for are very different from the values that we practice.

4B. The values that we say we stand for are taken very seriously as mandates and criteria for action and decisions at all levels.

5A. The values that are really important here generally support authoritarian and dependent behaviors.

5B. The values that are really important here require participative behaviors from all people.

VALUES TOTAL:

Column A

Column B

SECTION TWO: STRUCTURES

6A. *We are a hierarchical organization in which one's position on the organization chart makes a lot of difference in what one does and is allowed to do.*

6B. *We are a flat organization. The organization's structure makes it easy to meet customer needs, because anyone has open access to anyone else at any time.*

7A. *Departments and teams are structured functionally, and work is divided up to make it easy to manage and coordinate.*

7B. *Departments and teams are structured in the best way to get the work done, even if that means mixing levels and functions.*

8A. *The formal, administrative boss is the key decision maker in performance reviews.*

8B. *The people who must use what individuals or teams produce or deliver participate directly in performance reviews and have real influence in them.*

9A. *Job descriptions define what people can and cannot do. Team roles are relatively fixed.*

9B. *Work and group structures allow and support multiskilling and flexible work assignments for team members. Assignments are based on current workload, skills, and development priorities.*

10A. *People doing the day-to-day work report to supervisors and managers, who make and control the final decisions.*

10B. *Teams are designed and empowered to manage their own day-to-day activities and make their own operational decisions.*

STRUCTURES TOTAL:

Column A

Column B

SECTION THREE: LEADERSHIP

☐ **11A**. *Formal leaders use their positions for personal gain, power, and prestige.*

☐ **11B**. *Formal leaders are stewards of the organization's stakeholders and work actively to optimize the interests of all stakeholders.*

☐ **12A**. *Formal leaders expect people and systems to adapt quickly and rationally to change.*

☐ **12B**. *Formal leaders expect people to go through a period of adjustment, even of resistance, as part of any change process. They facilitate and guide emotional transitions.*

☐ **13A**. *Formal leaders behave autocratically. When others work with them, it is clear who is boss and who is subordinate.*

☐ **13B**. *Formal leaders behave participatively. They involve other people and readily defer to better ideas and expertise.*

☐ **14A**. *Formal leaders have an attitude of "I know" or "I have the answers."*

☐ **14B**. *Formal leaders admit when they don't have answers or when they need to learn, even from those "below" them.*

☐ **15A**. *Leadership is static. It is the prerogative of people who have formal authority.*

☐ **15B**. *Leadership in day-to-day work moves from person to person, depending on the task and the competencies required.*

LEADERSHIP TOTAL:

☐ *Column A*

☐ *Column B*

SECTION FOUR: MANAGEMENT PROCESSES

16A. Managers do the business planning and budgeting and conduct the business reviews.

16B. Staff at all levels are actively involved in business planning, budgets, and business reviews.

17A. Personal and team performance management—goal setting and performance feedback—are primarily processes for the personnel department. People play games with them in order to get better pay, recognition, and promotion.

17B. Personal and team performance management—goal setting and performance feedback—are credible business processes that are applied with the same nonnegotiable discipline and consistency as budgets and business plans.

18A. Decisions at all levels are highly controlled. Senior management often overrides decisions or requires approvals.

18B. Everyone is considered a decision maker within his or her area of performance. Approval levels exist only when they add value.

19A. Financial staff and senior management determine and control budgets.

19B. People everywhere have meaningful influence in the development of their own budgets. Senior management and financial staff play a supportive and coaching role.

20A. Senior management restricts distribution of business plans and strategies and provides information selectively to those who "need to know."

20B. Business plans and strategies are broadly distributed and widely discussed.

MANAGEMENT PROCESSES TOTAL:

Column A

Column B

SECTION FIVE: INFORMATION

21A. Executives treat business strategy and performance data as confidential, to be discussed and known only by a select few.

21B. Information about the bigger business picture is available to and openly discussed with everyone in the organization.

22A. Job performance data are designed for management use. Managers use the information to determine the areas that workers will act on and improve.

22B. Information systems and reports are designed to help the people who do the work to take action and solve problems.

23A. Data-processing and information systems specialists define information system requirements. Workers and line managers rely on them to determine the information that will be provided and how it will be formatted.

23B. People actively and deliberately define their own information needs. They actively use data for continuous improvement.

24A. People either try to hide their mistakes, or they look for someone on whom they can blame them.

24B. People openly admit their mistakes and use information and experiences for learning and improvement, not for punishment and blame.

25A. Functional staff manage and use most of the information related to their specialty. Workers and line managers depend on staff for decisions about budgets; human resource decisions, such as staffing; and the like.

25B. Everyone has access to basic financial, human resource, and marketing data and uses the data to make decisions in day-to-day work.

INFORMATION TOTAL:

Column A

Column B

SECTION SIX: RELATIONSHIPS

26A. *People address and talk to each other in ways that reflect relatively fixed superior-subordinate relationships.*

26B. *People work together productively and respectfully regardless of levels and functions and without inappropriate use of formal power or position.*

27A. *People are often taken by surprise by decisions that affect their work lives directly.*

27B. *People are involved in decisions that affect their work life.*

28A. *People who do the work (including workers, union leaders, and suppliers) pursue their own agendas regardless of the needs of customers or of the other stakeholders in the business.*

28B. *People who do the work fully appreciate and take responsibility for the role that their work plays in the organization's success.*

29A. *People do not face their own dissatisfaction or abuses of their relationships, or they deal with them in indirect ways that do not resolve issues constructively.*

29B. *People raise relationship issues and deal with them openly so that these issues can be resolved constructively.*

30A. *People compete with each other in the belief that appearing to know more than others is important.*

30B. *People learn openly from one another, regardless of level or status.*

RELATIONSHIPS TOTAL:

Column A

Column B

SECTION SEVEN: COMPETENCIES

31A. Only managers are expected to be competent in business and financial matters.

31B. All stakeholders—employees, managers, union officials, suppliers, customers—have the business and financial knowledge that they need in order to be effective business partners.

32A. Self-management actions are often seen as insubordination.

32B. The development of self-management capacity and the ability to act responsibly are key and visible goals in the organization.

33A. Only managers receive development in interpersonal skills and decision making so that they can give feedback, communicate, and control conflict.

33B. People everywhere in the organization actively develop key interpersonal abilities for communication, learning, and decision making.

34A. Disagreement and critical thinking rarely happen or are not encouraged.

34B. People throughout the organization are actively developing their ability to recognize, explore, and solve problems, and they discuss and appreciate issues from a variety of points of view.

35A. People's learning focuses on the tasks of their specific job.

35B. People's learning deliberately goes beyond their specific job so that they can understand larger customer and business issues and see their work in context.

COMPETENCIES TOTAL:

Column A

Column B

SECTION EIGHT: CONTROLS

36A. Management develops and implements the organization's measures, policies, rules, and other controls.

36B. People at all levels, or their legitimate representatives, help to develop the organization's measures, policies, rules, and other controls.

37A. Managers control and oversee the work of task forces and teams and require them to be highly coordinated.

37B. Managers encourage ad hoc groups to form around important problems. They expect informal coordination and politics to occur, and they are reluctant to impose unnecessary constraints while the groups learn and build support for new directions.

38A. Management control focuses on maintaining predictability and eliminating surprises.

38B. Management control focuses on keeping the appropriate tensions between stability (doing things as planned) and learning (experimenting and deviating from plans). Managers see the tension as an important form of control.

39A. People in the organization often break the spirit of the rules while observing the letter of the law.

39B. People respect the rules and controls because they understand and accept the need for them. They may consciously decide to break the letter of the law in order to preserve its spirit.

40A. People behave in different ways when management is watching and when they are working on their own.

40B. People treat their goals and job responsibilities as commitments whether or not authorities are watching.

CONTROLS TOTAL:

Column A

Column B

SECTION NINE: PAY

☐ **41A.** Pay and extrinsic rewards are used as motivators and to shape and influence performance.

☐ **41B.** The work itself and opportunities to be involved and to influence are key motivators.

☐ **42A.** Bonuses are based on individual achievement. The amount of extra pay is determined by formulas and ranking systems.

☐ **42B.** Through profit sharing and other group and team processes, people throughout the organization share in the wealth that they help to create.

☐ **43A.** A punitive and blaming climate prevails in the organization. People try to win and to look good at the expense of others.

☐ **43B.** An appreciative climate prevails in the organization. People feel acknowledged and acknowledge each other for their contributions.

☐ **44A.** The pay system is designed by specialists. Much about how it works and applies to individuals is secret.

☐ **44B.** The pay system was developed with input from all key stakeholders. It is an open system that everyone understands.

☐ **45A.** More people are dissatisfied with the pay system than are satisfied that it is fair.

☐ **45B.** People feel that the pay system is fair and that it is applied fairly.

PAY TOTAL:

☐ **Column A**

☐ **Column B**

GRAND TOTALS

☐ **Column A**
(Total Authoritarian Score)

☐ **Column B**
(Total Participative Score)

References

Adizes, Ichak. *Corporate Life Cycles: How and Why Corporations Grow and Die and What to Do About It.* Englewood Cliffs, N.J.: Prentice-Hall, 1988.

Argyris, Chris, and Schon, Donald A. *Theory in Practice: Increasing Professional Effectiveness.* Reading, Mass.: Addison-Wesley, 1974.

Bartlett, John. *Familiar Quotations: A Collection of Passages, Phrases, and Proverbs Traced to Their Sources in Ancient and Modern Literature* (16th ed., ed. Justin Kaplan). Boston: Little, Brown, 1992.

Belasco, J. A., and Stayer, R. C. *Flight of the Buffalo: Soaring to Excellence, Learning to Let Employees Lead.* New York: Warner Books, 1993.

Berg, Peter, Appelbaum, Eileen, Bailey, Thomas, and Kalleberg, Arne. "The Performance Effects of Modular Production in the Apparel Industry." Paper presented at What Works at Work: Human Resource Policies and Organizational Performance Conference, Washington, D.C., January 1995.

Blanchard, Kenneth, Carew, Donald, and Parisi-Carew, Eunice. *The One-Minute Manager Builds High-Performing Teams.* New York: William Morrow, 1990.

Blinder, Alan S. (ed.). *Paying for Productivity: A Look at the Evidence.* Washington, D.C.: Brookings Institution, 1990.

Block, Peter. *Stewardship: Choosing Service Over Self-Interest.* San Francisco: Berrett-Koehler, 1993.

Boroughs, Don L. "Amputating Assets." *U.S. News and World Report,* May 4, 1992, pp. 50-52.

Brookfield, Stephen. *Developing Critical Thinkers: Challenging Adults to Explore Alternative Ways of Thinking and Acting.* San Francisco: Jossey-Bass, 1987.

Charkham, Jonathan. *Keeping Good Company.* Oxford: Clarendon Press, 1994.

Covey, S. R. *The Seven Habits of Highly Effective People: Powerful Lessons in Personal Change.* New York: Fireside Books, 1989.

Delaney, J.T., Lewin, D., Ichniowski, C., "Human Resource Management Policies and Practices in American Firms," Report to the U.S. Department of Labor, September 1988.

Dunlop, John, and Weil, David. "Diffusion and Performance of Human Resource Innovations in the U.S. Apparel Industry." Paper presented at What Works at Work: Human Resource Policies and Organizational Performance Conference, Washington, D.C., January 1995.

Etzioni, Amitai. *A Responsive Society: Collected Essays on Guiding Deliberate Social Change.* San Francisco: Jossey-Bass, 1991.

Forum Corporation. *Influence: Achieving Results Through Collaboration.* Boston: Forum Corporation, 1991.

Fox, Matthew. *The Coming of the Cosmic Christ.* San Francisco: Harper, 1988.

Garvin, David A. *Managing Quality.* New York: Free Press, 1988.

Hallstein, Richard. *Memoirs of a Recovering Autocrat: Revealing Insights for Managing the Autocrat in All of Us.* San Francisco: Berrett-Koehler, 1993.

Hawking, Stephen. *Black Holes and Baby Universes and Other Essays.* London: Bantam Press, 1993.

Hayashi, Shuji. *Culture and Management in Japan.* Tokyo: University of Tokyo Press, 1988.

Helper, Susan R., and Leete, Laura. "Human Resource Policies and Performance in the Automotive Supply Industry." Paper presented at What Works at Work: Human Resource Policies and Organizational Performance Conference, Washington, D.C., January 1995.

Huselid, M. A. "The Impact of Human Resource Management Practices on Turnover, Productivity, and Corporate Financial Performance." In press, Academy of Management Journal, 1995.

Huselid, M. A., and Becker, B. E. "The Strategic Impact of Human Resources: Evidence from a Panel Study." Paper presented at What Works at Work: Human Resource Policies and Organizational Performance Conference, Washington, D.C., January 1995.

Ichniowski, Casey, and Shaw, Kathryn. "Human Resource Management and Competitive Performance in the Steel Industry." Paper presented at What Works at Work: Human Resource Policies and Organizational Performance Conference, Washington, D.C., January 1995.

Kearns, David T., and Nadler, David A. *Prophets in the Dark: How Xerox Reinvented Itself and Beat Back the Japanese.* New York: Harper Business, 1992.

Kennedy, Paul. *Preparing for the Twenty-First Century.* New York: Random House, 1993.

Kohn, Alfie. "Why Incentive Plans Cannot Work." *Harvard Business Review,* September-October 1993, pp. 54-63.

Koopman, A. D., Nasser, M. E., and Nel, J. *The Corporate Crusaders.* Johannesburg, South Africa: Lexicon Publishers, 1987.

Kotter, John, and Heskett, James. *Corporate Culture and Performance.* New York: Free Press, 1992.

Kravetz, Dennis. *The Human Resources Revolution.* San Francisco: Jossey-Bass, 1988.

Kübler-Ross, Elisabeth. *On Death and Dying.* New York: Macmillan, 1969.

Lao-tzu. *Tao Te Ching* (trans. D. C. Lau). Baltimore, Md.: Penguin Books, 1963.

Lao-tzu. *Tao Te Ching* (trans. Gia-fu Feng and Jane English). New York: Vintage Books, 1972.

Lawler, Edward E., III. *Strategic Pay: Aligning Organizational Strategies and Pay Systems.* San Francisco: Jossey-Bass, 1990.

Levine, David I., and Tyson, Laura D'Andrea. "Participation, Productivity, and the Firm's Environment." In Alan S. Blinder (ed.), *Paying for Productivity: A Look at the Evidence.* Washington, D.C.: Brookings Institution, 1990.

Lewin, D. "Financial Dimensions of Workforce Management." Unpublished paper presented at Instructional Systems Association Conference, March 1989.

MacDuffie, J. P., and Pil, F. "Firm Performance and Human Resource Practices in the Automobile Industry." Paper presented at What Works at Work: Human Resource Policies and Organizational Performance Conference, Washington, D.C., January 1995.

McGregor, Douglas. *The Human Side of Enterprise.* New York: McGraw-Hill, 1960.

Magnet, Myron. "The New Golden Rule of Business." *Fortune,* February 21, 1994, pp. 60-64.

Mintzberg, Henry. *Mintzberg on Management: Inside Our Strange World of Organizations.* New York: Free Press, 1989.

Mintzberg, Henry. *The Rise and Fall of Strategic Planning: Reconceiving Roles for Planning, Plans, Planners.* New York: Free Press, 1994.

Mitchell, Daniel J. B., Lewin, David, and Lawler, Edward E., III. "Alternative Pay Systems, Firm Performance, and Productivity." In Alan S. Blinder (ed.), *Paying for Productivity: A Look at the Evidence.* Washington, D.C.: Brookings Institution, 1990.

Nair, Keshavan. *A Higher Standard of Leadership: Lessons from the Life of Gandhi.* San Francisco: Berrett-Koehler, 1994.

O'Reilly, Brian. "What's Killing the Business School Deans of America?" *Fortune,* August 8, 1994, pp. 64-68.

Peters, Tom. *Leadership Alliance.* Schaumburg, Illinois: Video Publishing House, 1988, videocassette.

Rice, Faye. "How to Make Diversity Pay," *Fortune,* August 8, 1994, pp. 78-86.

Sakaiya, Taichi. *The Knowledge Value Revolution, or a History of the Future.* New York: Kodansha International, 1991.

Schuster, Jay R., and Zingheim, Patricia K. *The New Pay: Linking Employee and Organizational Performance.* New York: Lexington Books, 1992.

Semler, Richard. *Maverick! The Success Story Behind the World's Most Unusual Workplace.* New York: Warner Books, 1993.

Stayer, Ralph. "How I Learned to Let My Workers Lead." *Harvard Business Review*, November-December 1990, pp. 66-93.

Stern, Sam. "The Relationship Between Human Resource Development and Corporate Creativity in Japan." *Human Resource Development Quarterly*, 3(3), 1992, 215-234.

Stewart, Thomas A., "Managing in a Wired Company." *Fortune*, July 11, 1994.

Tarnas, Richard. *The Passion of the Western Mind: Understanding the Ideas That Have Shaped Our World View.* New York: Ballantine Books, 1991.

Toffler, Alvin. *Future Shock.* New York: Random House, 1970.

Tully, Shawn. "Your Paycheck Gets Exciting." *Fortune*, November 1, 1993, pp. 83-98.

Vroom, Victor H., and Yetton, Philip W. *Leadership and Decision Making.* Pittsburgh, Pa.: University of Pittsburgh Press, 1973.

Walton, Mary. *The Deming Management Method.* New York: Putnam/Perigee, 1986.

Welch, J. F. "To Our Shareholders." In *General Electric Company Annual Report.* Fairfield, Conn.: General Electric Company, 1991.

Wyatt Company. *Best Practices in Corporate Restructuring: Wyatt's 1993 Survey of Corporate Restructuring.* Quoted in "CrossCurrents," *At Work*, November-December 1993, p. 24.

Suggested Reading

THE GOVERNANCE SHIFT

Adizes, I. *Corporate Life Cycles: How and Why Corporations Grow and Die and What to Do About It.* Englewood Cliffs, N.J.: Prentice-Hall, 1988.

DeSoto, H. *The Other Path: The Invisible Revolution in the Third World.* New York: Harper & Row, 1989.

Drucker, P. F. *The New Realities: In Government and Politics, in Economics and Business, in Society and World View.* New York: Harper & Row, 1989.

Drucker, P. F. *Managing for the Future.* Oxford: Butterworth Heinemann, 1992.

Etzioni, A. *The Moral Dimension: Toward a New Economics.* New York: Free Press, 1988.

Fox, M. *The Coming of the Cosmic Christ.* San Francisco: Harper, 1988.

Fox, M. *The Reinvention of Work: A New Vision of Livelihood for Our Time.* San Francisco: Harper San Francisco, 1994.

Galbraith, J. K. *The Culture of Contentment.* Boston: Houghton Mifflin, 1992.

Halberstam, D. *The Next Century.* New York: William Morrow, 1991.

Hawking, S. *Black Holes and Baby Universes and Other Essays.* London: Bantam Press, 1993.

Hawrylyshyn, B. *Road Maps to the Future: Towards More Effective Societies—A Report to the Club of Rome.* Oxford: Pergamon Press, 1980.

Hayashi, S. *Culture and Management in Japan* (trans. F. Baldwin). Tokyo: University of Tokyo Press, 1988.

Kennedy, P. *Preparing for the Twenty-First Century.* New York: Random House, 1993.

Lewin, R. *Complexity: Life at the Edge of Chaos.* London: J. M. Dent, 1993.

Maynard, H. B., Jr., and Mehrtens, S. E. *The Fourth Wave: Business in the Twenty-First Century.* San Francisco: Berrett-Koehler, 1993.

Olson, M. *The Rise and Decline of Nations: Economic Growth, Stagflation, and Social Rigidities.* New Haven: Yale University Press, 1982.

Peck, M. S. *A World Waiting to Be Born: Civility Rediscovered.* New York: Bantam Books, 1993.

Peters, T. *Liberation Management: Necessary Disorganization for the Nanosecond Nineties.* New York: Knopf, 1992.

Peters, T. *Thriving on Chaos.* New York: Knopf, 1987.

Sakaiya, T. *The Knowledge Value Revolution, or a History of the Future.* New York: Kodansha International, 1991.

Schaef, A. W., and Fassel, D. *The Addictive Organization: Why We Overwork, Cover Up, Pick Up the Pieces, Please the Boss, and Perpetuate Sick Organizations.* San Francisco: Harper & Row, 1988.

Smuts, J. C. *Holism and Evolution.* Cape Town, South Africa: N & S Press, 1987.

Tarnas, R. *The Passion of the Western Mind: Understanding the Ideas That Have Shaped Our World View.* New York: Ballantine, 1991.

Thurow, L. *Head to Head: The Coming Economic Battle Among Japan, Europe, and America.* New York: William Morrow, 1992.

Toynbee, A. *Change and Habit: The Challenge of Our Time.* Oxford: One World, 1992 (originally published 1966).

STRUCTURES

Davenport, T. H. *Process Innovation: Reengineering Work through Information Technology.* Boston: Harvard Business School Press, 1993.

Davidow, W. H., and Malone, M. S. *The Virtual Corporation: Structuring and Revitalizing the Corporation for the Twenty-First Century.* New York: Edward Burlingame Books/Harper Business, 1992.

Hammer, M., and Champy, J. *Reengineering the Corporation: A Manifesto for Business Revolution.* New York: Harper Collins, 1993.

Johansson, H. J., McHugh, P., Pendlebury, A. J., and Wheeler, W. A., II. *Business Process Reengineering: Breakpoint Strategies for Market Dominance.* Chichester, England: John Wiley & Sons, 1993.

Katzenback, J. R., and Smith, D. K. *The Wisdom of Teams: Creating the High-Performance Organization.* New York: Harper Business, 1993.

McLagan, P. A. "Flexible Job Models: A Productivity Strategy for the Information Age." In J. P. Campbell, R. J. Campbell, & Associates, *Productivity in Organizations: New Perspectives for Industrial and Organizational Psychology.* San Francisco: Jossey-Bass, 1988.

Parker, G. M. *Team Players and Teamwork: The New Competitive Business Strategy.* San Francisco: Jossey-Bass, 1990.

Tomasko, R. M. *Rethinking the Corporation: The Architecture of Change.* New York: AMACOM, 1993.

VALUES

Hampden-Turner, C. *Corporate Culture: From Vicious to Virtuous Circles.* London: *Economist* Books/Hutchinson, 1990.

Pirsig, R. M. *Lila: An Inquiry into Morals.* London: Bantam Press, 1991.

Snyder, N. H., Dowd, J. J., Jr., and Houghton, D. M. *Vision, Values, and Courage: Leadership for Quality Management.* New York: Free Press, 1994.

Weisbord, M. R. *Discovering Common Ground.* San Francisco: Berrett-Koehler, 1992.

LEADERSHIP

Bennis, W. *Why Leaders Can't Lead: The Unconscious Conspiracy Continues.* San Francisco: Jossey-Bass, 1990.

Block, P. *Stewardship: Choosing Service Over Self-Interest.* San Francisco: Berrett-Koehler, 1993.

Bracey, H., Rosenblum, J., Sanford, A., and Trueblood, R. *Managing from the Heart.* Atlanta: HEART Enterprises, 1990.

Charkham, J. *Keeping Good Company.* Oxford: Clarendon Press, 1994.

Covey, S. R. *Principle-Centered Leadership.* New York: Fireside Books, 1992.

DePree, M. *Leadership Jazz.* New York: Doubleday Currency, 1992.

Greenleaf, R. K. *Servant Leadership: A Journey into the Nature of Legitimate Power and Greatness.* New York: Paulist Press, 1977.

Hallstein, R. *Memoirs of a Recovering Autocrat: Revealing Insights for Managing the Autocrat in All of Us.* San Francisco: Berrett-Koehler, 1993.

Kelly, R. *The Power of Followership.* New York: Doubleday Currency, 1992.

Kouzes, J. M., and Posner, B. Z. *The Leadership Challenge: How to Get Extraordinary Things Done in Organizations.* San Francisco: Jossey-Bass, 1987.

McClelland, D.C. and Burnham, D.H. "Power is the Great Motivator," *Harvard Business Review*, March-April 1976. Harvard Business School Press.

McLagan, P. A. "The New Era of Leadership." Parts I and II. *The President*, February 1993, pp. 1-8; March 1993, pp. 1-8.

Nair, K. *A Higher Standard of Leadership: Lessons from the Life of Gandhi.* San Francisco. Berrett-Koehler, 1994.

Wheatley, M. *Leadership and the New Science.* San Francisco: Berrett-Koehler, 1992.

Wills, Garry. *Certain Trumpets.* New York: Simon & Schuster, 1994.

MANAGEMENT PROCESSES

McLagan, P. A. "Performance Management: Can It Work?" *Human Resource Management,* September 1994, pp. 23-25.

McLean, G. N., Damme, S. R., and Swanson, R. A. (eds.). *Performance Appraisal: Perspectives on a Quality Management Approach: Theory-to-Practice Monograph.* Alexandria, Va.: American Society for Training and Development Press, 1988.

Mintzberg., H. *The Rise and Fall of Strategic Planning.* New York: Free Press, 1994.

Mohrman, A. M., Jr., Resnick-West, S. M., and Lawler, E. E., III. *Designing Performance Appraisal Systems: Aligning Appraisals and Organizational Realities.* San Francisco: Jossey-Bass, 1989.

Vroom, V. H., and Jago, A. G. *The New Leadership: Managing Participation in Organizations.* Englewood Cliffs, N.J.: Prentice-Hall, 1988.

Vroom, V. H., and Yetton, P. W. *Leadership and Decision Making.* Pittsburgh, Pa.: University of Pittsburgh Press, 1973.

Watkins, K. E., and Marsick, V. J. *Sculpting the Learning Organization.* San Francisco: Jossey-Bass, 1993.

INFORMATION

Bodenstab, C. A. "Flying Blind," *INC Magazine,* May 1988, pp. 141-142.

Bodenstab, C. A. "Keeping Tabs on Your Company," *INC Magazine,* August 1989, pp. 131-132.

Masuda, Y. *The Information Society as Postindustrial Society.* Tokyo: Institute for the Information Society, 1981.

Rheingold, H. *The Virtual Community: Finding Connection in a Computerized World.* London: Secker & Warburg, 1994.

Toffler, A. *Power Shift: Knowledge, Wealth, and Violence at the Edge of the Twenty-First Century.* New York: Bantam Books, 1990.

Zuboff, S. *In the Age of the Smart Machine: The Future of Work and Power.* New York: Basic Books, 1984.

RELATIONSHIPS

Fisher, R., Ury, W., and Patton, B. *Getting to Yes: Negotiating Agreement Without Giving In.* New York: Penguin Books, 1991 (originally published 1981).

Forum Corporation. *Influence: Achieving Results Through Collaboration.* Boston: Forum Corporation, 1991.

McGregor, D. *The Human Side of Enterprise.* New York: McGraw-Hill, 1960.

McLagan, P. A., and Krembs, P. *On the Level: Communicating About Performance.* Minneapolis: McLagan Learning Systems, 1995.

Noer, D. M. *Healing the Wounds: Overcoming the Trauma of Layoffs and Revitalizing Downsized Organizations.* San Francisco: Jossey-Bass, 1993.

Peppers, D., and Rogers, M. *The One-to-One Future: Building Relationships One Customer at a Time.* New York: Doubleday, 1993.

Ryan, K. D., and Oestreich, D. K. *Driving Fear Out of the Workplace: How to Overcome the Invisible Barriers to Quality, Productivity, and Innovation.* San Francisco: Jossey-Bass, 1991.

Ury, W. *Getting Past No: Negotiating with Difficult People.* London: Business Books, 1991.

COMPETENCIES

Covey, S. R. *The Seven Habits of Highly Effective People: Powerful Lessons in Personal Change.* New York: Fireside Books, 1989.

Senge, P. M. *The Fifth Discipline: The Art and Practice of the Learning Organization.* New York: Doubleday, 1990.

CONTROLS

Peck, M. S. *People of the Lie: The Hope for Healing Human Evil.* New York: Simon & Schuster, 1983.

Simons, R. "Control in an Age of Empowerment," *Harvard Business Review*, March-April 1995. Harvard Business School Press.

Stacey, R. D. *Managing the Unknowable: Strategic Boundaries Between Order and Chaos in Organizations.* San Francisco: Jossey-Bass, 1992.

Pascale, R. T. *Managing on the Edge: How the Smartest Companies Use Conflict to Stay Ahead.* New York: Simon & Schuster, 1990.

PAY SYSTEMS

Blinder, A. S. (ed.). *Paying for Productivity: A Look at the Evidence.* Washington, D.C.: Brookings Institution, 1990.

Kohn, A. "Why Incentive Plans Cannot Work." *Harvard Business Review,* September-October 1993, pp. 54-63.

Lawler, E. E., III. *Strategic Pay: Aligning Organizational Strategies and Pay Systems.* San Francisco: Jossey-Bass, 1990.

Mahoney, T. A. "Multiple Pay Contingencies: Strategic Design of Compensation." *Human Resource Management, 28*(3), 1989, 337-347.

Schuster, J. R., and Zingheim, P. K. *The New Pay: Linking Employee and Organizational Performance.* New York: Lexington Books, 1992.

GUIDING CHANGE AND TRANSITION

Argyris, C., and Schon, D. A. *Theory in Practice: Increasing Professional Effectiveness.* Reading, Mass.: Addison-Wesley, 1974.

Beer, M., Eisenstat, R. A., and Spector, B. *The Critical Path to Corporate Renewal.* Boston: Harvard Business School Press, 1990.

Bridges, W. *Transitions: Making Sense of Life's Changes.* Reading, Mass.: Addison-Wesley, 1980.

Drucker, P. F. *Innovation and Entrepreneurship.* London: Heinemann, 1985.

Etzioni, A. *A Responsive Society: Collected Essays on Guiding Deliberate Social Change.* San Francisco: Jossey-Bass, 1991.

Gleick, J. *Chaos: Making a New Science.* New York: Viking Press, 1987.

Land, G., and Jarman, B. *Breakpoint and Beyond: Mastering the Future Today.* New York: Harper Business, 1992.

Miller, L. M. *Barbarians to Bureaucrats: Corporate Life Cycle Strategies. Lessons from the Rise and Fall of Civilizations.* New York: Clarkson N. Potter, 1989.

Stayer, R. "How I Learned to Let My Workers Lead." *Harvard Business Review,* November-December 1990, pp. 66-93.

PARTICIPATION AND PARTICIPATIVE ORGANIZATIONS

Belasco, J. A., and Stayer, R. C. *Flight of the Buffalo: Soaring to Excellence, Learning to Let Employees Lead.* New York: Warner Books, 1993.

Bellah, R.N., Madson, R., Sullivan, W.M., Swidler, A., Tipton, S.M. *The Good Society.* New York: Vintage Books, 1991.

Davis, S. M. *Future Perfect.* Reading, Mass.: Addison-Wesley, 1987.

Johnson, K. *Busting Bureaucracy: How to Conquer Your Organization's Worst Enemy.* Homewood, Ill.: Business One Irwin, 1993.

Kearns, D. T., and Nadler, D. A. *Prophets in the Dark: How Xerox Reinvented Itself and Beat Back the Japanese.* New York: Harper Business, 1992.

Kotter, J., and Heskett, J. *Corporate Culture and Performance.* New York: Free Press, 1992.

Kravetz, D. *The Human Resources Revolution.* San Francisco: Jossey-Bass, 1988.

Lawler, E. E., III. *The Ultimate Advantage: Creating the High-Involvement Organization.* San Francisco: Jossey-Bass, 1992.

Lessem, R. *Developmental Management: Principles of Holistic Business.* Oxford: Basil Blackwell, 1990.

Lewin, D. "Financial Dimensions of Workforce Management." Unpublished paper presented at Instructional Systems Association Conference, March 1989.

McLagan, P. A. "Systems Model 2000: Matching Systems Theory to Future HRD Issues." In D. B. Gradous (ed.), *Systems Theory Applied to Human Resource Development: Theory-to-Practice Monograph.* Alexandria, Va.: American Society for Training and Development Press, 1989.

Nel, C. "Productivity: A 'True' Story." *People Dynamics,* September 1992, pp. 8-16.

Pinchot, G., and Pinchot, E. *The End of Bureaucracy and the Rise of the Intelligent Organization.* San Francisco: Berrett-Koehler, 1993.

Plunkett, L. C., and Fournier, R. *Participative Management: Implementing Empowerment.* New York: John Wiley, 1991.

Ravitch, D., and Thernstrom, A. *The Democracy Reader.* New York: Harper Collins, 1992.

Renesch, J. (ed.). *New Traditions in Business: Spirit and Leadership in the Twenty-First Century.* San Francisco: Berrett-Koehler, 1992.

Semler, R. *Maverick! The Success Story Behind the World's Most Unusual Workplace.* New York: Warner Books, 1993.

Skolimowski, Henryk. *The Participatory Mind: A New Theory of Knowledge and the Universe.* London: Arkana Penguin Books, 1994.

Stern, S. "The Relationship Between Human Resource Development and Corporate Creativity in Japan." *Human Resource Development Quarterly,* 3(3), 1992, 215-234.

Waterman, R. *The Frontiers of Excellence.* London: Nicholas Brealey, 1994.

Whiteley, R. C. *The Customer-Driven Company: Moving from Talk to Action.* Reading, Mass.: Addison-Wesley, 1991.

Index

Pat McLagan began her consulting career in 1969, just before the birth of her last child. Her focus then was on bringing participative learning processes into large corporations in Minnesota—Minnesota Mining and Manufacturing Company (3M), Honeywell, Control Data, General Mills, and Sperry Univac. It was not long before General Electric Company found out about her work and invited her to begin an odyssey of management and organization development that spread to the National Aeronautics and Space Administration (NASA), American Telephone & Telegraph (AT&T), Tektronix, Prudential, Citibank, the Internal Revenue Service, and other large and changing organizations in the United States. Her consulting work, which included work with the American Society for Training and Development (ASTD) to define the human resource development (HRD) profession of the future, led to speaking and consulting opportunities around the world. Today she is widely known for her pioneering work on competency-based human resource systems, leadership development, change management, and participative governance.

In 1984, she began a series of regular consulting and speaking engagements in South Africa that deepened her commitment to and interest in participation and in the difficult change processes needed to move to participative governance.

Called by her colleagues an insatiable learner and a persistent force for change, Pat has worked as a volunteer leader on many professional and community projects. The author of a broad array of programs, ranging from a computer-based learning-to-learn program to participative leadership and programs on consulting and change, she has written many books and articles on a variety of topics related to managing, working, learning, and communicating at the dawn of the participative age.

She has received many awards, including the Larry Wilson Leadership Award and the Gordon Bliss Award as outstanding U.S. human resource development professional. She is the fifteenth person and the second woman to be inducted into the HRD Hall of Fame. An honorary professor at RAU University in Johannesburg, South Africa, and a member of the American Society for Training and Development council of governors, she has served on the ASTD's national board of directors, the executive committee of the Instructional Systems Association, and the cabinet of the Minneapolis United Way, and in collaboration with the U.S. Department of Labor she led a national project to prepare high school students for the world of work. She spends much of her time today training change agents, assisting organizations with the change from authoritarian to participative governance, and speaking on topics related to participation, human resource strategy, human resource development, and change.

Pat is founder of McLagan International, a U.S.-based consulting firm. Working out of South Africa, she collaborates with McLagan Learning Systems and McLagan Consulting Group in the United States.

Christo Nel has spent the past fifteen years focusing on the role of business in change. An Afrikaner, he belongs to the group of indigenous white Africans who have lived in Africa since the late 1600s.

He rejected the apartheid system at an early age, but he felt powerless to do much about it as an individual. However, he became convinced that business and organizations within the productive system could have the change impact that isolated individuals could not. Above all else, he became increasingly convinced that organizations could play a key role in the transformation of society.

Between 1984 and 1986, he led Project Free Enterprise. This nationwide initiative drew together more than three thousand managers from more than one hundred of South Africa's largest organizations. The final report called for a fundamental transformation of South African society as a prerequisite for economic survival and growth, and it called on organizations to introduce participative systems of governance as the primary driving force for improved productivity.

In 1987, he was approached by a group of South Africa's most prominent business leaders to explore the establishment of relationships with banned popular leaders and organizations, including the

African National Congress. With this goal in mind, he cofounded the Consultative Business Movement (CBM) in 1988. The CBM dedicated itself to the establishment of democracy as a prerequisite for ensuring South Africa's economic viability. Over a period of three years, Christo gained the support of more than a hundred of the country's top business leaders in this cause as well as of key leaders in the Black community. The dialogues and trust that the CBM's efforts began to build, combined with pressure on the government from business, were forces that helped to break open society in preparation for the unique and peaceful national transformation to political democracy. Later, the CBM became the secretariat for the national negotiations that finally led to the removal of the apartheid system.

Christo has been at the forefront of exploring ways of transforming business and organizations into participative systems. He works with people across the entire spectrum of society and in the productive sector to build trusting relationships with executives, union leaders, and staff in all areas of work. He has been deeply involved in several efforts to introduce participative governance to major corporations in South Africa. Colleagues cite his relentless belief in the human spirit and his faith in the ability of everyone to learn.

One of South Africa's most sought-after speakers and consultants, Christo is a director of the ITISA consulting firm in Johannesburg.

Pat and Christo met in South Africa and married in 1993. They are cofounders of the Democracy and Work Institute, a research and application center dedicated to assisting organizations in the public and private sectors to move into the Age of Participation.